"Student ministry is c̲ _ _ _ _ g̲.̲_̲_̲.̲ _̲.̲._̲._̲._̲ _̲.̲._̲._̲.̲._̲ _̲.̲_̲._̲.̲_̲_̲ in North America, and for that matter, the world. Making disciples of this vast harvest field will be essential for the life and vitality of the church in the twenty first century. Doing it well is what *Navigating Student Ministry* is all about. This is the book those who want to reach teenagers for Christ have long needed. Now it is here! Dive in and reap its fruit."

—**Daniel L. Akin**, president, Southeastern
Baptist Theological Seminary

"My friend, Tim McKnight, has produced another must-have book! *Navigating Student Ministry* is relevant, practical, and helpful for everyone interested in reaching and mobilizing students with the gospel. These are ministry helps from practitioners with years of experience. I highly recommend this book."

—**Shane Pruitt**, national next gen director,
North American Mission Board

"As I read through Tim McKnight's new book, I can conclude he is an artist. He turned a blank canvas into a work of art. First, he sketched out objects on the canvas. Those objects are the concepts and content areas of student ministry. The table of contents in the new book reveals the artistic way all those elements are laid out. Then, he picked up the pallet to choose the colors that would fill those objects. Those colors are the authors. The colors are vibrant and beautiful because they represent some of the most valuable thought leaders in student ministry today. The finished art, *Navigating Student Ministry*, will be required reading in my student ministry courses. That is the strongest recommendation I can give to a book."

—**Richard Ross**, professor of student ministry,
Southwestern Baptist Theological Seminary

"Student ministry is a key, kingdom-influencing element in life of the local church. *Navigating Student Ministry* addresses vital areas of this important work. I would encourage anyone in or pursuing ministry with students to read it and be reminded of the important task that lies before us of reaching the culture for Christ at this critical crossroad of life."

—**Todd Sanders**, Falls Creek program director,
Oklahoma Baptists

"The gospel—knowing it, living it, sharing it, and equipping teens to do the same—is at center stage in this comprehensive and culturally relevant guide to leading students. *Navigating Student Ministry* rightly portrays evangelism and discipleship as vital and intertwined components of any youth program (as I often say: 'If you want them to grow, you have to get them to go') and outlines practical steps for implementing both. I highly recommend this book to every up-and-coming student minister and any student-ministry veteran who could use a refresher or a course correction."

—**Greg Stier**, founder, Dare 2 Share Ministries

"I'm passionate about longevity in youth ministry because I believe youth ministry is healthier when its leaders last. By compiling the thoughts of many lead thinkers in youth ministry, *Navigating Student Ministry* helps to lay a solid foundation that will lead to healthier and more seasoned youth pastors."

—**Chris Trent**, next gen catalyst,
Georgia Baptist Mission Board

NAVIGATING
STUDENT MINISTRY

NAVIGATING
STUDENT MINISTRY

CHARTING YOUR COURSE
FOR THE JOURNEY

Editor
TIM McKNIGHT

B&H
ACADEMIC
NASHVILLE, TENNESSEE

Navigating Student Ministry
Copyright © 2022 by Timothy McKnight

Published by B&H Academic
Nashville, Tennessee

ISBN: 978-1-4627-7336-7

Dewey Decimal Classification: 259.24
Subject Heading: LEADERSHIP \ CHURCH
WORK WITH STUDENTS \ STUDENTS

Unless otherwise noted, all Scripture quotations are taken from the
Christian Standard Bible®, Copyright © 2017 by Holman Bible
Publishers. Used by permission. Christian Standard Bible® and CSB®
are federally registered trademarks of Holman Bible Publishers.

Scripture quotations marked "NKJV" are taken from the
New King James Version®. Copyright © 1982 by Thomas
Nelson. Used by permission. All rights reserved.

Scripture quotations marked "ESV" are taken from the ESV®
Bible (The Holy Bible, English Standard Version®), copyright
© 2001 by Crossway, a publishing ministry of Good News
Publishers. Used by permission. All rights reserved.

Scripture quotations marked "NIV" are taken from THE
HOLY BIBLE, NEW INTERNATIONAL VERSION®,
NIV® Copyright © 1973, 1978, 1984, 2011 by Biblica, Inc.®
Used by permission. All rights reserved worldwide.

The web addresses referenced in this book were live and correct at
the time of the book's publication but may be subject to change.

Cover design by Brian Bobel.
Cover images: Emre Kuzu/Pexels and neyro2008/iStock.

Printed in the United States of America

27 26 25 24 23 22 VP 1 2 3 4 5 6 7 8 9 10

To the student ministers of the future preparing for ministry and to the student ministry veterans faithfully serving in churches.

Therefore, since we also have such a large cloud of witnesses surrounding us, let us lay aside every hindrance and the sin that so easily ensnares us. Let us run with endurance the race that lies before us, keeping our eyes on Jesus, the pioneer and perfecter of our faith. For the joy that lay before him, he endured the cross, despising the shame, and sat down at the right hand of the throne of God. Heb 12:1–2

CONTENTS

FOREWORD

Thirty-five years is a long time to do anything. It's staggering to think that's how long I've been in student ministry. If I were calculating this in dog years, I would be 245 years old. But as so many youth pastors will attest, doing ministry with and among teenagers can have two simultaneously dazzling effects: it can age you while at the same time keeping you young. If I were to sum up in simplistic terms the crux of ministering to students in America right now, it would be a combination of these two realities. We need the wisdom and insight that only decades of mistakes and missteps and hard-won battles can teach us, while at the same time pulling energy from a veritable fountain of youth, since we all know you have to be in really great shape or drink copious amounts of caffeine to keep up with a roomful of adolescents.

That's what Tim does here in *Navigating Student Ministry*. He doesn't so much attempt to "balance" the requirements that one would need to faithfully disciple teenagers as much as he "harmonizes" the various elements necessary for the task. And make no mistake, it is a task, to be sure. But it's a joyful task, more like an adventure than a tedious job. More akin to figuring out an intricate plot to a compelling movie while you're watching it than studying formulas in a classroom to regurgitate on a test. If you've ever so much as volunteered for a youth event at your church, you know that serving kids takes equal amounts of courage, humor, patience, toughness, tenderness, theology, and tenacity with a splash of luck and a dash of risk . . . all fueled by the Holy Spirit.

Tim marks out an approach to student ministry that is remarkably harmonized. He refuses to get caught up in the (needless) debate on whether evangelism or discipleship is more important and shows how, theologically and practically, they are two sides of the same coin. He avoids trite and shallow formulas for reaching lost students as well as for teaching Christian kids. Instead, he approaches the adventure of student ministry more circumspectly; namely from a doctrinal framework that centers all ministry activity around the good news of the gospel and the local church. Even the order of the chapters and the subject matter makes total sense, as you can see from even a cursory glimpse at the table of contents and chapter titles. Simply put, it's a brilliant approach to a subject that so many books and blogs and conferences have attempted to tackle.

Let me say that personally, Tim McKnight is one of my closest friends. He's a trusted brother in Christ with whom I have shared many meals and conversations. He's a soul winner. He preaches the gospel in his church and he shares the gospel one-on-one with people. He teaches classes about youth ministry at Anderson University, but he also disciples his own teenagers in his home alongside his wife. This is a man who models ministry. The words in this book reflect the life that Tim leads on Tuesday afternoons, not just Sunday mornings.

I began preaching to teenagers when I was a teenager. Now as I approach the ripe young age of fifty, I glance around my house and see my own teenage sons and a dozen of their friends laughing, eating (how do they eat so much?), wrestling on my wife's new couch, and making more noise than a political debate on cable TV. And yet they wind up on the back porch, circled up with their Bibles and their notebooks, singing worship songs and praying for each other and for their lost friends at their schools. And right there in that moment, I realize that technology and culture and politics have changed so many things from just thirty years ago when I was a student—while at the same time so many things have remained the same. They love being together. They crave community. They want to belong to a family. They are not hostile toward faith; they just won't tolerate hypocrisy or weak, superficial religiosity. They need moms and dads (biological and spiritual) to care about them and model life with Christ for them. They respond to love, correction, coaching, and compassion. They don't run away from theology.

They're not impossible to reach. They're not a lost generation or a lost cause. For those of us who love them and feel called to teach them how to follow Jesus, we just need a helpful resource from a tested and trusted voice to guide us. Tim McKnight is that voice and this book is that resource. I commend it to you with great enthusiasm and a third cup of coffee because I have to keep up with these kids somehow.

Clayton King
Founder and President, Crossroads Camps and Conferences
Pastor at Newspring Church, Anderson, South Carolina
Author and Evangelist

ACKNOWLEDGMENTS

Thanks to Chris Thompson, who asked me if I had any ideas for a manuscript while he met with our faculty at our annual retreat for the College of Christian Studies at Anderson University. As my contact with B&H Academic, he helped me turn an outline for a student ministry textbook into a book contract. Thanks, Chris!

Michael Duduit, my boss, friend, and the dean of the Clamp Divinity School and College of Christian Studies at Anderson University, offered consistent encouragement throughout this project. He is also a great supporter of student ministry and shares our vision of equipping men and women called to student ministry to reach the next generation.

Thanks to each contributor who agreed to write chapters for this project. You wrote, finished, and submitted your work in the middle of a global pandemic. You balanced teaching and serving in your ministries during this trying time with finishing these chapters. I am thankful for your hard work!

Thanks to my wife, Angela, and children, Noah, Micah, Karissa, and MaryAnna. I thank God for the blessing that you are to me and for the love you show. It is an honor to be your husband and father. God is so good to bless me with such a great family!

To my Lord and Savior Jesus Christ, I am nothing without You. Thank You for Your grace, mercy, and love!

Preparing for Your Journey

• TIM McKNIGHT •

I sat on the floor of the auditorium that we affectionately named "the big red bedroom" and stared at the map and protractor the sergeant had just issued me.[1] I was a second lieutenant in the United States Army and a student at the United States Army Chaplain Center and School's Officer Basic Course. We would complete the first phase of our training in a week with a field exercise at Fort Dix, New Jersey. There, we would conduct day and night land navigation, low- and high-crawl drills, night infiltration exercises, and, the highlight of the week, the gas chamber. On this day, they began teaching us the skills we needed to conduct land navigation so we'd be prepared to take the map, protractor, and compass and navigate through various points throughout Fort Dix.

It was the first time I had used one of the army's topographical six-digit grid maps. There were lines and numbers all over the map.

---

[1] The auditorium derived its name from the fact that it had red brick walls and was the site of numerous briefings in which we had to fight falling asleep after waking up at four in the morning and hiking five miles with a fifty-pound pack.

There was a key on the side designed to serve as a guide, but it was hard for me to interpret. I was not sure how to make sense of it all. I worried I wouldn't be able to know where I was or where I needed to go using only the map, terrain reference points, and the army-issued compass.

Fortunately, I was not alone. Seeing my confusion, two veteran officers patiently explained to me how to use my protractor, map, and compass to navigate in the field. They taught me all the vital information I needed to know about the map, so I could use it to pinpoint where I was and how to get to where I was going. Without those two officers, I am not sure I could have completed the mission.

A Youth Pastor without a Map

I wish I had had such veteran advice three years earlier as I sat in my office at my new church. Located only a quarter-mile from the college I attended at the time, the church had called me to serve as their new student pastor. I was twenty-one years old with no experience. I had previously served as a counselor and program director at an interdenominational youth camp, but I had no ministry experience in the local church.

I did not know where to start or where to go with the student ministry. I had no idea how to relate to parents of teenagers. I felt nervous talking with them because I had never raised a teenager. In fact, I had only recently been a teenager myself! This was only one of the many problems I faced. I did not even know where to begin in discipling the students. How would I pick the topics for our Bible studies? What material(s) would I use? How does adolescent development relate to how I would teach middle school and high school students? How would I relate to the staff? Could they tell that I was absolutely clueless about what I was doing?

These questions raced through my head as I stared at the blank computer screen. I wanted to call someone experienced in student ministry and get some advice, but the town was so small that our church was one of the few that could afford to hire a student minister. There was no other student minister I could call! There were no veteran ministers there to give me advice. I was a young college senior who had answered a call to ministry. I had a heart to reach students with the gospel. I was starting on what should be an exciting journey, but I did not feel the excitement. I felt afraid and alone. I did not want to fail the Lord, the church, the parents, or the students, but I didn't know what to do. I was lost.

A Map for Youth Ministry

Perhaps you can relate to this story. Maybe you are an adult volunteer who loves the Lord and loves students, but you do not know where to start with student ministry. You might be a college or seminary student taking your first class in student ministry. Maybe you are a pastor who wants to help your church develop a student ministry and bought this book to get information on where to start. Or it could be you are reading this as a veteran student minister who purchased this book as a resource to share with your student ministry team.

Wherever you are in navigating this journey of student ministry, you will find this book helpful. It contains advice from veteran academicians and practitioners in student ministry who have more than one hundred years of combined experience. Just as the two officers from my army days aided me, the advice from the student ministry experts in this book can help you successfully navigate student ministry. They wrote each chapter from their unique perspectives and within their areas of expertise. You may choose to read this book in sequence or read chapters on specific topics of interest. Either way, consider this book a resource (or map!) you can carry with you on your student ministry expedition.

Where We're Going

Because the Bible is God's Word and our authority regarding all matters of faith and life—including student ministry—the first chapter focuses on biblical foundations for student ministry. After discussing biblical revelation and authority, chapter one examines Scripture's emphasis on parents and the community of faith sharing the responsibility of discipling the next generation. It gives advice on establishing hermeneutical and theological foundations for students.

Chapter two includes a conversation of the call to student ministry. It explores the biblical foundation for the concept of calling. This is followed by a discussion about how individuals can discern if they are called to ministry. This chapter emphasizes the importance of internal and external confirmations of one's call to ministry. It concludes with an examination of the qualifications for ministry.

Our discussion then transitions to the life of the student minister in chapter three. This chapter focuses on the student minister's holistic health—including spiritual, physical, mental, and emotional health—and presents best practices for promoting health in each of those areas.

One way that student ministers relieve stress is by delegating ministry to others. The fourth chapter offers guidance for creating a plan to develop leaders in the student ministry. This plan includes practical steps for delegating tasks, releasing responsibility, and developing leaders who in turn reproduce themselves. The goal is to help student ministers equip a growing group of adult and student leaders to share ministry.

Chapter five touches on leadership in describing the student minister's relationship with the student ministry team. It includes a conversation about spiritual gifts and how each member of the church is called to serve a function in the body of Christ. It describes how student ministers should work with the congregation, staff and church leaders, parents, adult leaders, and student leaders to fulfill their mission.

We then shift our focus from the student ministry to the students. Chapter six provides helpful information regarding adolescent development such as the physical and mental changes students are experiencing, how family and peers influence their development, and some practical steps youth ministries can take to help teens navigate these changes and challenges.

Chapter seven defines the terms *culture* and *subculture* and explores the cultural norms of teenagers around the world. It offers guidance on how youth ministries can use the knowledge of youth culture to reach students for Christ.

Chapter eight explores the relationship between student ministry and the family, and it unpacks how the family relates to redemption's biblical metanarrative. It proposes that the family is the appropriate context for discipleship and offers invaluable instruction on how youth ministries can support and supplement the family's role in discipleship.

In chapter nine, the dialogue shifts from the family to the practical application of student ministry. We explore how evangelism relates to student ministry. This chapter unpacks how students must understand what biblical evangelism is, and it presents practical steps to help students know how to do it.

As evangelism and discipleship are the two sides of the same coin, it follows that a discussion of evangelism should be followed by one on discipleship. Chapter ten studies Jesus's command to make disciples and then explains what disciple-making is and how it's done.

The final chapters of the book begin a transition into the future. In chapter eleven, we discuss the relationship between student ministry and technology. This chapter explores the question of whether introducing technology into the student ministry will benefit or harm students. It includes a conversation regarding the relationship between identity, technology, and intimacy in students' lives along with suggestions for implementing technology in the student ministry strategy.

Chapter twelve predicts that student ministry's future will involve addressing weaknesses in current student ministry by emphasizing relationships regarding salvation, biblical teaching, and mobilizing students for missions. In light of these predictions, chapter twelve then provides student ministers with the means for evaluating their current student ministry strategy so they're equipped to make the changes necessary to engage what the future will bring.

Our concluding chapter outlines student ministry philosophy and strategy development. It explains the philosophy's elements of mission, core values, vision, and strategy. The chapter describes how student ministers can use each chapter in this book to help develop their strategy. It also reviews how the student minister, parents, adult leaders, and student leaders relate to the plan.

Two appendices then follow. The first appendix explores how catechism classes and other age-organized ministries throughout church history offer a strong precedent for age-organized gatherings of youth in the church. This discussion counters critics of student ministry who argue that youth's age-organized classes are a recent innovation in the church. The second appendix discusses the relationship between student ministry and parachurch ministries. It describes how parachurch ministries can help student ministers grow student leaders who can then help them implement their student ministry strategy in the church.

The chapters in this book as well as the appendices are written by student ministry veterans who are voices of wisdom and encouragement, and they can help you navigate student ministry in your respective context. If you listen to these voices and apply what they tell you, it will help you on your journey.

Are you ready to start? Let's go!

Biblical and Theological Foundations for Student Ministry

• TIM McKNIGHT •

I looked down at the luminescent dashes and digits of my army-issued lensatic compass. Rain clouds obscured the moonlight, and it started to drizzle on our heads. My group consisted of students at the Army Chaplain's School and Center conducting a night land-navigation course they needed to pass in order to graduate. We had completed the day land-navigation course earlier that afternoon. Now our task consisted of using a map, compass, and a list of bearings to find five license plates nailed to five trees somewhere in the vast forest at Fort Dix, New Jersey.

In the daytime, we had found that even if we strayed somewhat from the compass bearing, we might arrive closely enough to the tree to still see the license plate nailed to it. Night navigation was not so forgiving. We did not have the benefit of seeing the plate from a distance if we strayed off course. To avoid missing the license plate, we had to frequently check our compasses. The term we used for checking the compass frequently was "checking your azimuth." It was imperative that we check our azimuth frequently to stay on course during the night land-navigation exercise.

Biblical Foundations for Student Ministry

Checking our azimuth reminds me of the role that God's Word plays in student ministry. Before I would rely on my azimuth to point me to the desired destination, I had to be confident in my compass. Was it accurate and reliable? Was it calibrated to true north? Could I consider my compass trustworthy?

Before we turn to Scripture as our authority and foundation for student ministry, we must first believe that the Bible is reliable, trustworthy, and authoritative. Why should we consider the Bible our authority in the Christian life and student ministry? How do we know that Scripture is trustworthy? We must first answer such questions before we will consider Scripture our authority for student ministry and a foundation upon which we can build such ministry. These questions relate to the realm that theologians call "the revelation and authority of Scripture."

Biblical Revelation and Authority

The Bible is authoritative because it is the Word of God. In Paul's letter to Timothy, he wrote, "All Scripture is inspired by God and is profitable for teaching, for rebuking, for correcting, for training in righteousness, so that the man of God may be complete, equipped for every good work" (2 Tim 3:16–17). The Greek word for "inspired" in this passage is *theopneustos*. It means "God-breathed." Paul claimed that the Holy Spirit breathed out the words of Scripture through the biblical authors. Church historian Geoffrey Bromiley wrote the following in regard to how the early church fathers saw the relationship between the inspiration and authority of Scripture:

> As the Word of God given by the Spirit of God, Scripture had for the Fathers the status of a primary authority in the life, teaching, and mission of the church. Deriving from God and enshrining the truth of God, it had indeed the authority of God himself. This applied to the Old Testament in virtue of its prophetic testimony to the Christ who was still to come. It applied to the New Testament in virtue of its apostolic witness to the Christ who had already come in fulfillment of the promises.[1]

Through Scripture, God reveals who he is, through the Old Testament, culminating in the miraculous incarnation of Jesus in the New Testament. He unfolds his plan to redeem humankind from the beginning of creation in Genesis to the return of Christ in Revelation. The written Word introduces the incarnate Word through the witnesses of the Gospels. We see the good news of the gospel regarding the life, death, resurrection, ascension, and second coming of Jesus Christ in the words of the New Testament. Only through the Bible can we begin to learn who God is and how we might be reconciled to him through the gospel of Jesus Christ.

---

[1] Geoffrey W. Bromiley, "The Church Fathers and Holy Scripture," in *Scripture and Truth*, eds. D. A. Carson and John D. Woodbridge (Grand Rapids, MI: Baker Books, 1992), 207.

Because Scripture is God's Word, it bears his authority. If we follow Jesus Christ as Lord, we will seek to apply his Word to our lives. Christ-followers should submit to Scripture in all matters of faith and life. The Bible is the source of authority for believers. As such, all ministries of the church, including student ministry, are founded on the authority of Scripture.[2]

Although the Word of God is more than a compass, the Bible does provide direction for believers and churches. If we are going to navigate student ministry well, we must look to our compass to guide us in the right direction. With that in mind, what is the biblical foundation for student ministry?

Foundations in Deuteronomy

Listen, Israel: The LORD our God, the LORD is one. Love the LORD your God with all your heart, with all your soul, and with all your strength. These words that I am giving you today are to be in your heart. Repeat them to your children. Talk about them when you sit in your house and when you walk along the road, when you lie down and when you get up. Bind them as a sign on your hand and let them be a symbol on your forehead. Write them on the doorposts of your house and on your city gates. Deut 6:4–9

This passage of Scripture begins with the *Shema,* Israel's declaration of faith, which identified Israelites as God's chosen people and differentiated them from their surrounding polytheistic neighbors. In reciting the *Shema,* the people of Israel acknowledged the sovereignty of Yahweh over their lives. Through this confession, they remembered

---

[2] For an excellent discussion of revelation and authority, see D. A. Carson and John D. Woodbridge, eds., *Scripture and Truth* (Grand Rapids, MI: Baker Books, 1992); and Carl F. H. Henry, ed., *Revelation and the Bible: Contemporary Evangelical Thought* (Grand Rapids, MI: Baker Books, 1958).

who God is and the ways he sovereignly worked on their behalf. In turn, through the inspiration of the Holy Spirit, Moses charged them to love God for who he is and for what he has done.

Regarding this passage, Michael McGarry, in his book *A Biblical Theology of Youth Ministry*, writes, "God's people ought to be marked by love: love of God that is so life-transforming others are loved more than oneself. In the same way that Israel embraced the Shema as their identity marker, Christians live according to the gospel of grace."[3] There is a biblical foundation for student ministry in the call of this passage for parents and the faith community to help students love God with their hearts and souls.

Moses admonished the assembly of Israelites to teach the accounts he shared with them regarding God's faithful provision on behalf of the people of Israel to the next generation. Notably, he called for Hebrew parents to teach their children who God is and what he has done with the goal of their loving God and placing their faith in him.[4] The responsibilities and goals of teaching given to parents in this passage make clear that a biblical student

---

[3] Michael McGarry, *A Biblical Theology of Youth Ministry* (Nashville: Randall House Publications, 2019), 22–23.

[4] Regarding Moses's admonishment to parents, Old Testament scholar J. A. Thompson writes, "The demand of love toward God implies all other demands, and the disposition of love toward God implies the disposition both to obey his commandments and to impart these to the children of the following generations, so as to maintain an attitude of love and obedience among the people of God from age to age (7a, 20ff). The book of Deuteronomy attaches a special importance to this task of teaching the family (4:9b; 6:20–25; 11:19). But the demands of Yahweh's covenant are to be the subject of conversation at all times in the home, by the way, by night and by day. Israel is to *teach them diligently, talk of them constantly, bind them as a sign* on various parts of the body, and *write them*. God's love and his covenant demands were to be the central and absorbing interest of a man's whole life." J. A. Thompson, *Deuteronomy*, Tyndale Old Testament Commentaries, ed. D. J. Wiseman (Downers Grove, IL: InterVarsity Press, 1974), 123.

ministry must involve parents as the primary disciplers of their students. Deuteronomy 6:4–9 clearly teaches that parents are primarily responsible to lead the next generation to love God, remember him, and keep his commandments. Biblical student ministry must, therefore, involve parents.

Biblical student ministry also involves the church, student pastors, and adult student leaders. Moses spoke those words of admonishment to the entire faith assembly of Israel, not just to parents. The entire faith body of Israel carried the responsibility of passing on a love for God and his commandments to the next generation. The Levites, leaders in the faith community, helped parents to teach their children the commands of Yahweh. The people of faith shared in their responsibility to raise children of faith.

Such an admonishment to the community of faith in Moses's time provides a biblical foundation for the conviction that the church is responsible for helping parents teach their students to love God and keep his commandments. Pastors, student pastors, and adult student leaders should come alongside parents and help them to disciple their students. Some students in our churches do not have parents who believe in God and follow Christ. Adults in the church are responsible to teach those students to love God and follow his Word.[5] Like the Levites, church leaders, including student ministers, should shepherd their students through teaching the Word of God and nurturing them in the faith.

These words from Moses to parents and the faith community of Israel regarding passing on a love for God and faith in Yahweh to Israel's covenant children help lay a biblical foundation for student

---

[5] I chose here to focus on Deuteronomy; however, there are also examples from the New Testament in Titus 2 and Ephesians 4 that refer to the role of adults in the church in discipling younger believers.

ministry. They call families and the family of God to raise children who love the Lord and keep his commandments. As Christ-followers, however, we know that this covenant will foreshadow a new covenant that Jesus Christ will establish.

Foundations in Matthew

The eleven disciples traveled to Galilee, to the mountain where Jesus had directed them. When they saw him, they worshiped, but some doubted. Jesus came near and said to them, "All authority has been given to me in heaven and on earth. Go, therefore, and make disciples of all nations, baptizing them in the name of the Father and of the Son and of the Holy Spirit, teaching them to observe everything I have commanded you. And remember, I am with you always, to the end of the age." Matt 28:16–20

People place great weight upon their last words spoken at the end of their time on this earth. Jesus is no different. In this passage of Scripture, he met the disciples back where his ministry began in Galilee. During this last meeting with them, Jesus fulfilled the promise he made to them when they started following Him, "'Follow me,' he told them, 'and I will make you fish for people'" (Matt 4:19). His final words to them showed them what he meant by this promise.

First, in this passage, we see that the Great Commission is based on the authority of Jesus Christ (28:18). Jesus is the sovereign Lord through whom all things were created (John 1:1–4; Col 1:16–17). As Lord of all heaven and earth, Jesus's authority extends over the object of this command—his disciples, which include students, parents, and church leaders. The Great Commission given to the disciples on that day still applies to every Christ-follower today.

The scope of the Great Commission also relates to student ministry. It calls Christ-followers to make disciples of *panta ta ethne*—"all nations" (Matt 28:19). Jesus wants his followers to reach people from every ethnic group and every generation with the gospel. Students across the world fit easily within this scope. According to the United Nations Population Fund, there are 1.8 billion people who are between ten and twenty-four years old.[6] This comprises 23 percent of the world's population. These students need to hear the life-changing gospel and become followers of Jesus Christ.

There is only one imperative in this command from Jesus: "make disciples." The words we translate as "go," "baptizing," and "teaching" are all participles in the original language. A rough translation of the imperative and participles in the passage would read "as you are going," "make disciples," "baptizing," and "teaching."[7] The point is this: Christ-followers are to make disciples as they are going about their daily life. While they are at work, school, or home, or are performing tasks in their communities, Jesus calls them to make disciples. Disciple-making should be a part of their everyday lives. For the purpose of our focus, parents should disciple their students as they are going about their daily and weekly routines. Student pastors and church leaders should come alongside families and help them disciple their teenagers. If there are any teens who do not have believing parents, then the student ministers and leaders in the church must evangelize and disciple them.

---

[6] United Nations Population Fund, "Adolescent and Youth Demographics: A Brief Overview," accessed October 17, 2020, https://www.unfpa.org/sites/default/files/resource-pdf/One%20pager%20on%20youth%20demographics%20GF.pdf.

[7] For reference to the commentaries, I used to study this passage. For more commentary, I recommend Craig L. Blomberg, *Matthew*, The New American Commentary, vol. 22, ed. David S. Dockery (Nashville: Broadman Press, 1992); D. A. Carson, *Matthew* in *The Expositor's Bible Commentary*, vol. 8, ed. Frank E. Gaebelein (Grand Rapids, MI: Zondveran, 1984); R. T. France, *Matthew*, Tyndale New Testament Commentaries, vol. 1 (Grand Rapids, MI: Eerdmans, 1985).

This focus on the church relates to Jesus's mention of baptism in his description of the disciple-making process in this passage. Baptism implies that the individual has already become a disciple through repentance and faith. A peer, parent, or student ministry leader shared the gospel with the student, and he or she began, through repentance and faith, the life of a disciple. The next step for this new believer is to make his or her faith in Christ public by following Christ's example and being baptized. As one who maintains believer's baptism, I hold that baptism unites the new disciple into the local church. In their public profession of faith through baptism, Christ-followers are identifying with a local congregation. The congregation, in turn, is affirming this believer's confession of faith as legitimate and commits to helping the new believer grow in Christ as the scriptural phrase in the first sentence of the next paragraph shows.

This emphasis on spiritual growth relates to Jesus's admonition for disciple-makers, "teaching them to observe everything I have commanded you" (Matt 28:20). Notice that he did not say, "teaching them everything I have commanded you." Disciple-making is not merely leading students to make a "decision" for Christ through the presentation of the gospel. It is not just an information dump of biblical knowledge and facts. It involves showing, through teaching and example, how to live the life of the disciple; how "to observe everything [he has] commanded" (28:20). In student ministry, we want parents, student ministers, adult leaders, and peers to instruct by teaching and to show by example how new believers should apply the Word of God to their lives and follow Jesus. Student ministry leaders must help parents disciple their students this way. For students who do not have believing parents, student ministers and adult leaders must act as spiritual parents of sorts and provide the teaching and example for these students to follow. We are not satisfied with teenagers merely trusting in the grace of Jesus, but also helping them live in obedience to the commands of Jesus.

Darren DePaul, student ministry practitioner and author, is correct in his assertion, "Here is my basic, biblical assumption: *the primary role of the youth pastor and the student ministry in the local church is to make disciples of Jesus Christ.*"[8] We can only claim that we have made a disciple when we see the new believer, in turn, making disciples.[9] At that point, we can say that we have taught them to observe Jesus's commands—including the Great Commission.

The Great Commission's call to make disciples applies to students in cultures around the globe. This call to disciple-making forms a foundation for student ministry that seeks to come alongside parents to help them lead their children to Christ and disciple them in hopes that they would learn the ways of Christ and join the church in the Great Commission's work of making more disciples.

Foundations in 1 Corinthians

Although I am free from all and not anyone's slave, I have made myself a slave to everyone, in order to win more people. To the Jews I became like a Jew, to win Jews; to those under the law, like one under the law—though I myself am not under the law—to win those under the law. To those who are without the law, like one without the law—though I am not without

---

[8] Darren DePaul, "Making Disciples Who Make Disciples" in *Gospel-Centered Youth Ministry*, eds. Cameron Cole and Jon Nielson (Wheaton, IL: Crossway, 2016), 39.

[9] Regarding the relationship between evangelism and discipleship, Craig Blomberg writes, "Evangelism must be holistic. If non-Christians are not hearing the Gospel and not being challenged to make a decision for Christ, then the church has disobeyed one part of Jesus's commission. If new converts are not faithfully and lovingly nurtured in the whole counsel of God's revelation, then the church has disobeyed the other part." Blomberg, *Matthew*, 433.

God's law but under the law of Christ—to win those without the law.
To the weak I became weak, in order to win the weak. I have become all
things to all people, so that I may by every possible means save some. Now
I do all this because of the gospel, so that I may share in the blessings. 1
Cor 9:19–23

In this passage from Paul's letter to the church in Corinth, we see
a glimpse into his strategy of missions and evangelism. He was willing to build bridges to the people with whom he shared the gospel by
adopting particular cultural characteristics through which he could
communicate the gospel message. He never changed the message but
expressed a willingness to change his methods to fit his cultural context. Missiologists call this method of using cultural characteristics as
means through which one can communicate the "gospel contextualization." Missiologist Daniel R. Sanchez writes:

> Contextualization can be defined as making concepts and
> methods relevant to a historical situation. From this definition,
> missiological contextualization can be viewed as enabling the
> message of God's redeeming love in Jesus Christ to become
> alive as it addresses the vital issues of a sociocultural context
> and transforms its worldview, its values, and its goals.[10]

We see a great example of contextualization in Paul's encounter
with the philosophers on the Areopagus in Athens.[11] He engaged
the group of philosophers who gathered there daily to share the good
news of the resurrection with them. In his conversation with them,
Paul made reference to an altar to an unknown god that stood on the

---

[10] Daniel R. Sanchez, "Contextualization and the Missionary Endeavor,"
in *Missiology*, ed. John Mark Terry (Nashville: B&H Publishing Group,
2015), 281.

[11] John B. Polhill, *Acts*, The New American Commentary, vol. 26, ed.
David S. Dockery (Nashville: Broadman Press, 1992), 365–78.

grounds of Mars Hill (Acts 17:23). He used this religious symbol as a means to segue to a presentation about the God of Scripture. In addition to this cultural/religious reference, Paul also quoted from Greek philosophy to build a bridge for the gospel in his conversation with them (Acts 17:28). The apostle used both aspects from Greek culture (religious idols and Greek philosophy) to place the gospel into their context.

Notice that Paul did not advocate changing the message of the gospel, either in his letter to the church in Corinth or in his encounter with the philosophers in Athens. Through contextualization, he built bridges to the culture he engaged over which the gospel could travel. Although he quoted Greek philosophy in his encounter at the Areopagus, Paul did so to introduce the news of the resurrection of Jesus Christ. We know he did not sacrifice the content of the gospel because of the philosophers' response to this aspect of the gospel. Regarding this response, Luke recorded, "When they heard about the resurrection of the dead, some began to ridicule him, but others said, 'We'd like to hear from you again about this'" (Acts 17:32).

This biblical model of contextualization forms a key foundation for student ministry. Students throughout the world have their own subcultures within their cultures. They possess their own language, dress, music, means of communication, etc. Student ministry exists as a means to follow Paul's example of adapting methods and means to carry the gospel to a particular culture. Student ministers and church leaders study teenage culture to build bridges over which the gospel can travel to that culture. Biblical student ministry does not change the message of the gospel to reach teenagers. It simply contextualizes the gospel, as Paul exercised and advocated, to reach students with the saving message of Jesus Christ. Regarding this focus on reaching teenagers with the good news of the gospel, Cameron Cole rightly asserts, "The proclamation of the gospel constitutes one of the most

pivotal functions of youth ministry."[12] Biblical contextualization provides student ministry a means to proclaim the gospel in ways that
students understand.

The Biblical Metanarrative of the Gospel

The biblical metanarrative, or overarching story of the gospel, also
forms a foundation for student ministry. This narrative delineates
God's mission of the redemption of humanity—the *missio Dei*, the
mission of God. Regarding the metanarrative of Scripture, missiologist Christopher Wright writes:

> This has often been presented as a four-point narrative: *cre-
> ation, fall, redemption,* and *future hope.* This whole worldview
> is predicated on teleological monotheism: that is, the affir-
> mation that there is one God at work in the universe and
> in human history, and that this God has a goal, a purpose, a
> mission that will ultimately be accomplished by the power
> of God's Word and for the glory of God's name. This is the
> mission of the biblical God.[13]

This metanarrative begins with Creation. God created human
beings in his image (Gen 1:26–27). Men and women have inherent
value because they bear the image of God (*imago Dei*). Teenagers
as well are image-bearers. Like every human being, God creates
teenagers "remarkably and wondrously" in their mothers' wombs

---

[12] Cameron Cole, "The Gospel at the Heart of All Things," in *Gospel-
Centered Youth Ministry*, eds. Cameron Cole and Jon Nielson (Wheaton, IL:
Crossway, 2016), 33.

[13] Christopher J. H. Wright, *The Mission of God: Unlocking the Bible's
Grand Narrative* (Downers Grove, IL: InterVarsity Press, 2006), 64.

(Ps 139:14). God creates every human being to have a relationship with him.

Human beings' problem is the fall. Adam and Eve disobeyed God because they wanted to be like him (Genesis 3). The fall brought death to creation and the human race. As a result of the fall, every human being is also born with a sin nature (Rom 5:12–21). Left in our sin, humans are dead spiritually, followers of Satan, and under God's wrath (Eph 2:1–3). By nature, we want to rebel against the God who created us. In our sin, we justly deserve God's eternal condemnation and punishment; therefore, apart from Christ, we would suffer eternal punishment for our sin (Matt 25:41, 46; 2 Thess 1:9).

However, God does not leave humans in their sin but provides a way of redemption through his Son, Jesus Christ. Jesus Christ was fully human and fully divine (John 1:1–14). God sent Christ to live a perfect life in our place that we could not live and to die a death in our place that we deserve (Matt 5:17–20; Heb 4:15; 1 John 2:1–2). He sent Jesus to save people from all over the world from their sins (John 3:16; 1 John 2:1–2). Jesus paid the ransom for the sins of those who would believe in him through his blood shed on the cross (Matt 20:28; Acts 20:28; Eph 1:7; Col 1:13–14). On the cross, Jesus willingly and lovingly bore the wrath of God for our sin on our behalf (Isa 53:10–11; Gal 3:13). God satisfied his demand for justice over our sin by sacrificing his only Son in our place (Rom 3:21–26). After Jesus's death, his followers buried him in a tomb. He rose from the dead, showing that he was whom he claimed to be—God in flesh (Matt 12:28–40; Rom 1:1–4; 1 Cor 15:12–19). Christ then ascended into heaven, where he intercedes to the Father on behalf of the saints (Rom 8:34; Heb 7:23–28). Jesus left his followers to share the message of his life and work to people around them and make disciples (the Great Commission). Now, Jesus's message is that anyone who repents of their sins and trusts in him as Lord will experience salvation, redemption, forgiveness of their sins (Rom 10:9–13), and eternal life. These followers of Jesus also look forward to his return.

The final part of the metanarrative is the consummation of the kingdom. Jesus Christ will return to earth to raise the dead, both righteous (to glorified bodies; 2 Cor 15:2) and unrighteous, for the final judgment. At the judgment, Jesus Christ will hold everyone to account for their lives. People who know Christ by following him through repentance and faith will receive their eternal reward for the faithful lives they lived, enter into the joy of their salvation, and reign with him over a new heaven and a new earth (Matt 25:23; 1 Cor 3:14; 2 Cor 5:10; 2 Tim 4:8; Rev 5:9–10; 7:15–17; 21:1–5; 22:3). Regarding the resurrected dead who are not Christ-followers, the Bible states that, during the judgment, they are thrown into the lake of fire, a place of eternal suffering, along with Death, Hades, and Satan (Rev 20:10–15). At the consummation of his kingdom, Christ raises his church to reign with him forever and vanquishes evil.

Students, along with every human being, play a part in this metanarrative of the gospel. They are created in the image of God and to have a relationship with him. Like everyone else, students bear a sin nature that leads them to worship themselves rather than God and places them at enmity with him. Christ lived a perfect life and died a sacrificial death in place of teenagers. Any student who repents and believes in the Lord Jesus Christ can become one of his followers. As Christ-followers, students can look forward to the hope that Christ will return, raise them from the dead with glorified bodies, reclaim his church, vanquish evil and death, and live eternally in relationship with them as they reign over a new heaven and a new earth. In short, students need to hear the gospel and how the metanarrative of God's redemptive work in Scripture relates to their lives.

Summarizing the Biblical Foundations for Student Ministry

The Bible provides a foundation for the existence and practice of student ministry. God's covenant with the people of Israel in the Old Testament admonishes parents and Israel's faith community to pass on faith in God and knowledge of his character and work to the next generation. The Great Commission admonishes Christ-followers, including parents and church leaders, to make disciples of all peoples, including teenagers, who live with trust in and obedience to Jesus. Paul's words and example regarding contextualization of the gospel provide biblical support for student ministry. Finally, the metanarrative of the gospel throughout the Bible applies to students as it helps them see their place within the rescue story of God.

Hermeneutical and Theological Foundations for Student Ministry

Having established some of the biblical foundations for student ministry, it is essential that we also establish our student ministries upon a sound interpretation of Scripture and sound theology. Biblical interpretation and theology form the principles upon which we build our student ministry. If either is weak, we will develop unhealthy or unbiblical student ministries.

Hermeneutics and Student Ministry[14]

In his letter to the young pastor Timothy, the apostle Paul admonished, "Be diligent to present yourself to God as one approved, a

---

[14] The scope of this chapter does not allow for an exhaustive treatment of the subject of hermeneutics. An excellent resource to introduce youth leaders,

worker who doesn't need to be ashamed, correctly teaching the word of truth" (2 Tim 2:15). He stressed the importance of working hard to interpret Scripture rightly. Timothy's interpretation of Scripture would have a direct impact on his teaching and preaching, and the same is true for those ministering to students. Student ministers and leaders must possess keen hermeneutical skills and equip their parents, leaders, and students to develop a sound interpretation.

What does hermeneutics mean? Biblical hermeneutics refers to the exercise and discipline of biblical interpretation. Describing the components of hermeneutics, New Testament scholar Robert Stein writes, "These three components are the *Author*, the *Text*, and the *Reader*, or, as linguistics tend to say, the *Encoder*, the *Code*, and the *Decoder*."[15] In hermeneutics, we ask: Who was the author of this book/passage of Scripture? What was the author's intent for writing the passage? When did the author write the book? What is the genre of the passage (historical, poetic, apocalyptic, prophetic, wisdom)? What does the passage mean? What is the linguistic structure of the passage? What are the keywords in the passage? How does this passage fit into the overall context of the book/Bible? Who was the audience for this passage? What was their context? What did the passage mean to its original audience? All of these questions relate to biblical hermeneutics.

Student ministries need student pastors who possess strong hermeneutical skills. If given the opportunity, ministers in student

---

parents, and students to biblical interpretation is Matt Rogers's and Donny Mathis's *Seven Arrows: Aiming Bible Readers in the Right Direction* (Spring Hill, TN: Rainer Publishing, 2017). An excellent introduction to hermeneutics for college and seminary students is Robert H. Stein's *A Basic Guide to Interpreting the Bible: Playing by the Rules* (Grand Rapids, MI: Baker Books, 1994).

[15] Stein, 18.

ministry should learn the biblical languages. They should study hermeneutics in a formal setting under teachers well versed in the discipline. Such student pastors will possess more tools to equip their adult leaders, parents, and students to become interpreters of the Bible who rightly divide God's Word.

Theology and Student Ministry

Hermeneutics is crucial because it focuses on the right interpretation of the revelation of God in Scripture. As mentioned previously, God reveals himself in the incarnate Word, who is Jesus Christ, and in God's written Word—the Bible. Theology focuses on the study of God. It involves using Scripture as our source of authority to understand who God is and what he does. The study of theology helps us to understand various aspects of the gospel of Jesus Christ. This chapter's scope does not allow for an exhaustive treatment of every theological doctrine or facet related to student ministry.[16] This section simply provides an overview of the various types of theology that student ministers may utilize to formulate a robust theological foundation for student ministry.

---

[16] There are some excellent books on theology available to people involved in student ministry. For an introduction to biblical theology accessible to adult leaders and students, I recommend Graeme Goldsworthy, *According to Plan: The Unfolding of God in the Bible* (Downers Grove, IL: InterVarsity Press, 1991). For an introduction to systematic theology, see Wayne Grudem, *Bible Doctrine: Essential Teachings of the Christian Faith* (Grand Rapids, MI: Zondervan Academic, 1999). For systematic theologies written for college and seminary students, see Daniel Akin, *A Theology for the Church* (Nashville: B&H Academic, 2007); Louis Berkhof, *Systematic Theology* (Carlisle, PA: The Banner of Truth Trust, 2003); Herman Hoeksema, *Reformed Dogmatics* (Grand Rapids, MI: Reformed Free Publishing Association, 1966); and Robert Reymond, *A New Systematic Theology of the Christian Faith* (Nashville: Thomas Nelson Publishers, 1998).

Biblical theology concentrates on the progressive revelation of God throughout Scripture. Theologian Wayne Grudem defines biblical theology, stating, "Biblical theology gives special attention to the teachings of *individual authors and sections* of Scripture, and to the place of each teaching in the *historical development* of Scripture."[17] The focus of this discipline of theology is on doctrines within the context of a particular passage or book of Scripture. For example, biblical theologians might study how the doctrine of God develops in the book of Exodus. At the same time, biblical theology also looks at the metanarrative of Scripture and how doctrines progress through the Bible. Biblical theology lays the foundation for systematic theology.

Systematic theology categorizes theology by doctrine. It takes the doctrine first, then focuses on how the entire Bible relates to that particular doctrine. For example, systematic theologians might study the doctrine of sin and list passages from the Old and New Testament that relate to particular aspects of that doctrine. Systematic theology is helpful because its doctrinal focus allows Christians to see what the whole Bible teaches about a particular subject. There is a rich history of systematic theologians from which student ministers and leaders can draw to help them build a solid theological foundation for their ministries and their students.

Practical or pastoral theology has to do with how doctrine relates to the everyday lives of students and their families. Theologian Graeme Goldsworthy writes, "Pastoral theology occupies itself with the way the Word of God touches people where they are and in whatever condition they are. It is concerned with the practical

---

[17] Wayne Grudem, *Systematic Theology: An Introduction to Biblical Doctrine* (Grand Rapids, MI: Zondervan, 2000), 22.

application of the gospel to Christians in every aspect of their life."[18]
Through such application of theology, student ministers help students and their families understand how the rich doctrines related
to the gospel relate to their everyday lives. Pastoral theology helps
ministers to shepherd their students through the hardships and
challenges they face.[19]

Conclusion

There is a clear biblical foundation for student ministry involving parents and the faith community in both the Old and New Testaments.
Biblical interpretation and robust background in theology are necessary for healthy student ministry. Hermeneutics and theology impact
methodology. If the biblical and theological foundations of a student
ministry are weak, that ministry will be unhealthy and will produce
students who lack a firm foundation in doctrine. Lack of sound
theology also leads to problematic methodology. It is like using a
bad compass bearing during the land-navigation course. Failure to
refer back to the compass will lead you to stray off course. On the
other hand, when student ministers align with parents to help equip
them to disciple their students with a strong biblical and theological
grounding, student ministries will begin to produce students who
graduate with a resolute faith that will carry them into college or a
career. They refer back to their compass, the Word of God, and it
keeps their ministries and lives on course.

---

[18] Goldsworthy, *According to Plan*, 31.

[19] For excellent resources related to pastoral theology, I recommend the
Puritans. They are historically known as being physicians of the soul.

The Call to Student Ministry

• SAM TOTMAN •

What Is a Call to Ministry?

Sensing a call to ministry? Unsure? How does one know that God is calling them into ministry, and what does it mean? What are the qualifications and expectations? If God calls, what steps should the recipient take moving forward? As individuals wrestle with the call to ministry, these questions can become overwhelming. Thankfully, Scripture has much to say about the issue of calling and the questions around it.

A survey of both the Old and New Testaments offers several examples of calling, which highlight its intangible nature and the effect it has on its recipients. Common reactions of those called include feelings of confusion, fear, doubt, and more. Before one says with Isaiah, "Here I am, Lord, send me," he or she quite often must wrestle with the seemingly oppressive responsibility and challenges that lie ahead. This chapter helps students navigate the call of the student minister and how it relates to his or her call to ministry. It will include a discussion focused on the key elements involved in discerning a call to ministry. It will also describe how a call to student ministry differs from a call to other types of ministry.

Step One: Understand That No One Responds to God's Calling the Same

The first step in navigating one's call to student ministry is to think about where they are in life. Recognizing the call of God can leave one in a precarious position. Perhaps the individual already has a plan and direction for his or her future. When the spirit of God begins to put those plans into question, one can lose that sense of direction. Experiencing lostness is disorienting. The world that once felt familiar now no longer makes sense. Unresolved fear and doubt can evolve into panic, leaving one paralyzed to make the best decision.

When the Israelites found themselves in the grip of their oppressors, they would often cry out to God for direction. In one such instance, the Midianites were pressing in on Israel, consuming their crops and attacking their people, leaving God's people poverty-stricken. Like the rest of the Israelites, Gideon had a plan. Stay out of sight. Hide. One evening, God spoke into his hiding place—"The Lord is with you, valiant warrior" (Judg 6:12). For anyone else this affirmative title might fit, but for Gideon it made no sense and only raised more questions. How could he be a "valiant warrior" if he is hiding in a ditch from the enemy? "Go in the strength you have," the Lord continued, "and deliver Israel from the grasp of Midian. I am sending you!" (Judg 6:14). Gideon had no sense of direction because he was lost, directionless, paralyzed by his fear. Why would

God send him? Where was he sending him? One can only imagine the thoughts that went through his mind at that moment.

God's call can come in the darkest moments of one's life when one least expects it. This disorienting experience leaves some spinning, struggling to find their starting point. If there is a lesson to be learned from Israel, it is to cry out to God in prayer and ask for direction when one feels lost. Fortunately, the Spirit of God directs God's people and empowers them to accomplish the tasks God sets before them.

Step Two: Understand Different Callings God Gives

The calling of God begins with the call to salvation. As Matthew Barrett explained, this involves two calls: the gospel call and the effectual call of God.[1] In the gospel call, God calls all people to repent and turn away from sin and trust in the life, death, and resurrection of Jesus Christ.[2] God so loved the world that he sacrificed his only son, so that anyone who placed their trust in him would not spend eternity apart from him but instead live eternally in fellowship with him in heaven (John 3:16). The call of the gospel is offered to all people and can be accepted or rejected. The effectual call, on the other hand, is the call of God given to the elect. It is based purely on the righteous and wise will of God and not on man's good character, works, or intentions, lest anyone should have any reason to boast.[3] While many may resist and reject the gospel call, the effectual call of God transforms a person's heart, whereby they possess a holy inclination to seek, love, and follow the Lord in joyful obedience. Apart from

---

[1] Matthew Barrett, "Effectual Calling," n.d., https://www.thegospel coalition.org/essay/effectual-calling/

[2] 2 Cor 7:10; Matt 11:28.

[3] Barrett, "Effectual Calling"; see John 6:44; Rom 8:28–30; Eph 2:8–9.

saving faith that comes from the effectual call of God, no individual will ever desire to please God or live in right fellowship with him.

One of the most disturbing passages in all of Scripture is Matt 7:21–23, which states, "Not everyone who says to me, 'Lord, Lord,' will enter the kingdom of heaven, but only the one who does the will of my Father in heaven. On that day many will say to me, 'Lord, Lord, didn't we prophesy in your name, drive out demons in your name, and do many miracles in your name?' Then I will announce to them, 'I never knew you. Depart from me, you lawbreakers!'" Notice the great deeds these individuals referenced: prophesying, driving out demons, and performing miracles. By any standards, these actions qualify as ministry, and yet God took no pleasure in any of it. They said all the right words: "Lord, Lord!" They looked the part, prophesying, driving out demons, performing miracles. Today, one might highlight preaching, teaching, making hospital visits, generally serving others, and yet, apart from a saving relationship with Jesus Christ, no one can please God. Before one can answer the call to ministry, he or she must first answer the call to salvation.

Step Three: God's Calling to Priesthood

Next, one must acknowledge God's call to all Christians into ministry as members of God's priesthood of believers.[4] Paul wrote in Eph 4:11–13, God provided specific individuals to train "the saints for the work of ministry, to build up the body of Christ, until we all reach unity in the faith and in the knowledge of God's Son, growing

---

[4] James M. George, "The Call to Pastoral Ministry," in *Rediscovering Pastoral Ministry: Shaping Contemporary Ministry with Biblical Mandates*, ed. John MacArthur Jr. (Dallas: Word Publishing, 1995), 103.

into maturity with a stature measured by Christ's fullness." Scripture paints a beautiful portrait of the New Testament church, not an elite group of spiritual leaders and their underlings, but a body of believers, trained and disciplined to perfectly illustrate the love and freedom found only in a loving God. Every disciple who trusts in Jesus Christ, who exalts Jesus to lord over their life, has been committed by God to a life of service. Paul wrote in Eph 2:10, "we are his workmanship, created in Christ Jesus for good works, which God prepared ahead of time for us to do." This call to service does not necessitate a vocational office in a church or ministry, but instead takes place in everyday life. Paul wrote of this everyday ministry believers are called to in Eph 4:15–16: "speaking the truth in love, let us grow in every way into him who is the head—Christ. From him the whole body, fitted and knit together by every supporting ligament, promotes the growth of the body for building itself up in love by the proper working of each individual part." Every member of God's family should actively pursue ministry as God has gifted them to do, to do their part for the proper working of God's church.

Step Four: Be Open to a Specific Call

Though God calls all people to salvation and all believers to ministry within the church, he also calls specific people to ministry. Ephesians 4:11–12 states that God "gave some to be apostles, some prophets, some evangelists, some pastors and teachers, to equip the saints for the work of ministry, to build up the body of Christ." Jesus is the head of the church, and he calls certain individuals to serve the church in special ways.

God's specific call can be made to a particular people or area of service. Paul opened many of his letters by identifying himself as an apostle set apart by the will of God.[5] Paul's call to ministry is undoubtedly unique. The trajectory of Paul's life radically changed the moment Christ first confronted him on the road to Damascus. Ironically, for God to give Paul a vision for reaching the Gentiles, God chose to remove his sight in a blinding light. One can only imagine the initial fears that ran through Ananias as the Lord shared with him that this known persecutor of Christians needed his help. Ananias did what most people naturally do when God gives them a challenging command: make God aware of the danger. "Lord, people talk about how bad this guy is. He is known to kill Christians. Those he does not kill, he puts in prison. Are you sure?" The Lord then clearly shared with Ananias Paul's new mission: to take God's name to the Gentiles, kings, and Israelites (Acts 9:13–16). In this instance, the Lord wanted Paul to seek the aid of Ananias, to find orientation, the starting point of his mission. After a brief time of preparation, in Paul's own words, "He who formerly persecuted us now preaches the faith he once tried to destroy" (Gal 1:21–24).

Paul's call to ministry was dramatic and specific, his mission clear—to extend the good news of the gospel to the uncircumcised, the gentiles. God directs specific individuals to serve a particular area, need, or people group. When God called Gideon, he called him to a particular task—to deliver Israel from Midian. Directly speaking, the call to student ministry is the specific call to serve students, though, as any experienced minister would attest, ministry in the trenches is far from simple. As other contributors to this book will confirm, a holistic approach to student ministry reaches beyond the students and takes into consideration the various connections that influence

---

[5] See Rom 1:1; 1 Cor 1:1; 2 Cor 1:1; Gal 1:1; Eph 1:1; Col 1:1; 1 Tim 1:1; 2 Tim 1:1; Titus 1:1.

their live—family, peers, and culture. Each of these areas can and will significantly impact the spiritual, social, and psychological paths of adolescents. Although Paul had a clear vision to evangelize the Gentiles, he spent the rest of his life fleshing out this calling, as will everyone whom God calls into this type of service.

Do all ministry leaders have these kinds of conversion and calling experiences? No, but as extreme as Paul's conversion and calling might seem, even Paul had questions. Surrounded by a blinding light, falling to the ground, and hearing a voice from the heavens, Paul still asked, "Lord, who are you?" So why does the call to ministry elicit questions, doubts, and concerns?[6] Perhaps Moses overreacted when God told him to take on the most powerful nation in the known world. Surely, Gideon should have known that his army of three hundred was perfectly capable of taking on ten thousand trained soldiers. Why did Samuel not know that God was speaking to him in the middle of the night? Maybe the real question is, What person in their right mind would not have problems, doubts, and concerns? To participate in the divine plan of God is an incredible privilege. Left to one's own devices, skills, and talents, who is capable of accomplishing the will of God? When God asks so much of the believer, how can he or she know for sure of their calling? Oswald Chambers noted that one's call might be similar to Paul's, a Damascus experience, or it might come gradually in time, but in every case, the process will be guided and directed by the prompting of the Spirit of God.[7] While God engages his servants in various ways, he never forsakes them to determine and accomplish his goals alone.

---

[6] See Exod 3:11; Judg 6:13; 1 Sam 13; 16:2; Jer 1:4–7; Isa 6:5.

[7] Oswald Chambers, *My Utmost for His Highest*, in *The Complete Works of Oswald Chambers* (Grand Rapids, MI: Discovery House, 2013), 828.

How Do You Know if You Are Called to Ministry?

Paul often emphasized that his role as an apostle was by the will of God and not man, but how does one go about having such confidence? How does one know the difference between the will of God and their own? Gideon proposed several tests of God to make sure God was going to follow through on his promises. Gideon's method of determining God's will is neither a positive nor prescriptive example of what we should do, but is instead a negative example that put Gideon's lack of faith on full display. Scripture provides several more productive and God-honoring ways in which one can discern the call to ministry.

Inward Passion

First, one possible indicator of God's calling is an inward passion for a particular area, need, or people group. As one reads through Paul's accounts of his missionary journeys, his love for the Gentiles becomes undeniable. Whether it is a burden for the people of southeast Asia or a group of teenagers in South Carolina, the Holy Spirit stirs the heart of the minister to such an extent that he or she sacrifices the comforts of their alternative choices and commits their life to service. This passion is an essential component of God's plan as it is one of the driving forces that undergird the strength of their resolve in the face of challenge.

In 2007, digital writers for the *Wall Street Journal* and co-producers of the D: All Things Digital Conference, Kara Swisher and Walt Mossberg hosted a panel discussion with Steve Jobs of Apple Inc. and Bill Gates of Microsoft. After their informative talk, audience members had an opportunity to ask their questions of Jobs and Gates. Rob Killion, an audience member, asked the two technology leaders what the single most valuable piece of advice they could give the audience to help them build their own companies to the stature of Apple and Microsoft. Gates answered the question saying that successful leaders were passionate leaders. Jobs reiterated the value of passion. Without passion, any rational person would give up because there are more reasons to quit than continue. Any sane person, Jobs continued, would quit because the work is too challenging, the time requirements too demanding, and opposition too oppressive. The people who had a passion for their work succeed, and the ones that did not love it, quit.[8] Both Gates and the late Jobs arguably built the two leading technology companies in the world. Paul knew the passion of which these two contemporaries spoke. Paul wrote, "I am compelled to preach—and woe to me if I do not preach the gospel!" (1 Cor 9:16). Howard Sugden and Warren Wiersbe wisely say that ministry is too demanding and challenging without a robust inward inclination of calling.[9] Erwin Lutzer wrote that ministers lacking conviction often lack courage, always carrying their resignation letter in hand, poised to leave at the first sign of conflict.[10]

Paul had plenty of reasons to give up on his mission to evangelize the Gentiles. Paul's suffering came to define his ministry. God told Ananias that Paul would experience much suffering in his name.[11] In 2 Cor 11:24–29, Paul recounts his pain. The Jews whipped him with thirty-nine lashes on each of five separate occasions. He was

---

[8] Steve Jobs and Bill Gates, interview by Kara Swisher and Tom Mackey, D: All Things Digital Conference, May 30, 2007, http://allthingsd .com/20070531/d5-gates-jobs-transcript.

[9] Howard F. Sugden and Warren W. Wiersbe, *When Pastors Wonder How* (Chicago: Moody, 1973), 9.

[10] Erwin W. Lutzer, "Still Called to the Ministry," *Moody Monthly* 83, no. 7 (March 1983), 133.

[11] Acts 9:16.

beaten with rods three different times and stoned. He experienced three shipwrecks. He faced danger from both his people as well as the people group he sought to serve. Paul endured hardship and toil, sleepless nights, and hunger. What was it that kept him going? Paul endured suffering because of his passion and love for God and the church. Paul knew everything he suffered was for the benefit of others so that God's grace could extend to as many people as possible (Acts 20:24; 2 Cor 4:15–18).

Modern-day ministers might not face the same difficulties as Paul, but they will experience their own set of challenges. Youth ministers likely trade shipwrecks for broken-down buses; and whippings, beatings, and stoning for verbal lashings from pastors, deacons, parents, and even the students they serve. If sleepless nights are not in the student minister's job description, they should be. Effective student ministers will pour out themselves to engage students and participate in God's grand plan to bring about change in their life. Ministry is difficult work that demands the minister, like Paul, have a passion for it that will strengthen them amid hardship and sustain them for the long haul. The call to ministry requires passion, but passion alone can be misleading and is not always the best indicator of God's will.

Spiritual Disciplines

One cannot rely on passion alone; he or she must buttress that passion by other means. How can one know the will of God? Romans 12:2 states, "Do not be conformed to this age, but be transformed by the renewing of your mind, so that you may discern what is the good, pleasing, and perfect will of God." How can one avoid conformity and transform their mind? In discerning God's call to ministry, Alice Cullinan noted, one cannot underestimate the value of reading

Scripture and prayer.[12] The Holy Spirit uses these spiritual disciplines to instruct the believer and reveal God's plan for his or her life. Transformation of the mind takes place as the reader engages God's Word, and the Spirit brings about conviction. Scripture provides the foundation upon which all ministry is constructed. It is the lens through which one can evaluate his or her decisions and plans.[13] Jason Allen of Midwestern Baptist Theological Seminary noted teaching and preaching the Word of God is the defining qualification of a minister regardless of the place of ministry or the office he or she holds.[14] The minister of God must be a student of the Word if he or she is to communicate the truths of the gospel effectively.

Some have tried to separate the twin tasks of shepherding and teaching, feeling that their call is simply to teach and preach and not to involve themselves in the pastoral work of ministry. Derek Prime and Alistair Begg highlight that Eph 4:11 does not allow for separation between these two essential tasks. Both are included in the role of the ministry leader.[15] Upon understanding how to shepherd the flock, Prime and Begg argue that only then can the men or women of God effectively teach and present the Word of God in a way that their people can understand and apply to their lives.[16] Therefore, as individuals follow their sense of calling, each should serve in a variety of areas to inform their decision and develop as potential ministers of God.

---

[12] Alice R. Cullinan, *Sorting It Out: Discerning God's Call to Ministry* (Valley Forge, PA: Judson Press), 29–30.

[13] Cullinan, 29.

[14] Jason K. Allen, *Discerning Your Call to Ministry: How to Know for Sure and What to Do About It* (Chicago: Moody, 2016), 22.

[15] Derek J. Prime and Alistair Begg, *On Being a Pastor: Understanding Our Calling and Work* (Chicago: Moody, 2004), 31.

[16] Prime and Begg, 32.

Additionally, people should seek God in prayer and continue to pursue his direction as they flesh out their calling. James taught, "If any of you lacks wisdom, he should ask God—who gives to all generously and ungrudgingly—and it will be given to him" (Jas 1:5). Prayer is how people commune with their God. What a great privilege a believer has that he or she can kneel before the throne of the righteous God; raise his or her questions, concerns, and doubts; and get a response.[17] The reoccurring theme throughout Scripture is that God answers the prayers of his people, especially the individuals he has called into kingdom work.

External Confirmation

The call to ministry may begin with an inner voice, but this desire should be tested and affirmed by other mature believers. Jeff Iorg wrote about three types of individuals, particularly crucial to individuals pursuing a call to ministry.[18] First, one should consider the input of spiritual leaders such as other pastors, student ministers, and small-group leaders. Since these individuals are likely to understand the spiritual implications of one's pursuit, one should listen carefully to their concerns and reservations. Second, Iorg suggested one should seek his or her family's guidance, but he qualified this suggestion noting that not everyone has a Christian family on which to lean.[19] Individuals who lack the support of believing family members can rely on the guidance of their spiritual mentors. Paul's words to Timothy are essential to note here as he referred to Timothy as his true son in the faith. He called on Timothy to remember the sincere

---

[17] 1 John 5:14–15, Ps 37:4–5.

[18] Jeff Iorg, *Is God Calling Me? Answering the Question Every Believer Asks* (Nashville: B&H, 2008), 61–63.

[19] Iorg, 62.

faith that first dwelt in his grandmother and his mother and convinced Timothy that he possessed it as well. He called on Timothy to fan into a flame the fire of God. Paul served as a spiritual father to Timothy, and now God was using Paul to equip Timothy for the challenges of ministry (1 Tim 4:14). Paul also served as a model Timothy could emulate and follow.[20] Third, Iorg noted that those who are married should consult their spouse.[21] If God has genuinely called one into ministry, he or she will have begun the process in the spouse as well. Individuals who do consider and communicate with their spouses about entering the ministry set themselves up for heartache and frustration when they deal with the inevitable conflict between their spouse's desires and their ministry's demands.

A fourth source of confirmation to seek would be one's own local church. The local church is well-suited to confirm one's ministry calling as it observes the spiritual life and ongoing ministry of the individual. Charles Spurgeon wrote, "The will of the Lord concerning pastors is made known through the prayerful judgment of his church. It is needful as a proof of your vocation that *your preaching should be acceptable to the people of God*."[22] Prime and Begg noted that as the individual becomes aware of his or her calling, the local church can come alongside the individual to recognize calling and giftedness.[23]

In Acts 13:2–3, Luke wrote, "As they were worshiping the Lord and fasting, the Holy Spirit said, 'Set apart for me Barnabas and Saul for the work to which I have called them.' Then after they had fasted, prayed, and laid hands on them, they sent them off." Several elements of this passage are essential to explore. First, the church

---

[20] 1 Tim 1:2–7, 13–14.

[21] Iorg, 63.

[22] Charles Spurgeon, *Lectures to My Students* (1875; repr., Grand Rapids, MI: Baker Books, 1980), 29.

[23] Prime and Begg, *On Being a Pastor*, 24.

leaders understood that this message was from the Holy Spirit, but they had also already observed the success of Saul's and Barnabas's service. The church was perfectly poised to send out these ministers with confidence because of their own experience and the confirmation of the Spirit.[24] Individuals exploring a call to student ministry should make that journey known to church leadership. Additionally, he or she should seek every opportunity to explore that calling in their local student ministry. Once one has made this acknowledgment, the local church should come alongside the individual and begin equipping him or her to serve in ministry effectively.

The Qualifications of the Called

When is one ready to start serving in ministry? Should he or she wait until after he or she has received proper training and send-off? Since God calls all believers to begin serving others upon conversion, then all of God's people should actively seek opportunities to minister regardless of their level of training. As they're actively serving, they'll begin to realize their own passions and gifts, and the church will have much opportunity to observe and confirm any calling they might receive. Ultimately, the local church is in the best position to help individuals determine God's call on their lives. By serving within the local church, believers can gain a deeper sense of calling for themselves that can be confirmed by the informed and loving counsel of their church family. Serving in and support from the local church will help solidify one's resolve and prepare them to face the challenges of ministry with confidence.

---

[24] Brian Croft, *Prepare Them to Shepherd: Test, Train, Affirm, and Send the Next Generation of Pastors* (Grand Rapids, MI: Zondervan, 2014), 36–37.

When Paul faced opposition, he pointed his sending as an acknowledgment of his calling. In Galatians 2, Paul could have allowed a group to continue influencing public opinion in a negative way; he could have looked the other way, but, instead, he rightfully defended his ministry. He wrote:

> they saw that I had been entrusted with the gospel for the uncircumcised, just as Peter was for the circumcised, since the one at work in Peter for an apostleship to the circumcised was also at work in me for the Gentiles. When James, Cephas, and John—those recognized as pillars—acknowledged the grace that had been given to me, they gave the right hand of fellowship to me and Barnabas, agreeing that we should go to the Gentiles and they to the circumcised. (Gal 2:7–9)

Paul anchored his resolve in recognition of the spiritual leaders who had sent Paul and the other apostles through the laying on of hands.

Paul's Qualifications to Timothy

Paul told Timothy, "If anyone aspires to be an overseer, he desires a noble work" (1 Tim 3:1). Scripture uses terms such as "overseer," "elder," and "bishop" interchangeably for the role of pastor. He then proceeds to outline for Timothy the qualifications of the overseer, which is distinct from any other position in the church. While most student ministers do not hold a pastoral office (i.e., they're not the authoritative leaders of the whole congregation), the biblical qualifications for overseers are still relevant standards. Roland Martinson once wisely commented, "The history of primarily calling inexperienced and inadequately trained young people to do youth ministry reflects the myth that youth ministry is a beginner's job that doesn't require much education, experience, or skill. Nothing could be farther from the truth."[25] Overlooking the biblical qualifications for ministerial leadership will lead to disastrous outcomes for the youth ministry and the church at large. Having a love or passion for teenagers is not enough. Paul offered more substantive qualifications for those desiring influential ministry roles, and the church would be wise to make them their own.

Student Ministers Must Have Good Standing

First, for Paul, an overseer, without question, above all other items on the list must be "above reproach" (1 Tim 3:2). Paul continued in 1 Tim 3:7, adding one's reputation was especially important regarding those outside of the church. In other words, young Timothy, people are watching. Every action one takes, every choice one makes matters. According to Croft, "above reproach" does not merely mean the minister avoids evil, but even the appearance of evil.[26] Basil Manly Jr. writes, "No amount of talent, no extent of education, no apparent brilliancy of fervor, should even be allowed to gain admission into the ministry for one whose piety there is a reason to doubt, or who has not a more than ordinarily active and consistent holiness."[27] Since one of the primary roles of youth leaders is to engage and develop deep relationships with minors, they must put in place extraordinary measures to ensure that they avoid any chance of accusation, including avoiding reputation killers such as drunkenness and impropriety.

---

[25] Cited by Mark DeVries, *Sustainable Youth Ministry: Why Most Youth Ministry Doesn't Last and What Your Church Can Do about It* (Downers Grove, IL: InterVarsity Press, 2008), 29.

[26] Croft, 46.

[27] Basil Manly, "A Call to the Ministry," accessed July 13, 2021, https://www.9marks.org/article/call-ministry/.

To avoid this, it is imperative a student minister consider personal barriers such avoiding being alone with members of the opposite gender who are not their spouse or thinking carefully about appropriate displays of affection. While some actions are not evil in and of themselves, those desiring to lead in ministry must be diligent to avoid even the appearance of evil. Student ministers must seek to be above reproach.

Student Ministers Must Have Self-Control

Next, Paul exhorts Timothy that ministers are to be self-controlled, sensible, respectable, and hospitable.[28] Knowing that self-discipline does not typically characterize youth leaders, those desiring ministry roles should live in such a way to help correct this perception.

Self-control is more than just saying no to public taboos; it means making choices that bring honor and glory to God. Filling up the baptismal with Orbeez might seem like a good idea for a social media post, but these actions are not likely to lead to prolonged tenure. Slipping the whitewater rafting guide a twenty-dollar bill to give the kids an experience they will never forget might have unintended consequences resulting only in tragedy. These types of choices, unfortunately, happen in student ministry. Careers end. Students get hurt physically, emotionally, and, worse, spiritually. Youth ministers who actively pursue opportunities to demonstrate their maturity in ministry build respect over time. Qualified leaders are individuals who have demonstrated discipline, temperance, and wisdom.

---

[28] 1 Tim 3:2.

Student Ministers Must Have Led Others Faithfully

Paul includes other qualities of a minister, including managing his household with dignity.[29] Youth ministers might or might not have a spouse or children at the stage of life in which they consider entering into the ministry. In terms of evaluation, one might need only look at how he or she treats his or her own family. Has he demonstrated a healthy respect for his parents? Does she have her family's blessing to proceed in ministry? Unfortunately, not all individuals have believing parents or even supportive parents. These exceptions aside, Paul's exhortation here seems to concern more of a demonstration of one's ability to lead. He questions, "If anyone does not know how to manage his own household, how will he take care of God's church?" (1 Tim 3:5). In this case, church leadership can provide opportunities for the individual to serve and gain experience through leading others. Regardless of family situation, these opportunities should allow the individual to demonstrate his or her ability to lead.

Student Ministers Have an Ability to Teach

Out of all the qualifications, the one attribute that stands out from the rest is the ability to teach.[30] A student minister must be able to communicate the truths of God's Word effectively. Later, Paul exhorted Timothy to "pay close attention to your life and your teaching; persevere in these things, for in doing this you will save both yourself and your hearers" (1 Tim 4:16). Further, Paul told Timothy, "I solemnly charge you before God and Christ Jesus, who is going

---

[29] 1 Tim 3:4–5.
[30] 1 Tim 3:2.

to judge the living and the dead, and because of his appearing and his kingdom: Preach the word; be ready in season and out of season; correct, rebuke, and encourage with great patience and teaching" (2 Tim 4:1–2). Paul made such an assertion to Timothy because ministers must defend against intentional or unintentional heresy. Teenagers need ministers who have a passion and ability to teach the Word of God faithfully.[31]

The Paradox of Readiness

One should note that even if he or she meets all of the qualifications for ministry, one might still feel disoriented and face doubts. James Bryant and Mac Brunson note, "You would think that the closer a man comes to God, the cleaner and holier he will feel. In fact, just the opposite is true. No serious preacher of the Gospel feels worthy of the call to preach."[32] One of the most frequent questions in Scripture upon receiving God's call goes along the lines of "Who am I that you would consider me?" When God spoke to Moses from a burning bush, Moses asked, "Who am I that I should go to Pharaoh and that I should bring the Israelites out of Egypt?" (Exod 3:11). When God called to Gideon on the threshing floor, he asked God, "How can I deliver Israel? Look, my family is the weakest in Manasseh, and I am the youngest in my father's family" (Judg 6:15). Even Paul, arguably the most exceptional leader of the first-century church, did not cast himself in such a positive light. Paul challenged Timothy to follow in his teaching, but he also acknowledged that he was an imperfect model apart from the

---

[31] Ezra 7:10.

[32] James W. Bryant and Mac Brunson, *The New Guidebook for Pastors* (Nashville: B&H Academic, 2007), 11.

grace of Christ. He wrote, "'Christ Jesus came into the world to save sinners'—and I am the worst of them. But I received mercy for this reason, so that in me, the worst of them, Christ Jesus might demonstrate his extraordinary patience as an example to those who would believe in him for eternal life" (1 Tim 1:15–16). In 1 Cor 15:9–10, Paul noted that he felt like the least of the apostles, not even worthy of being called an apostle. He never forgot his persecution of the church and his actions as before his conversion. His hope was not founded in his righteousness but in the knowledge of God's grace, and he used that understanding as a springboard for his ministry. He continued in 1 Cor 15:10, "But by the grace of God I am what I am, and his grace toward me was not in vain." Paul demonstrated how God could use and radically transform even a murderous persecutor to accomplish his divine plan. Those sensing the call to ministry may question why the Lord would choose them over all the other options available to him. As one prepares to enter the ministry, he or she might develop an acute awareness of his or her shortcomings. Possessing a biblical understanding of God's grace and mercy will help to overcome these feelings. That being said, those called to ministry have a great responsibility, more so than anyone else in the church, to demonstrate righteousness.

Next Steps

Discerning a call to ministry demands much prayer and a sensitivity to the Spirit of God. With the support and affirmation of the local church, individuals have much help available for determining God's call into vocational ministry. Chuck Fuller, from Anderson University, suggested the local church should focus on the following areas: (1) identifying character flaws that would hinder ministry, (2) determining spiritual maturity and readiness for service,

(3) discerning spiritual giftedness, (4) refining leadership skills, (5) developing preaching and communication, and (6) gaining experience in a variety of ministries.[33] As prayerful attention is given to one's inward sense and one's outward confirmation toward ministry, one is bound to gain great confidence in answering the question, "Am I called?"

---

[33] Kristopher Barnett et al., *Called: Understanding the Call to Ministry* (Anderson, SC: AUMinistry Press, 2018), 20–21.

The Life of the Student Minister

• TIM McKNIGHT •

In the chapter on biblical and theological foundations, I mentioned my experiences as a second lieutenant in the United States Army's land-navigation course. This course equips soldiers with the skills needed to accomplish their missions. When it comes down to the most critical aspect of mission completion, the public probably focuses on the sophisticated hardware that the army possesses. While there is definitely a cool factor related to military equipment and weapons, especially gear used by special operations forces, mission completion depends on the health, skills, and proficiency of the United States Army soldier—the software. If soldiers are not practicing self-care or soldier care, they cannot successfully complete the mission.

If self-care is essential on the physical battlefield, it is far more critical for followers of Jesus Christ, who fight spiritual battles every day "against the rulers, against the authorities, against the cosmic powers of this darkness, against evil, spiritual forces in the heavens" (Eph 6:12). Church leaders—in our context, student ministers—bear an even more significant burden in this struggle, as they carry the weight of leadership and the accountability of shepherding students in their ministries. When ministers fail to care for themselves, the stresses of ministry can have a devastating impact on their physical, mental, and spiritual health.

Pastors and student pastors risk burnout, health issues, family problems, and moral failure when they fail to exercise self-care. Ministry is a stressful endeavor. Student ministers have very hectic schedules. They balance expectations of church members, tasks and deadlines, communication with parents and students, study and preparation for teaching and discipling, planning and scheduling, unexpected crises, and their own personal soul care. With such pressures, it's no wonder that "75 percent of pastors report being 'extremely stressed' or 'highly stressed.'"[1] At times, the stresses of ministry can seem overwhelming. A study from Lifeway Research reveals that "48 percent of pastors agree they often feel the demands of ministry are greater than they can handle," and "54 percent of pastors agree the role of pastor is frequently overwhelming."[2]

---

[1] Bill Gaultiere, "Pastor Stress Statistics," Soul Shepherding, accessed October 27, 2020, https://www.soulshepherding.org/pastors-under-stress/.

[2] Lifeway Research, "Reasons for Attrition Among Pastors Quantitative Report Pastor Protection Research Study," Lifeway Research, accessed October 27, 2020, http://lifewayresearch.com/wp-content/uploads/2015/08/Reasons-for-Attrition-Among-Pastors-Quantitative-Report-Final1.pdf.

Unfortunately, ministers sometimes use unhealthy coping mechanisms to deal with the stresses of ministry. Some pastors and student ministers turn to pornography as a coping mechanism. The Barna Group reports, "Most pastors (57 percent) and youth pastors (64 percent) admit they have struggled with porn, either currently or in the past."[3] Some ministers reach the tragic conclusion that they cannot cope any longer and commit suicide.

All of the above statistics drive home the point that self-care is imperative for people serving in student ministry. They prompt questions such as: How do I promote my physical, emotional, and spiritual health while serving in ministry? What time-management tools should I implement to balance my time well and avoid over-commitment? What role do spiritual disciplines play in the life of the student minister? How can people serving in student ministry build positive relationships with their friends and family members? This chapter will focus on such questions and how student ministers can develop healthy lives and life habits to sustain them as they navigate student ministry.

Caring for the Whole Person

When a scribe asked Jesus about the greatest commandment, Jesus responded, "Listen, Israel! The Lord our God, the Lord is one. Love the Lord your God with all your heart, with all your soul, with all your mind, and with all your strength" (Mark 12:29–30). His answer indicates that we are multifaceted beings. This chapter's scope does not

---

[3] The Barna Group, "The Porn Phenomenon," The Barna Group, accessed October 28, 2020, https://www.barna.com/the-porn-phenomenon/#.VqZoN_krIdU.

permit an exhaustive discussion regarding the various components that make up individuals.[4] For this chapter's purposes, we will focus on the health of the body (physical and mental) and soul (spiritual).

Spiritual Health: Caring for the Soul

When I first arrived at the United States Army Chaplain Center and School, I could not run a mile. I possessed the stamina in my legs; however, I had not yet built up the lung capacity to sustain me to run that distance. I needed to train. Out of sheer discipline (I hate running), I began to run for longer times and distances. With each training session, I developed more stamina, endurance, and strength. I had to discipline myself to conduct my daily workouts to develop into a better runner.

Developing spiritual health is similar to developing physical health; it takes discipline. For this reason, the apostle Paul compared spiritual development to physical training. He wrote, "But have nothing to do with pointless and silly myths. Rather, train yourself in godliness. For the training of the body has limited benefit, but godliness is beneficial in every way, since it holds promise for the present life and also for the life to come" (1 Tim 4:7–8). The New American Standard Bible translates the word for "training" as "discipline." Much like techniques and drills that help athletes develop and grow in their strength and abilities, spiritual disciplines help believers grow in their spiritual health and maturity as they seek to follow Christ. The Puritans called the spiritual disciplines "means of grace." They are God-given means through which the Holy Spirit matures us and brings us closer to Jesus Christ. While this chapter's

---

[4] For a helpful discussion on this topic, see Grudem, *Systematic Theology*, 472–77 (see chap. 1, n. 17).

scope does not permit a full delineation of every spiritual discipline, we will examine a few that are most critical to the spiritual health of student ministers.[5]

Bible Reading/Study

Regarding the reading and study of Scripture, Christian scholar Donald Whitney writes, "No Spiritual Discipline is more important than the intake of God's Word. Nothing can substitute for it. There simply is no healthy Christian life apart from a diet of the milk and meat of Scripture."[6] Reading and studying the Bible is the primary way that we feed ourselves spiritually. In the passage mentioned previously, Paul encouraged Timothy to be "nourished by the words of the faith" (1 Tim 4:6). Without a daily diet of God's Word, we will starve and stunt our spiritual growth. Such neglect of God's Word is harmful to followers of Jesus Christ but devastating to student ministers and other such leaders in churches. God calls ministers to provide an example of a disciple for others to follow; that includes parents, adult leaders, and students. We also minister out of the overflow of our intake of God's Word. Failure to receive a steady diet of the Word of God each day produces spiritual anemia that will dry up a minister's ability to care for his or her people. You cannot give what you don't have! We need a steady diet of God's Word to maintain healthy and growing spiritual health and healthy ministries.

---

[5] There are several excellent books available on the spiritual disciplines. Two I recommend are Dallas Willard, *The Spirit of the Disciplines: Understanding How God Changes Lives* (San Francisco: HarperCollins, 1991); and Donald S. Whitney, *Spiritual Disciplines for the Christian Life* (Colorado Springs: NavPress, 2014).

[6] Whitney, *Spiritual Disciplines*, 22.

In addition to providing sustenance and growth, God's Word also helps student ministers to fight the spiritual battles they face on a daily basis. Scripture helps us to fight against temptation in our lives. David wrote about how memorizing and meditating on God's Word protects faithful followers against sin (Ps 119:11). We know that while he was in the wilderness, Jesus resisted temptation from Satan by quoting Scripture (Matt 4:1–11). Paul encouraged believers in Ephesus to put on the armor of God and to take up the Word of God as the only offensive weapon with which they could fight their spiritual battles (Eph 6:10–20). As leaders, student ministers endure focused attacks from the enemy. We must read, memorize, and meditate on the Word of God to help us to fight against evil and temptation.

One temptation we face as followers of Jesus and leaders in the church is to fall into false doctrine. A daily diet of Scripture helps us to build and retain a firm foundation on truth that protects us from drifting into or being deceived by false teaching. Paul repeatedly emphasized in his letter to Timothy the importance of studying the Word of God and Scripture's inspiration, authority, reliability, and sufficiency to protect against false doctrine and to equip disciples (2 Tim 2:15; 3:16–17; 4:1–5). We do not depend on ourselves to gain this grounding in the truth. Thankfully, Jesus left behind for us the Holy Spirit to teach us through the very Word he inspired (John 16:12–15).

Although there are other reasons for and benefits of reading and studying the Bible, the last purpose on which we will focus is that Scripture reveals God and his gospel to us. From beginning to end, the Bible is a beautiful message of who God is and how he has worked and is working his redemptive plan for humanity. In Scripture, we discover the life-changing news of the gospel of Jesus

Christ. The written Word of God directs us to the incarnate Word of God—Jesus Christ. Daily intake of God's Word helps ground us in the gospel and reminds us of the metanarrative of God's mission to establish the kingdom of God. This is the very gospel we seek to hold out to our family members, friends, and students.

Prayer

One of my heroes of the faith is Billy Graham. During his life, he preached the gospel to millions of people around the world. He held counsel with numerous presidents of the United States and leaders from around the globe. When asked if he would change anything about his ministry, Graham replied, "If I had it to do over again, I'd spend more time in meditation and prayer and just telling the Lord how much I love him and adore him and [am] looking forward [to] the time we're going to spend together for eternity."[7] When I heard this response from someone who God used in a powerful way to advance his kingdom, I resolved to spend more time in prayer and meditation as well; however, his comment begs the question, "Why is prayer so important?"

Prayer is communication with the God who created us and sent his Son to provide a way for us to have redemption and a personal relationship with Him. Indeed, we can only enter into the presence of God, in prayer, through the great high priest, Jesus Christ, who shed his blood to atone for our sins (Heb 4:14–16). When we converse with God through prayer, it is a dialogue. We speak to God in

---

[7] Erin Roach, "Billy Graham in TV Interview, Reflects: 'My Time Is Limited,'" *Baptist Press*, December 21, 2010, accessed October 30, 2020, https://www.baptistpress.com/resource-library/news/billy-graham-in-tv-interview-reflects-my-time-is-limited/.

our prayers and listen for his response. Such an answer most often comes by God speaking through his Word, his people, or circumstances. As we read God's Word and pray, we also know God more fully and grow in our love toward him.

Prayer offers student ministers an opportunity to seek God's direction and wisdom in their lives and ministries. James wrote believers scattered during the Diaspora, encouraging them to pray to the Lord for wisdom (Jas 1:5). Prayer involves acknowledging God in our plans and decisions. When we rely on him in this way, the Bible teaches that he will direct us in the way he wants us to go (Prov 2:1–6; 3:5–6). Life and ministry can be confusing. At times, we might not know what decisions to make or what to do in a particular situation. Prayer provides us the opportunity to seek God's face and the promise that he will answer and give wisdom and direction.

One simple tool that I have found helpful in my prayer life is the ACTS acrostic (Adoration, Confession, Thanksgiving, Supplication). It provides structure and focuses my prayers. As we focus on adoration, we remember that, through prayer, we are communicating with the God of the universe who is holy and worthy of our worship and our lives (Matt 6:9). Through confession, we repent and confess our sins seeking God's forgiveness (Matt 6:12). It is also vital in our prayers that we give God thanks for who he is and what he has done (Phil 4:6; 1 Thess 5:16–18). Thanksgiving reminds us of the faithfulness of God in our lives and our ministries. Finally, supplication involves lifting our concerns and requests for others and ourselves to the throne of God (Matt 6:10, 11, 13; Phil 4:6; 1 Pet 5:6–7). Our prayers of supplication carry the promise and confidence that God cares for us, is sovereign and in control, and can act in his power on our behalf. Such assurance helps to reduce our anxiety and concern for our lives, families, and ministries (Phil 4:6–7).

Journaling

Many great saints practiced the spiritual discipline of journaling in daily walks with Christ. I have benefited from reading the journals of David Brainerd, George Whitefield, and Jim Elliot.[8] From these accounts, we learn about how God worked in the lives of these saints. They wrote about their progression in the faith, families, struggles, prayer concerns, and victories. We see God's providential hand in their lives through their reflections on how he worked in them.

Journaling is a spiritual discipline that relates to both Bible reading and prayer. It is often beneficial to write down one's reflections and questions regarding a particular passage that is the focus of that day's devotional reading. These reading reflections help disciples to process what God is teaching them through his Word. Journaling also helps student ministers to meditate on particular parts of the passage that the Holy Spirit impresses on them. Through journaling, disciples can also reflect on how their reading of Scripture relates to a growth area of their spiritual health, a circumstance occurring in ministry, or individuals with whom they interact in daily life and ministry. Student ministers can look at their journals throughout time and see how God uses his Word to help them to grow in the faith and in their ministries.

---

[8] For journals from these three men, see David Brainerd, "The Life and Diary of the Rev. David Brainerd," in *The Works of Jonathan Edwards*, ed. Jonathan Edwards (Edinburgh: The Banner of Truth Trust, 1995), 2:313–447; George Whitefield, *George Whitefield's Journals* (London: The Banner of Truth Trust, 1960); and Jim Elliot, *The Journals of Jim Elliot*, ed. Elisabeth Elliot (Grand Rapids, MI: Fleming H. Revell, 1978).

Journaling also relates to the prayer life of the student pastor. Followers of Christ can use prayer journals to write down and keep track of specific prayer requests they have on a daily basis. They also can categorize these requests in various areas of their lives: family, finances, church, friends, people with whom they are having gospel conversations, etc. As they pray through these requests, student ministers can use their journals to keep track of how God is answering their prayers. In this way, prayer journals can serve as a great reminder of God's faithfulness in the life of student ministers and an encouragement in their ministries.

Summary Thoughts on Spiritual Health

While this treatment of the spiritual disciplines is not an exhaustive one, it does mention the primary disciplines necessary for student ministers to develop spiritual health. Bible intake and prayer are essential in the lives of believers, especially those disciples leading in student ministry. Journaling helps student ministers to reflect on Scripture and track the faithfulness of God through their prayer lives. Leaders who implement these basic spiritual disciplines will develop spiritual health and a strong foundation on which to incorporate some of the other means of grace into their lives.

Physical and Mental Health

I will never forget the feelings of shock and grief I experienced when I read the post on Facebook. Our state announced that one of our pastors committed suicide. He felt like he could not deal with the stresses of ministry any longer, so he took his own life. About a year prior to his death, he messaged me on Facebook as a result of a conversation in a pastors' group. He shared with me about the opposition he experienced in his congregation and wanted my advice on how to deal with it. I remember thinking about how common his situation was becoming. A pastor wishing to rekindle the fire for evangelism in his congregation, but the church folks did not want to reach their community and opposed the pastor. Leading change through such a body of church members can feel exhausting and heartbreaking. The stresses of ministry overwhelmed my fellow pastor, and he killed himself. When I read about his death, he was one of seven pastors in my state who had committed suicide in the last seven years—an average of one a year.

In addition to stresses and mental health issues in ministry, many ministers also suffer from physical issues. Stress harms the body physically as well as mentally. Stress can physically contribute to high blood pressure, cardiac disease, diabetes, gastrointestinal problems, and chronic musculoskeletal issues.[9] Student ministers must mitigate stress in their lives through healthy coping mechanisms to avoid health issues. An unhealthy diet can also harm ministers' physical health. A shocking number of pastors are either overweight or obese.[10] This combination of stress and weight problems is devastating to the physical health of ministers.

----

[9] American Psychological Association, "Stress effects on the body," American Psychological Association, November 1, 2018, accessed November 2, 2020, https://www.apa.org/topics/stress-body.

[10] An article in *Facts and Trends* reports that "more than 75 percent of American preachers are overweight, many to the point of obesity." Robert Alford, "Pastors Are Digging Their Graves with Their Teeth," *Facts and Trends*, April 19, 2018, accessed November 2, 2020, https://factsandtrends .net/2018/04/19/pastors-are-digging-their-graves-with-their-teeth/. The Hartford Institute for Religion Research claims that "78 percent of clergy are either overweight (48 percent) or obese (30 percent)." The Hartford Institute of Religion Research, "Fast Facts About American Religion," The Hartford Institute of Religion Research, accessed November 2, 2020, http:// hirr.hartsem.edu/research/fastfacts/fast_facts.html.

Stress in ministry will always exist. Ministry needs never go away; they are always present. There is, however, only one of you. God created you unique and called you to student ministry. How can you develop habits that will enable you to do student ministry for the long haul? What are some positive coping mechanisms with which you can deal with stress? What are some ways that you can develop good mental health? How can you guard your physical health as you minister to students, parents, and the churches? The following sections will list some tips you can use to promote physical and mental health in your life and ministry.

Physical Health

The Bible teaches that we are stewards of our bodies and accountable to the Lord for how we take care of them (1 Cor 3:16–17; 6:19–20; 10:31). Our goal should be to care for them well to serve the kingdom as long as possible. While the following suggestions for physical health might seem like common sense, understand that the above discussion's statistics indicate that many ministers are not applying them to their lives to care for their bodies. Here are some tips for promoting physical health:

1. **Get good doctors.** Even if you are in your early twenties, seeing your doctor is essential for promoting physical health.[11] Regular visits to your doctor can save your life. There are preventive tests that physicians prescribe that screen for diseases and other health issues that affect specific

---

[11] The Iowa Clinic, "Even the Young and Healthy Need to See a Doctor on the Regular," The Iowa Clinic, May 2, 2018, https://www.iowaclinic.com /primary-care/even-the-young-and-healthy-need-to-see-a-doctor-on-the -regular/.

demographic segments of a population. Your doctor can help you see if you might be susceptible to these health conditions. If you have a medical problem, quick treatment is essential. If you are not seeing your physician regularly, you will not know about underlying issues that might exist. Your physician can also advise you on reducing stress, eating healthy, losing weight, and taking measures to promote a healthy life.

2. **Eat good food.** The Centers for Disease Control and Prevention (CDC) reports, "Adults who eat a healthy diet live longer and have a lower risk of obesity, heart disease, type 2 diabetes, and certain cancers."[12] Student ministry is not known as an environment that promotes healthy eating. It usually involves picking up fast food during the day or eating large quantities of pizza with students. Intentionality is the key. Find ways to incorporate healthy eating into your day and the student ministry events you schedule. A healthy diet will help keep you in the game as a student minister.

3. **Get good exercise.** Most physicians recommend that people exercise at least 30 minutes per day. Mayo Clinic suggests 150 minutes of aerobic exercise and at least two strength-training sessions per week.[13] Regular exercise helps to prevent heart disease and other chronic diseases such as cancer and diabetes. It also relieves stress. Furthermore, physical

---

[12] National Center for Chronic Disease Prevention and Health Promotion, "Poor Nutrition," National Center for Chronic Disease Prevention and Health Promotion, accessed November 2, 2020, https://www.cdc.gov/chronicdisease/resources/publications/factsheets/nutrition.htm.

[13] Mayo Clinic Staff, "Exercise: 7 Benefits of Regular Physical Activity," Mayo Clinic, accessed November 2, 2020, https://www.mayoclinic.org/healthy-lifestyle/fitness/in-depth/exercise/art-20048389.

activity builds up the immune system. Student ministers who exercise will be healthier and live longer than people who do not.

4. **Get good rest.** Our bodies need rest. There is a reason that the Lord called for us to observe a sabbath in our week. Lack of sleep can lead to serious health problems. The National Heart, Lung, and Blood Institute reports, "Ongoing sleep deficiency is linked to an increased risk of heart disease, kidney disease, high blood pressure, diabetes, and stroke."[14] Rest allows our bodies and minds to recuperate from daily stress and exertion. If we want to maintain healthy bodies in student ministry, we must take time to rest.

Taking the steps mentioned above will help you to maintain your physical health and promote longevity in student ministry. On the contrary, failure to practice healthy habits regarding our bodies dishonors the Lord and risks the chance of chronic health conditions that will inevitably affect our ministries for the worse.

Mental and Emotional Health

Our mental and emotional health are also important in student ministry. Scripture reminds us consistently of the importance of our minds and our thought life. The Greatest Commandment calls us to love God with all our mind (Mark 12:30). Paul admonished the church in Rome to renew their minds (Rom 12:2). What we focus on mentally has spiritual implications, so we should focus on that which

---

[14] National Heart, Lung, and Blood Institute, "Sleep Deprivation and Deficiency," National Heart, Lung, and Blood Institute, accessed November 3, 2020, https://www.nhlbi.nih.gov/health-topics/sleep-deprivation-and-deficiency.

is God honoring (Phil 4:8). In addition, failure to maintain healthy mental and emotional well-being can have a devastating impact on our lives, our families, and our ministries to students. The following suggestions are some steps we can take to promote mental and emotional health:

1. **Educate yourself about yourself.** It is helpful to learn about ourselves, our personalities, strengths, and weaknesses. God makes everyone different with unique personalities. Become an expert regarding your personality. The Myers-Briggs Type Indicator and DISC assessment are two tools that can help you determine your personality type and characteristics.[15] Knowing our personalities helps us to leverage our strengths and compensate for our weaknesses when interacting with others. This knowledge also enables us to understand better how we process things mentally and emotionally. Such self-awareness helps promote mental and emotional health in student ministry.

2. **Pray.** Prayer has a positive impact on our mental and emotional health as well as our spiritual health.[16] The Bible mentions prayer to counter anxiety in our lives (Phil 4:6–7; 1 Pet 5:6–7). God wants us to lift our anxiety and fears to him through prayer. When we do so, the Bible promises that "the peace of God, which surpasses all understanding, will guard your hearts and minds in Christ Jesus" (Phil 4:7). Prayer has a positive influence on our mental and emotional health.

---

[15] There are free versions of both of these personality assessment tools online. Simply type their names in a search engine, and you will find them.

[16] Rob Whitley, "Prayer and Mental Health," *Psychology Today*, December 3, 2019, https://www.psychologytoday.com/us/blog/talking-about-men/201912/prayer-and-mental-health.

3. **Speak truth to your emotions.** It is problematic when we allow our emotions to dictate our thought life. It helps to take the Word of God and apply it to our feelings. Memorizing Scripture is a great way to help our mental health. God's Word brings healing, truth, and peace to our broken lives (Ps 119:105, 165; John 17:17). Daily time reading and meditating on the Word of God is a great habit to help our mental health.

4. **Rest.** Just as rest supports our physical health, resting well also benefits our mental and emotional health. Taking relaxation breaks during work helps to reduce stress. Going for a walk to enjoy nature can provide a restful break from stress. Getting enough sleep is vital to physical, mental, and emotional health. Rest and relaxation are an important part of a student minister's mental health.

5. **Relationships.** Healthy relationships with mature believers who support you and pray for you also promote mental and emotional health. God created us for relationship. He established the church with many members who are interdependent and mutually supportive (Rom 12:3–8; 1 Cor 12:12–30; Eph 4:11–13; Heb 10:24–25). These relationships allow us to share our feelings, concerns, joys, and struggles with people we love and trust. Such life-giving relationships with other believers help student ministers maintain mental and emotional health.

This chapter's scope does not allow for a full delineation of practices that can promote mental and emotional health in student ministers; however, if they follow the above suggestions, they will safeguard their minds and emotions.

Summary Thoughts on Physical and Mental Health

If student ministers desire to serve in student ministry for the long term, they must pay attention to their physical, mental, and emotional health. The suggestions mentioned in this chapter are a few ways to help them maintain health in these areas. Failure to address these needs in their lives can have a devastating impact on the student minister. We honor God when we attend to these physical, mental, and emotional needs. It is foolish to neglect them.

The Student Minister and Time Management

Student ministers and leaders who desire to maintain holistic health while conducting effective ministry must practice good stewardship of their time. Scripture calls us to exercise good time management. David prayed that God would help him to remember that his days are short and life is brief (Ps 39:4–5). Moses asked the Lord to teach us to number our days so that we spend our time wisely (Ps 90:10–12). In the book of Proverbs, the writer praised the person who makes plans and condemned individuals who are slothful and reckless with their time (Prov 13:4; 21:5). In the New Testament, Jesus said that we should spend our time and energy with a kingdom focus (Matt 6:19–21, 33). Paul admonished the church in Ephesus to make the most of their time and use it wisely (Eph 5:15–17). He reminded the Colossian believers to interact with other people being mindful of the urgency of the time and their need for the gospel (Col 4:5). The writer of Hebrews warned believers of the shortness of our days as they relate to the need to affirm that we have genuine faith in Christ Jesus (Heb 3:13–15). Finally, James encouraged Christ-followers to make plans with God's will as their overarching desire (Jas 4:13–15). Both the Old and New Testaments teach the truth that we have a finite number of days in which to live our lives; therefore, we must manage and spend our time as a gift from God that we must use for his glory.

If we are to practice good stewardship of time in our lives and ministries, it is important that we adopt effective time-management practices. In the final pages of this chapter, we will discuss basic skills that will help us manage our time well, in a way that honors the Lord and promotes holistic health.

Establish a Good Calendar and Keep Track of It

The first step to managing our time well is maintaining consistent interaction with our calendars. Some student ministers prefer to organize their calendar digitally, while others prefer hard-copy calendars and planners. The best approach is one that works best for you! Use the calendaring method that best fits your skills and preferences; however, if you are comfortable using digital calendars, they carry the advantage of mobility and interactivity. Most digital calendars synchronize between computers, tablets, and smartphones. This can help you keep track of appointments and activities when you are away from the office. Student ministers can also share their digital calendars with their teams utilizing various calendar programs and platforms. This interactive capability allows for better communication and collaboration.

When managing your calendar, it is vital to track it by year, month, week, and day. Posting tasks and scheduled events in each of these segments of time helps student ministers to track progress toward goals over time and promotes the accomplishment of assignments on time. Digital calendars allow users to switch between each of these time segments on their calendars so that they can go from tasks or activities for a particular day and see how they fit into the weekly, monthly, or yearly calendar.

Digital calendars also often have alerts that users can set to ensure they are at an appointment on time or have notice of an upcoming deadline. These alerts can synchronize across devices, ensuring that ministers receive the alerts from their smartphones when they are on the go. This feature keeps users on schedule and gives them helpful reminders regarding events, tasks, or appointments.

Establish Goals or Tasks

It is beneficial for student ministers to plan goals or tasks they want to accomplish during a particular year. Student ministry planning teams can also plan events, tasks, or goals for the team as well. As this chapter focuses on the student minister, we will discuss their individual goals in this section; however, some of the principles and approaches mentioned here could apply to team planning as well.

Set Personal Goals for the Year

Perhaps you have a goal to lose weight. Maybe you want to write a book. In the coming year you plan on hiking in several state parks nearby. You want to memorize a verse of Scripture each week. Perhaps you want to set a reading goal of finishing a book per week or month. Set down the personal goals that you want to accomplish that year.

Set Goals for Your Family

If you are single, your family members are the people who are closest to you. Maybe you want to write an encouraging note each week to a family member or close friend. You could also plan to have at least one date per month with your spouse. There might be a vacation destination that your family really wants to visit that year. Take time to set goals for your family members or close friends so your most important goals don't get overrun by urgent tasks.

Set Goals for Your Ministry

Perhaps you want to recruit one new adult each month to help with the student ministry. The church's student ministry curriculum might not suit you, so you set the goal of picking a new discipleship curriculum for the students. Maybe instead of selecting new material, you decide to write your own and have it published. It might be the right year to go back to school and receive more education for student ministry.

A great time to set your personal, family, and ministry goals is during a personal planning retreat. Take a weekend to get away to a quiet place and spend time with the Lord praying over your coming year. Ask him to guide you as you formulate goals in each of these areas of your life and ministry. You will leave the weekend refreshed and focused on the coming year.

Backward Planning and Action Steps

Once you set your goals, it is time to place deadlines on the calendar for the accomplishment of those goals. You might set deadlines for events during this planning stage as well. After selecting the due date on the calendar, you begin the process of backward planning and creating action steps to achieve your goals.

Backward planning involves moving backward from the established deadline to the present and asking the question, "What steps need to occur between now and then for successful completion of the scheduled goal or event?" These steps are called "action steps." We must act to complete them to move toward the overall completion of the goal. The action steps break the goal into smaller tasks we must perform between now and the deadline. We must prioritize these action steps based on their importance for achieving the goal or completing the event.

Prioritizing Tasks and Action Steps

Successful time management and achievement of the tasks and action steps necessary to achieve a goal require that student ministers exercise wisdom and discernment to prioritize how they spend their time. A resource that I have found very helpful in my life and ministry is the book *Freedom from Tyranny of the Urgent* by Charles E. Hummel.[17] In his book, he mentions three categories to prioritize tasks or action steps when managing our time: Important—Urgent, Important—Not Urgent, Not Important—Urgent.[18]

Tasks that are important and urgent require our immediate attention. They are critical to achieving the desired goal or outcome and are also time-sensitive. These tasks demand that we drop anything else we are doing and give them our full attention. We might not have scheduled them, but they are critical to our lives and ministries. An example would be a hard deadline that cannot be postponed.

Action steps, or time commitments that are important but not urgent, do not require our immediate attention. These time commitments include the routine action steps that we scheduled over some time to complete our goal or scheduled task. Their deadline is not

---

[17] Charles E. Hummel, *Freedom from Tyranny of the Urgent* (Downers Grove, IL: InterVarsity Press, 1997).

[18] Hummel, *Freedom from Tyranny of the Urgent*, 38–39.

imminent, yet we must work on these items. Working on these tasks is less stressful because they are not urgent. Suppose student ministers spend most of their time focusing on things that are important but not urgent. In that case, they will avoid the stress of living perpetually in the important and urgent category of prioritization.

Tasks that are not important but urgent are at the lowest level of prioritization for time management. These tasks often might appear urgent to someone else; however, we do not share that individual's sense of urgency. An example of an item that is not important but urgent might be a routine text message we receive from a student or parent. Although they might expect we send an immediate response, we do not need to share their sense of urgency, as the text is routine and not a crisis. If we are not careful, we could let this category dominate our schedules, essentially allowing everyone around us to determine our priorities and focus.

Using Hummel's categories helps us to prioritize and schedule our tasks by their importance and urgency. Prioritization of tasks allows us to reduce stress and achieve the goals and action steps that we develop as we plan and backwards plan. Such prioritization is essential to effective time management.

Tasks versus Relationships

When discussing time management and planning, we must not allow tasks to overshadow relationships. People are more important than projects. As Christ-followers, we are called to love God and love our neighbors (Mark 12:29–31). It is not loving for us to neglect our relationships to achieve goals or scheduled tasks. Our students, parents, and adult volunteers should feel more important than tasks or plans on our calendar. This priority of people over projects is especially true regarding our families.

If you are a single person serving in student ministry, your family might consist of your immediate family members, or it might include your closest friends and fellow Christ-followers. Whoever they might be, you must prioritize spending time with these trusted people in your life. As mentioned previously, they help your mental and emotional health and can encourage you in ministry. At the same time, they desire to spend time with you as well.

Married student ministers must not neglect their spouses and children. Our spouses should not feel that tasks and activities take priority over them. We must prioritize spending time with our families. They should feel like they mean more to us than our ministries. One way to ensure that we are keeping balance in our schedules regarding our families is to include our spouses in the planning process. Including them in our planning and time-management processes helps us and communicates to them our love and acknowledgment of their value in our lives.

Conclusion

The Bible teaches that we should manage our time well. As we prioritize people over tasks, we must establish goals for our lives and our ministries. Prioritization and backward planning are helpful tools that can help us organize and schedule the action steps we create to accomplish our objectives. These necessary tools assist us in stewarding our time well.

Good time management also helps student ministers prioritize the steps necessary to promote their spiritual, physical, mental, and emotional health. If you apply the suggestions mentioned in this chapter, you will accomplish one of the critical elements to navigating student ministry—caring for yourself holistically.

Student Ministry and Leadership Development

• CHANDLER VANNOY •

When I stepped into my first student pastor role, I did not fully grasp the weight of the ministry to which I was called. I knew that I would be leading a student ministry, but I did not realize that I would also lead parents and leaders older than me.

I was overwhelmed. I didn't know where to start. Honestly, I felt lost. If you've ever been lost, in any context, you know the demoralizing effect. When you don't know where you're supposed to go or what you're supposed to do, you second-guess every decision you make and a feeling of lostness only deepens. Feeling lost is even worse when you are responsible for leading others, and you realize your confusion won't only affect you but could cause these others to lose their way, too. When it comes to navigating student ministry, the student pastor sets the direction. Even if you are stepping into uncharted territory, others will look to you for leadership and answers. In many ways, I felt like an inexperienced captain of a ship at sea trying to navigate through a dark, foggy night. I was in over my head.

As I look back on those days, I now see that God worked in my life and ministry to create for me a humility on which he could build my understanding of leadership. He stripped away pride and showed me my need for him to lead me. I did not want to say this at the time, but I can now echo Paul's words when he said, "I will most gladly boast all the more about my weaknesses, so that Christ's power may reside in me" (2 Cor 12:9). My weakness in leadership caused me to feel lost, and that forced me to look outside of myself to find my way. S. D. Gordon's words remind Christian leaders of our hope when we feel surrounded by fog:

> Let it once be fixed that a man's one ambition is to fit God's plan for him, and he has a North Star ever in sight to guide him steadily over any sea, however shoreless it seem. . . . He has a compass that points true in the thickest fog and fiercest storm, and regardless of magnetic rocks."[1]

It is in Christ that we find strength to lead. Not ourselves.

The aim of this chapter is to help you prepare for the weighty calling of leadership by defining leadership from a biblical perspective. This involves showing the importance of leadership development and providing a practical plan for developing leaders. My goal is to help you lead your ministry well enough so that your leaders and students may grow deeper in their relationship with Christ.

---

[1] S. D. Gordon, *Quiet Talks on Personal Problems* (Toronto: W. Briggs, 1907), 158.

A Biblical Definition of Leadership

One reason many church leaders feel lost when it comes to leadership is because they are looking at the wrong map. They look to the world for examples of how to lead and how to be successful, instead of looking to God himself. This does not mean that secular leadership principles and practices can never be helpful, but it means that, as undershepherds of Christ, our primary example and understanding of leadership must first come from Jesus Christ, not Mark Zuckerberg. As H. B. Charles once said:

> Lead as a pastor. You are not a CEO. You are not a business tycoon. You are not an expert in organizational leadership. You are a pastor. You are a shepherd. A gospel herald. Don't abandon that sacred role for anything or anyone.[2]

Pastors must find their definition of leadership by looking to God's Word. Our standard is Scripture. All other resources we use must first be filtered through a biblical lens, not the other way around. Business books can be helpful but cannot replace the Word of God. Deriving our understanding of leadership from the Word, and not the world, will bring us the confidence we need to lead like God would have us.

For pastors, our calling is deeper than others. Our goal is not to increase our company's profit. It is not even to grow our ministry numerically. Our goal is to grow mature disciples in Christ. And this goal requires us to not only be great leaders but also great teachers.

---

[2] H. B. Charles, *On Pastoring: A Short Guide to Living, Leading, and Ministering as a Pastor* (Chicago: Moody, 2016).

Gary Bredfeldt reminds us in his book *Great Leader, Great Teacher* that "the Biblical leader is first and foremost a bible teacher."[3] He goes on to say, "Teachers shape, challenge, and change people, and, in doing so, they lead. Great teachers are leaders and conversely, great leaders must be teachers."[4]

Leadership, in general, is a heavy responsibility. But pastoral leadership is even weightier because we are shaping people through our teaching and the example we set with our lives. Remember that Jas 3:1 says, "Not many should become teachers, my brothers, because you know that we will receive a stricter judgment." Famous leaders have always known this. Leadership is influence, the ability of one person to influence others to follow his or her lead.

John Maxwell famously said, "Leadership is influence—nothing more, nothing less."[5] John Piper adds to that definition when he says, ". . . spiritual leadership [is] knowing where God wants people to be and taking the initiative to get them there by God's means in reliance on God's power."[6]

With this influence and power comes a cost, though. J. Oswald Sanders reminds us that "to aspire to leadership in God's kingdom requires us to be willing to pay a price higher than others are willing to pay. The toll of true leadership is heavy, and the more effective the leadership, the greater the cost."[7] Because of this, we should not step into a student pastor role haphazardly. We should enter into any

---

[3] Gary Bredfeldt, *Great Leader, Great Teacher: Recovering the Biblical Vision for Leadership* (Chicago: Moody, 2006), 15.

[4] Bredfeldt, 13.

[5] John C. Maxwell, *21 Irrefutable Laws of Leadership* (Nashville: Thomas Nelson, 1998), 13.

[6] John Piper, "The Marks of a Spiritual Leader," *Desiring God,* January 1, 1995, https://www.desiringgod.org/articles/the-marks-of-a-spiritual-leader.

[7] J. Oswald Sanders, *Spiritual Leadership: Principles of Excellence for Every Believer* (Chicago: Moody, 2007), 139.

pastoral role with great care. We should count the cost of leadership. The role of church leader is honorable work and an honorable position, but, as Paul Tripp reminds us through the title of his book, it is a dangerous calling. Leadership is dangerous because, without Christ, we will use our honorable position for personal gain. Our hearts are full of sin and wired to abuse the power of leadership. Jeremiah 17:9 says, "The heart is more deceitful than anything else." We cannot trust ourselves.

In their book *Designed to Lead*, Kevin Peck and Eric Geiger examine how all things in creation can be used for destructive and selfish reasons, including leadership. Even things that do not seem bad on the surface can be manipulated and twisted into a power struggle and should be handled with caution. However, they also go on to note that "leadership, like everything else in creation, can and should be redeemed for God's glory."[8]

The Spiderman comic books are right when they say, "With great power comes great responsibility."[9]

Since leadership is such a great responsibility, we must steward it well. As pastors looking to lead others to Jesus, we must look to his example to make sure we are leading people in the right direction. As Sanders reminds us, "Jesus's master principle was that true greatness, true leadership, is found in giving yourself in service of others, not in coaxing or inducing others to serve you."[10]

Throughout the Gospels, Jesus served others. If the Son of God came to earth and served his own creation, we should follow in his footsteps. Jesus said in Mark 10:43–45, "Whoever wants to become great among you will be your servant, and whoever wants to be first

---

[8] Eric Geiger and Kevin Peck, *Designed to Lead* (Nashville: Lifeway Christian Resources, 2017), 55.

[9] Stan Lee, *Amazing Fantasy #15* (New York: Marvel, 1962).

[10] Sanders, *Spiritual Leadership*, 14.

among you will be a slave to all. For even the Son of Man did not come to be served, but to serve, and to give his life as a ransom for many." Servanthood is what makes Christian leadership unique and utterly distinct from the world. In the example of Jesus, leaders are called to follow him, deny themselves daily, and serve others. Jesus's example is a complete 180 from the world's idea of leadership. You won't find these characteristics in most organizations or companies. Truthfully, this type of leadership is actually against our very nature. The only way we can lead in this way is to daily spend time with Jesus so he can shape our life and leadership. A tough truth we must remember is that we cannot lead others to where we have not been ourselves. We must follow Christ to lead others to him. This is why Michael Wilder and Timothy Paul Jones remind us in their book *The God Who Goes Before You*, "Before we are leaders, we must be followers—followers of a God who goes before us."[11] In this book, they introduce the idea of followership being the key to leadership. For the Christian leader, followership means that everyone, even the leaders, is being led by Christ. And the only way we can effectively lead others to Christ is to daily pursue Christ in our own life.

Paul Tripp echoes this idea in his book *Dangerous Calling* when he says, "I am more and more convinced that what gives a ministry its motivations, perseverance, humility, joy, tenderness, passion, and grace is the devotional life of the one doing ministry."[12] Student ministry is not about how much theology we know or if we are caught up on the latest leadership trends. What matters is if the theology we study moves from our minds and changes our hearts and affects our lives. As pastors, our private devotional life fuels our public, pastoral

---

[11] Michael Wilder and Timothy Paul Jones, *The God Who Goes Before You* (Nashville: B&H Academic, 2018), 10.

[12] Paul David Tripp, *Dangerous Calling* (Wheaton, IL: Crossway, 2012), 35.

life. Once again, Jesus sets the example. Think about the Gospels and all the stories we read. How often did Jesus wake up early and spend time in prayer with the Father? Jesus led his disciples to do the same. They saw him retreating to pray. They heard him quote Scripture. They saw him live out his teachings.

J. Oswald Sanders states, "Spiritual leadership requires spirit-filled people."[13] We are called to be spirit-filled leaders who desire to develop spirit-filled students. If our ministries produce students who are not filled with his Spirit, our ministries are not fulfilling the Great Commission. That starts with us being spirit-filled people first and foremost. Before we can lead, we have to follow. If we rely on our own strength, we will always fall short.

A Conviction for Leadership Development

When I stepped into my first student pastor role, I was ready to invest in every student in our ministry, lead as many Bible studies as I possibly could, and disciple students every chance I could get. Outside of the work of the Holy Spirit, I truly thought that the success of our student ministry was solely based upon my capacity to minister to our students.

I quickly realized that not only was this untrue, but it was also impossible for me to be the only one pouring into students. Even more, some students didn't think I was cool and wanted nothing to do with me. I soon discovered what I needed was a ministry full of leaders who had a desire to care for and disciple students. The reality is one person can only effectively disciple ten to twelve students at a time, which limits the impact that we can have within our ministries, but if we focus on building up a team of leaders, the impact becomes

---

[13] Sanders, *Spiritual Leadership*, 91.

infinite. By just adding ten leaders, our reach goes from ten students being effectively discipled to one hundred and ten students.

Let's think about the idea of the captain of a ship. Even an inexperienced captain can be effective if he surrounds himself with the right crew. Think about it. The ships that work most effectively are the ones with the greatest crew, not just the best captain. A captain is only as good as the crew that is with him. The same is true for student pastors. When navigating the sea of student ministry, we need others on the ship to strengthen us where we are weak. There are others who are gifted where we are not. Our job is to identify where we are weak and then to empower others on the ship to use their gifts in that role and task. We were not meant to do ministry on our own. We were never meant to be the hero. We need a team around us.

Bob Russell writes, "[God] is more likely to work through us if we swallow our pride, admit our shortcomings, gather around us people who have strengths in the areas where we are weak . . . and quit trying so hard to be a hero to everyone."[14] Paul lays this idea out for us in Rom 12:3, 6 when he says, "I tell everyone among you not to think of himself more highly than he should think. . . . According to the grace given to us, we have different gifts: If prophecy, use it according to the proportion of one's faith."

Within the body of Christ, we all have different gifts. In our student ministry, we need leaders surrounding us with different gifts than our own. We have to stop trying to be the hero who does everything in our ministry. That is not going to work.

Paul lays the groundwork for the responsibility that God has given church leaders in Eph 4:11–13:

---

[14] Bob Russell, *After 50 Years of Ministry: 7 Things I'd Do Differently and 7 Things I'd Do the Same* (Chicago: Moody, 2016), 155.

And he himself gave some to be apostles, some prophets, some evangelists, some pastors and teachers, to equip the saints for the work of ministry, to build up the body of Christ, until we all reach unity in the faith and in the knowledge of God's Son, growing into maturity with a stature measured by Christ's fullness.

Paul reminds us that as pastors and church leaders, our work is not to do all the work of ministry ourselves. It is the development of God's people under our care. And there is nothing more sacred and strategic in his kingdom than equipping others to grow in their maturity in Christ and to serve in ministry.

God did not intend for his church to be a community with a gifted pastor and staff members who do all the ministry, but instead it was to be a community of gifted people equipped for the work of ministry. That's a big shift from how most churches view ministry.[15]

When we do all the work of the ministry instead of equipping others, we limit the effectiveness of the church. Oftentimes, it is for selfish and prideful reasons that we don't want to invite others into our ministry. We like feeling important. We like feeling in control.

As Russell says, "A lot of problems we get into in leadership are the result of ego. We like being needed. We like being in control. We like being the center of attention. We like thinking no one else can do it as well as we can."[16]

As we lead our student ministry, we must daily seek to let go of control, let go of our ego, and let go of the idea we are the only one who can do the work of the ministry.

---

[15] Todd Adkins, *Developing Your Leadership Pipeline* (Nashville: Lifeway Christian Resources, 2016), 3.

[16] Russell, *After 50 Years of Ministry*, 156.

Simply put . . .

Doing = building up ourselves

Equipping = building up the church

Eric Geiger and Kevin Peck sum this up perfectly when they say, "When pastors/teachers train and prepare God's people for ministry, the result is the body of Christ is built up."[17]

Since we should spend more time equipping than doing, that means we should focus time on training and developing the leaders in our ministry.

We see this in the life of Jesus. When we picture the day-to-day ministry of Jesus, our minds often jump to the time he spent in front of crowds. But when we read the Gospels and actually look at the life of Christ, we see that he spent more time with the Twelve than he did in front of the crowds.[18]

I serve on the leadership team at Lifeway Christian Resources. One of the exercises we take church leaders through during our leadership pipeline coaching is learning the Development Pie chart.[19] The chart provides a visual aid to help others see how Jesus spent his time. Look at the time he spent doing ministry himself compared to the time he spent on developing his disciples.

---

[17] Geiger and Peck, *Designed to Lead*, 35.

[18] Adkins, *Developing Your Leadership Pipeline*, 3.

[19] Lifeway Leadership, *90 Second Leadership – Development Pie: How Jesus Spent His Time*, November 3, 2017, leadership.lifeway.com/2017/11/03/90 -second-leadership-development-pie-jesus-spent-time/.

Jesus's Time

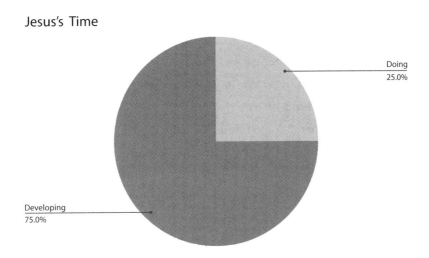

Doing
25.0%

Developing
75.0%

Now, when we compare the way Jesus spent his time to the way we spend our time in ministry, we will often begin to see some stark differences. If you are like many people, you likely spend half your time developing and half of your time doing, but even that is probably generous on the side of developing.

Our Time

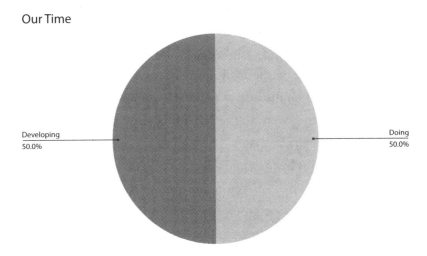

Developing
50.0%

Doing
50.0%

This simple comparison ought to instruct us on how we should manage our time in ministry. Todd Adkins reminds us, "We must develop leaders to do the work of the ministry, not just do the work of the ministry ourselves. We must make disciples, not just be disciples. We must build an army of leaders, not just an audience of listeners."[20] A general doesn't build an army by doing everything. He builds an army by training the men and women in his charge and allowing them to lead.

If we step into student ministry and do everything by ourselves, we are going to be tired, exhausted, and burned out because we are trying to do everything on our own. It does not work. And not only does it not work, that is not the way God designed it.

You might not be a National Basketball Association (NBA) fan, but you probably know who LeBron James is. During the playoffs a few summers ago, I remember watching LeBron and the Cavaliers in game 7 of the playoffs, where the winner would go on to the NBA finals and the loser would go home. There was a moment in game 7 when LeBron's coach tried to pull him out of the game to give him a little rest. LeBron looked straight at him and said, "I'm playing the whole game." He refused rest. He knew his team would lose without him on the court. He knew he had to score forty-five points just to make it a game. And he did. And they won. Then they went to the NBA finals and got swept in four straight games by the Warriors. They got swept because you cannot win championships by playing isolation basketball, or as many call it, by playing "hero ball." If you never give up the ball and want to have full control, you are going to come up short. This is because the game was designed to be played as a team. Michael Jordan

---

[20] Adkins, *Developing Your Leadership Pipeline*, 3.

himself said, "Talent wins games, but teamwork and intelligence wins championships."[21]

For student pastors, it is easy to try to play hero ball when it comes to leading a ministry and being involved in everything with all things running through us, but that is exhausting. It also stunts the growth of our ministry. God designed the church to thrive when we are equipping others to lead and when we don't care who gets the credit. We need to understand that if we want to strengthen our student ministries and see them thrive, we must become developers of people, not just doers of ministry. This conviction fuels everything else we do.

A Practical Plan to Develop Leaders

Believing in the importance of leadership development does not mean one will actually do the work of developing leaders. We can all agree that an important ingredient for a thriving student ministry is to develop leaders, but the reality is that many leaders don't actually have a plan to train and develop their people. Even with a conviction to develop leaders, it is not always easy to know where to start. LifeWay Research conducted a study with one thousand pastors, and it showed that an overwhelming majority of pastors affirm the importance of leadership development and training but less than 30 percent of churches have a plan in place to train and develop their people. Ninety-two percent of churches think they should train leaders, but only one in four have a plan.[22] That means almost every

---

[21] Michael Jordan, Mark Vancil, and Sandro Miller, *I Can't Accept Not Trying: Michael Jordan on the Pursuit of Excellence* (San Francisco: HarperSanFrancisco, 1994), 24.

[22] Lifeway Research, "CRD Training Project" (Nashville: Lifeway Christian Resources, 2012.)

single one of you reading this book would affirm Eph 4:11–13 and
the need to "equip the saints," but less than 30 percent of you know
where to start.

One thing I wish I had when I entered my first student ministry
position was more real-life ministry examples from which to learn.
That's why I want to offer three practical steps to help you move
toward becoming a developer of people.

1. Delegate Tasks

Most student pastors take ownership of everything and rarely delegate work. Unfortunately, leaders will never be developed if ministry
responsibilities aren't delegated.

To assess how you are doing in ministry, take a minute and write
the top twenty tasks you do on a weekly basis. After completing your
list, categorize each task into these two categories: (1) what I must do
and (2) what others can do.

There are certain tasks on your list that *only you can do* and you
have to make time for those. And if you are not careful, you won't
have time for them.

We allow ourselves to focus only on the tasks only we can do—
the ones that are our strengths—and by delegating tasks that we don't
need to have our hands on. And here's the amazing thing about this:
there are people who love to do the tasks that you hate to do. If event
planning and handling all of the details is not your sweet spot, there
is someone in your church who lives for that. Delegate event planning
to someone else. If hospitality is not your spiritual gift and is draining
to you, find someone who is energized by thinking through how to
welcome people warmly into your ministry and delegate the welcome
ministry to this person. If you can find someone who loves replying to

emails, then you should delegate your entire inbox. But sadly, I don't think anyone is wired that way. So, we will probably all be stuck with email. Delegating provides other believers with opportunities to serve in areas in which they're gifted and for which they have a passion.

As we are talk about delegating, some of us are scared because we like to control everything. Your palms are getting sweaty even thinking about giving up control. Because when we control everything, we feel the student ministry will be at its best. That it will be excellent.

And what happens is that we end up sacrificing leadership development on the altar of excellence. When we touch everything and control it beginning to end, we believe the final result will be excellent. It will be a ten out of ten. But if we equip someone else to do this, it would only be above average and a seven or eight out of ten. And it wouldn't be up to our standard. For example, if we were to lead the group discussion with our high school students, the conversation would be theologically rich and thought-provoking and awesome. But if, say, "Rick" were to lead that discussion, it wouldn't be as great. When we think this way and try to control everything, it leads us to put a lid on our growth and hinders us from developing others.

Bob Russell says, "I'm convinced the failure to effectively delegate is the primary reason most churches don't grow much beyond two hundred people."[23]

For student pastors, our goal should not be to grow beyond a certain number, but we should desire to have the greatest gospel impact possible. And a failure to delegate will limit our impact.

Yes, excellence is great, but that is not what Jesus called us to. He called us to equip the saints for the work of the ministry, not to be excellent.

---

[23] Russell, *After 50 Years of Ministry*, 156.

We see delegation in Jesus's life and also in the life of Moses in Exodus 18. Moses led the Israelites and served as the judge for all the people. Scripture says they stood around him from morning till evening. His plate was unbelievably full. His calendar was packed.

So his father-in-law stepped in and gave Moses some timely advice:

> What you're doing is not good. . . . You will certainly wear out both yourself and these people who are with you, because the task is too heavy for you. You can't do it alone. Now listen to me; I will give you some advice, and God be with you. You be the one to represent the people before God and bring their cases to him. . . . But you should select from all the people able men, God-fearing, trustworthy, and hating dishonest profit. Place them over the people as commanders of thousands, hundreds, fifties, and tens. (Exod 18:17–21)

Jethro told Moses to hand off tasks to others to make his load lighter so that he could focus on what only he could do.

I encourage you, just like Moses, to assess your regular tasks and see what you can delegate to lighten your load. More importantly, see how you can empower others to lead and grow in their faith by partaking in the ministry.

Now, this delegation might all sound great, but you might be sitting there asking yourself, *How do I actually hand off things to others?*

Well, that leads us to our second practical way to develop people.

2. Gradually Release Responsibility

Equipping and developing leaders requires both intentional time and effort. You can't simply empower someone through a text message or email. That's dumping responsibility on them. Development happens when people are engaged by the mission, equipped to do it, and accept the responsibility to carry it out. This is exactly how Jesus modeled leadership development.

If you think about it, Jesus rarely did the work of the ministry alone. Yes, he spent time alone, but when he ministered to others, his disciples were nearby. This was on purpose. Jesus wanted to make sure they were equipped before they took on all of the responsibility.

Early on, the disciples watched Jesus, but soon he asked them to serve with him. Then Jesus flipped the script and asked them to serve while he observed and helped. And even after he ascended into heaven, Jesus promised he would continue to observe and help by sending the Holy Spirit. During this shared ministry, Jesus wasn't throwing away his responsibility when he gave it to the disciples; he was equipping them by gradually handing off the responsibility and sharing it.[24]

The work of gradually giving away ministry responsibility can be summarized in four key phrases: intentional ministry, guided ministry, collaborative ministry, and equipped ministry.[25] As we look at it, this follows Jesus's example. It starts with "I do, you watch, then we talk." Then he moves to "I do, you help, we talk." And then it is "You do, I help, we talk." And finally, it is "You do, I watch, we talk."

In all of this, the biggest part is the "we talk" aspect. We need to dialogue with those we are leading about their experience and answer any questions they might have.

Let's look at this development approach through the scenario of equipping a new small group leader in your student ministry.

---

[24] Todd Adkins, *Succession at Every Level* (Nashville: Lifeway Christian Resources, 2017), 6.

[25] Adapted from Douglas Fisher and Nancy Frey, *Better Learning through Structured Teaching* (Alexandria, VA: ASCD, 2014), 3.

Say you have been leading an eighth-grade boys group, but you want to raise up another leader in your place to take over when this group gets to high school and you can launch another group.

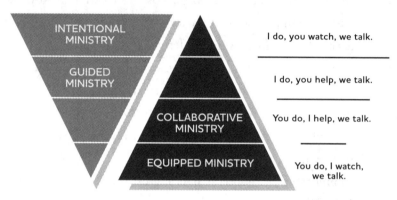

PASTOR'S RESPONSIBILITY

INTENTIONAL MINISTRY — I do, you watch, we talk.

GUIDED MINISTRY — I do, you help, we talk.

COLLABORATIVE MINISTRY — You do, I help, we talk.

EQUIPPED MINISTRY — You do, I watch, we talk.

LEADER'S RESPONSIBILITY

Intentional Ministry. You lead the group, and the new leader is watching. The key again is that you talk about and process what they watched. This will be the time they ask questions, and you walk through why you did what you did.

Guided Ministry. In this step, you and the new leader share the responsibility. You let them help lead some of the discussion, then the two of you talk about their experience of leading the discussion and some of their challenges.

Collaborative Ministry. At this point, the new leader leads the group on their own, but you're still available to help. You then discuss how it went and evaluate their leadership.

Equipped Ministry. The new leader now fully leads the group without your help. You may watch and observe and are still available to talk about how they can continue to grow and improve. This is the last step before they are ready to lead without you.

If your small groups meet once a week, this handing off of the ministry will take about four to six weeks, depending on the challenges and questions that arise throughout the process.

The beautiful thing about this model is that the new leader can repeat it. That means within the next year, this small group leader should be walking a new small group leader through this process. This model makes sure we are truly equipping leaders and not just dumping responsibility on them.

An applicable step for you is to choose one item on your list of regular tasks that you are currently doing and then walk someone else through this process. Begin to gradually hand off the responsibility to them and equip them for the work of the ministry.

Be aware they are not going to live up to your excellent standard of leading a small group right away. But they will never be equipped to lead if you don't walk alongside them and give them the opportunity to lead the group themselves.

So let's gradually hand off the responsibility to our leaders and equip them along the way.

If you follow the steps of delegating tasks and gradually releasing responsibility, you will begin to develop leaders.

Which leads us to our last practical step.

3. Multiply Leaders Who Multiply Leaders

I'm sure you would love to say, "We have too many leaders and too many volunteers in our student ministry. We don't need you to help this week." The reality is most church leaders weekly say almost the opposite: "We need more leaders. I wish we had more volunteers." This is a challenge that most churches face.

The problem is when we are playing hero ball, trying to control everything and delegating nothing, we become a bottleneck to growth and multiplication of our people. But when we delegate and equip others, we multiply our influence and leadership. This must be one of our main focuses as a leader: to reproduce ourselves and multiply leaders. Practicing leadership development impacts your ministry.

When you multiply leaders who multiply leaders, this is what the result will look like over time.[26]

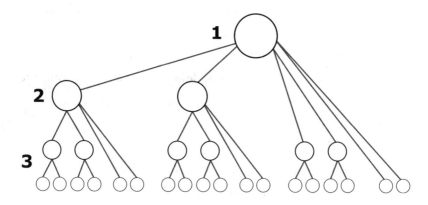

When we invest in a few leaders at a time, we create a culture of development and multiplication and encourage everyone to participate, not just the student pastor.

This idea is seen in Paul's instruction in 2 Tim 2:2: "What you have heard from me in the presence of many witnesses, commit to faithful men who will be able to teach others also." Paul not only taught Timothy Jesus's teachings and the gospel but demonstrated to him how to lay out the gospel on a daily basis. Here he instructed Timothy to follow his example and teach both the content of

---

[26] Todd Adkins, *Creating and Curating a Recruiting Culture* (Nashville: Lifeway Christian Resources, 2018), 13.

Scripture and then show how disciples live out the teachings of the Bible in their daily lives.

Geiger and Peck say, "Find those whose hearts are his and coach them on their competence. Invest in people who love the Lord and develop their skills. Pour yourself into people who have devoted themselves to him."[27]

When you focus on multiplying leaders and reproducing yourself, you'll begin to see leaders, who you've been praying for and asking to serve year after year, step out of their comfort zone and use the gifts that God has given them to serve the church. This is exactly the goal of Eph 4:13: ". . . we all reach unity in the faith and in the knowledge of God's Son, growing into maturity with a stature measured by Christ's fullness."

This idea of multiplication goes for your students, too. They can handle more than you think. As you lead your student ministry, don't be scared to call your students into leadership development as well. If they can handle calculus and chemistry while juggling extracurricular activities, they surely can handle some leadership in your ministry.

As leaders multiply and are developed, you will see your students and leaders grow in their maturity in Christ. Because they are no longer just showing up on a Sunday, they now understand what it means to be the church and serve and invest in the ministry.

When we are developing leaders, we are pulling others into God's mission and showing them their place to serve in the body of Christ, not letting them sit on the sidelines but equipping them to be a part of what God is doing. And helping them not just be a disciple but to make disciples as well.

This is why leadership development matters.

---

[27] Geiger and Peck, *Designed to Lead*, 25.

When we focus on developing others and inviting them to do the work of the ministry as well, we will see our students and leaders grow in their maturity in Christ. If we want to navigate student ministry well and see our ministries thrive, we must become developers of people, not just doers of ministry.

The Student Ministry Team

• TIM McKNIGHT •

One thing I have enjoyed the past two summers is rafting down the Ocoee River with students from First Baptist Church of Georgetown (Georgetown, SC). They invited me to preach at their summer camp held in Tennessee for the last two years. On the last day of camp, they'd graciously invite me to join them for some white-water rafting.

Whitewater rafting is no small task and cannot be done alone. It would be physically impossible for one person to whitewater raft successfully alone. Each raft needs the occupants on its left and right sides to paddle as a team. The guide steers the raft from the back and communicates directional commands to each side of the raft. Without the paddling team working on each side and present in the raft, the guide would not have enough weight or directional control to keep the river vessel facing the right direction. Rafting with a team is not a suggestion but a necessity.

Like whitewater rafting, student ministry is a team effort. Leaders cannot successfully navigate student ministry by themselves. The Bible teaches that believers serve as members of the body of Christ, each of them contributing to the overall body by functioning in their individual and unique roles as they exercise their spiritual gifts.

This chapter surveys the key groups of people that youth ministries must acknowledge and include as a part of their youth ministry team. The congregation is the umbrella under which the student ministry team serves and the body of which the student ministry team is a part. Members of the staff or leaders of ministry areas are an essential part of the student ministry team. Parents or legal guardians are a crucial component of the team, as they should be the primary ones discipling their students. Adult volunteers help student ministers to multiply themselves in ministry and serve a wider number and variety of students. Student leaders are vital to the team as they disciple their peers and serve using their spiritual gifts in the church. The following discussion focuses on student ministry teams, including their biblical foundation and composition.[1]

The Student Ministry Team and the Body of Christ

Biblical student ministry cannot be done in isolation. God did not design the church for ministers to serve as the "hired guns" who serve in ministry while everyone else watches them. As mentioned in the

---

[1] For more information on a comprehensive approach to student ministry involving the congregation, staff, parents, adult leaders, and student leaders, see Tim McKnight, *Engaging Generation Z: Raising the Bar for Youth Ministry* (Grand Rapids, MI: Kregel Academic, 2021).

previous chapter on leadership development, student ministers must also guard against refusing to delegate ministry to people in their congregation out of fear it would risk the failure of specific tasks or responsibilities. Trying to perform student ministry alone opposes the teaching of Scripture; it creates the potential for the student minister to be overwhelmed by responsibilities and suffer burnout.

The apostle Paul painted a strikingly different picture of the church in his instruction regarding spiritual gifts. He taught that every believer is given a gift by the Holy Spirit that should be exercised within the body of Christ (Rom 12:3; 1 Cor 12:11). Each disciple of Jesus Christ possesses a spiritual gift that serves a particular function in the body of Christ. No part of the body is insignificant. Every believer who serves is critical to the function of the body of Christ (Rom 12:4–5; 1 Cor 12:14–22). When any part of the body suffers, the entire body suffers (1 Cor 12:26). Every member of the body is significant and plays an important role.

Student ministers do not possess every spiritual gift, nor are they to attempt to perform every function needed in the student ministry. God calls student ministers to equip adult leaders, parents, and students to use their spiritual gifts serving in ministry (Eph 4:11–13). For student ministry leaders to fail to delegate ministry or disciple other adults and students to do ministry contradicts the clear teaching of Scripture regarding their responsibilities to equip and mobilize them for ministry. Such mobilization multiplies the student ministry, promotes unity, and provides the potential for gospel saturation and kingdom advancement.

According to the apostle Peter, the ultimate purpose for members of the body of Christ, including student ministry leaders, is to exercise their spiritual gifts to the glory of God. He wrote, "If anyone speaks, let it be as one who speaks God's words; if anyone serves, let it be from the strength God provides, so that God may be glorified through Jesus Christ in everything. To him be the glory and the power forever and ever. Amen" (1 Pet 4:11). We are to exercise our gifts in the church to point to Christ and not ourselves.

Student ministers should help their adult leaders, parents, and students discover their spiritual gifts and implement them in ministry. By encouraging and equipping believers to serve according to their giftedness, student ministers provide opportunity for church members to serve and, therefore, will significantly multiply their ministry's effectiveness.

The Student Ministry Team: The Congregation

As mentioned in our chapter on biblical foundations for student ministry, the faith community or the congregation has a responsibility to disciple students and help them to establish firm foundations in biblical doctrine. Unfortunately, student ministry in the past segregated students from the rest of the congregation. Describing this unhealthy approach to student ministry, Mark DeVries writes:

> Most "successful" youth ministries have their own youth Sunday school, youth missions, youth small groups, youth evangelism teams, youth worship, youth budget, youth interns, youth committees, youth offering, youth Bible studies, youth "elders" (like "jumbo shrimp"?), youth centers, youth choir, youth rooms, youth discipleship programs, youth conferences, youth retreats, youth fundraisers, and (my personal favorite) youth ministers.[2]

---

[2] Mark DeVries, *Family-Based Youth Ministry* (Downers Grove, IL: 2004), 41–42.

The more that student ministries duplicate ministries already existing in the larger congregation, the more they divide students from the larger church family. Student ministers who follow this strategy for student ministry are, in essence, creating a parachurch organization within the church.

Student ministers further separate the church's student ministry by creating and implementing mission statements, core values, and strategies that differ from those adopted by the entire congregation. The pastors, staff, deacon body, congregational leaders, and members of the congregation all play a role in developing the church's mission statement, core values, and strategy. When student ministers create guiding documents that differ from the church's, they essentially establish a parachurch organization within the congregation and further separate the student ministry from the rest of the church.

Thankfully, this pattern in student ministry of separating the students from the rest of the congregation is beginning to change. There is a growing emphasis on involving the students in as much of congregational life as possible while maintaining times when the students meet to worship or study Scripture in a way that best fits their developmental levels and culture. The following suggestions are ways that student ministers can ensure that student ministry is a part of the congregation:

1. **Share the church's mission, core values, and strategy.** Student ministers promote unity, cooperation, and collaboration in the congregation when they align the student ministry's guiding documents with the church's statements. They should also design the student ministry in a way that is guided by and reflective of the church's mission, values, and strategy. Such alignment helps parents, adult volunteers, and

students in the student ministry see how the student ministry relates to the larger congregation.

2. **Communicate, communicate, communicate.** Student ministers should communicate regularly with the congregation regarding key emphases and events in the student ministry. Student testimonies, whether live or via video, are powerful ways to help the congregation see what God is doing in the church's teenagers' lives. Meeting with key ministry teams such as the finance team, deacons, and personnel teams can also help communicate how God uses the student ministry concerning the church's mission, core values, and strategy.

3. **Invite members of the congregation to participate in the student ministry.** Create entry points into the student ministry for members of the congregation at every level of ministry. Some church members might simply support the students by attending student-led services or events in the church. Student ministry sponsors are church members who give financially to help the student ministry or a student attend summer camp. Adult volunteers serving in the student ministry as teachers, small group leaders, mentors, and other roles come from such invitations to participate in student ministry.[3]

4. **Involve students in ministry in the congregation.** When students use their spiritual gifts in the congregation, they develop multigenerational relationships while working alongside church members. They also exercise their spiritual gifts in ministry to help accomplish the mission and strategy of the church. Serving in the congregation also helps students develop a sense of belonging to the church body. One reason

---

[3] More will be said about adult volunteers later in the chapter.

students eighteen to twenty-six years of age left the church after graduating is that they never felt that they belonged to or had the freedom to serve in the larger congregation.[4]

Your student ministry team can discover other ways that the student ministry can engage the congregation. These are just a few suggestions to get you started on the path of engagement.

The Student Ministry Team: Staff and Church Leaders

Whether the student ministers are paid staff or volunteers, they will work with other church leaders or staff members on the church's ministry leadership team. This team often consists of pastors, ministry leaders, or volunteers helping to lead children, adult, or senior ministries. Even though student ministers might serve under a specific lead pastor or family pastor, it is still essential they do the good and hard work to communicate, coordinate, and collaborate effectively with this team.

One of the most helpful tools I encountered in my ministry on church staffs is a book by John Maxwell titled *360° Leader*.[5] Maxwell advocates that leaders need to lead upward, across, and down. They lead upward by helping their supervisors, across by serving their peers, and down by leading people following them in their area of responsibility. To better grasp how student ministers can work effectively with the church's leadership team, let's examine each of these in turn.

---

[4] David Kinnaman, *You Lost Me* (Grand Rapids, MI: Baker Books, 2011); Ed Stetzer, Richie Stanley, and Jason Hayes, *Lost and Found* (Nashville: B&H, 2009).

[5] John Maxwell, *360° Leader* (Nashville: Thomas Nelson, 2005).

Leading Up

Student ministers lead up by serving their pastors effectively and responsibly. They should seek to be trustworthy and trusted by their leaders. One way to do this is to constantly seek your own growth in needed areas. Work to proficiently interpret the Scriptures. Do what's needed to manage your time wisely. Be diligent to fulfill your responsibilities in your ministry area. Take a genuine interest in your pastor's ministry responsibilities. Discuss with them how they see the student ministry relating to the mission, core values, and strategy of the church. Explain to them your understanding regarding how the adult ministry and children's ministry relate to the student ministry, then listen for their response and feedback. Also a leader can lead up by offering help in appropriate areas. Ask your pastors the question, "How can I serve you?" Be someone to whom the pastor can hand off responsibility and not worry about whether it will be done or done well. Even more, lead up by involving your pastors. Offer them an open invitation to attend any student event on the calendar. Invite them to preach or speak to the students at least once a year. Discuss with your pastors how you can work together to reach and disciple your students' parents. Work with them regarding equipping parents to disciple their students. Explain to them your understanding regarding how the adult ministry and children's ministry relate to the student ministry, then listen for their response and feedback. Finally, at the very least, keep your pastors informed regarding what God is doing in your student ministry.

Now that we know what it means to lead up, I want to say a word to pastors who might read this chapter. Pastors, you are called to shepherd the flock you serve and lead (1 Pet 5:1–4). This responsibility involves shepherding your staff, including your student ministers. Whether your student ministers are young in life and ministry or are older and experienced student pastors, they need you to shepherd them well. Encourage them in the Word by focusing on their spiritual walk with Christ and not just the next event for which they are responsible on the church calendar. Understand that they not only need to possess and exercise skills in biblical interpretation, but also must communicate the profound truths of God to students in middle school and high school. Encourage them as they serve the congregation, staff, parents, adult leaders, and students. If they are young, they might need you to help them disciple parents or provide someone who can speak authoritatively regarding raising teenagers because they are not parents and have not raised any teens. They need your support and time to learn how to improve their ministry leadership. The students also need you to engage them. Support your student ministers by occasionally dropping in on a student event or function. It might surprise you that students stated that liking the pastor was the third most important factor for them concerning the church.[6]

Leading Across

Student ministers lead across in serving with the staff members or leaders who minister to the children and adult ministries. It is important that the leaders in the children's and student ministries communicate regarding their discipleship goals for children and students. Since the children's and student ministries are crucial in helping parents and the congregation develop orthodoxy (right belief), orthopathy (right emotions/affections), and orthopraxy (right practice) in the students,[7] they should discuss the transition between

---

[6] George Barna, *Real Teens: A Contemporary Snapshot of Youth Culture* (Ventura, CA: Regal, 2001), 139.

[7] For a thorough discussion of how to develop orthodoxy, orthopathy, and orthopraxy in students, see McKnight, *Engaging Generation Z*.

children and student ministry and how best to serve families during that transition. On a more practical level, student ministers should communicate with adult and children's ministers to ensure that they coordinate together regarding the church calendar. They must be careful not to plan events over each other. They should also not schedule so much on the calendar that they prevent families from spending time together in discipleship.

Student ministers must coordinate with the other church leaders to accomplish the mission and strategy of the church. To accomplish this, we have examined the crucial tasks leading up toward their supervisors and across to their ministry colleagues. Now, we move to examine the concept of leading down, which will bring us to a new ministry team to consider.

The Student Ministry Team: Adult Volunteers

Continuing John Maxwell's concept regarding 360° leadership, student ministers lead down by recruiting, discipling, and deploying adult volunteers in the student ministry. By leading down, this does not imply that there is a sense of superiority and inferiority between student ministers and adult leaders. Leading down actually refers to the student minister exercising servant leadership toward the adult volunteers in the student ministry. Good student ministers realize that their adult volunteers are the backbone of the student ministry. They help the student minister multiply ministry and bear great influence in discipling the students.

Adult leaders are ministry multipliers in your student ministry. The more adults you have serving in the ministry, the more students to whom you can minister. Each volunteer possesses different personalities and strengths. Student ministers will not always connect with every student. Perhaps there is too much of a personality difference, or the student does not open up to the student pastor. Having numerous adult volunteers ministering to the students increases the possibility that students will find a personality with which they can connect. In addition, as mentioned previously, student ministers do not have every spiritual gift. They need adult leaders who minister through a wide variety of gifts as they serve in the student ministry.

In addition to helping a ministry multiply, it's important to note the influence adult leaders have on students. Students look up to their adult leaders as mentors and examples to follow in ministry. For example, see how this dynamic is true regarding an adult leader's example of sharing the gospel. In a study they conducted regarding the influence of adult leaders on student evangelism, David Rahn and Terry Linhart write:

> When student leaders saw adults lead someone to Christ at least weekly, they reported leading more than eight friends to Christ themselves. If they observed adults evangelizing only monthly, student leaders were likely to lead fewer of their friends (four to eight) to Christ. Our research showed this to be a consistent trend. *The more often adults were observed leading others to Christ, the more often student leaders led their own friends to Christ.* When adults engaged in observable evangelistic practices less frequently, student leaders followed their pattern. The students who reported seeing adults only occasionally—if ever—evangelize were also likely to report not having led anyone to Christ.[8]

---

[8] David Rahn and Terry Linhart, *Evangelism Remixed: Empowering Students for Courageous and Contagious Faith* (El Cajon, CA: Youth Specialties, 2009), 25.

What a powerful illustration of the influence that adult leaders have on their students.

Adult leaders can affect students in both positive and negative directions. It is imperative that student ministers exercise great care and discernment in recruiting, discipling, and deploying adult leaders in the student ministry. If adult leaders are mature spiritually and proficient in their respective ministries, they can have a positive impact on the student ministry. On the other hand, adult leaders who are inept and spiritually immature can have a devastating impact on the students.

Practical Steps for Recruiting the Right Leaders

How can student ministers exercise care in recruiting the right adult leaders? The following suggestions are steps we can take in recruiting and discipling adult leaders.

1. **Offer personal invitations.** Announcements and impersonal invitations to service are not effective means by which to recruit adults to serve in the student ministry. Such unintentional invitations will not bring the quality of adult leaders that student ministries need. By focusing on personal invitations, student ministers approach adults about whom they have some knowledge regarding their story and their spiritual maturity. Student ministers should give the invitation to serve along with the understanding that the adult must go through the adult volunteer candidacy process for the student ministry. If they are not willing to go through this process, they should not serve in the student ministry.

2. **Conduct formal interviews.** Conduct a formal interview, application process, and background check.[9] The leadership team of the student ministry should conduct in-person interviews of every adult who applies to serve in the student ministry. They should hear the faith journey of every candidate and discuss the prospective adult volunteer's spiritual gifts and where they feel led to serve in ministry. Student ministers should practice due diligence in checking references that candidates list on their applications. They should also ask these references for other references. In addition, the student ministry leadership should conduct background checks on every adult volunteer candidate.[10] The emphasis on this process is to recruit quality adult volunteers who are growing in their faith and pose no threat to the students' safety.

3. **Provide a role model.** Have the adult volunteer shadow another veteran volunteer in the student ministry. After determining the volunteer candidate's spiritual gift, have them shadow an adult volunteer who serves in an aspect of the student ministry that matches the particular gift. For example, if the volunteer candidate's spiritual gift is teaching, they can shadow a small group leader who has taught for years in the student ministry. They will observe the volunteer

---

[9] For more on a volunteer application process, including application templates, see Doug Fields, *Purpose-Driven Youth Ministry* (Grand Rapids, MI: Zondervan, 1998); and Mike Work and Ginny Olson, *Youth Ministry Management Tools 2.0: Everything You Need to Successfully Manage Your Ministry* (Grand Rapids, MI: Zondervan, 2014).

[10] Student ministers can contact state and local law enforcement for low-cost background checks within those jurisdictions. Parachurch organizations that conduct federal, state, and local background checks are available online.

for a while. Then the candidate will have an opportunity to teach while the veteran observes. After a debriefing, the adult volunteer candidate may start teaching a small group if the veteran and the student ministry leadership team believe he or she is ready.

4. **Equip leaders regularly.** Offer weekly equipping meetings with adult volunteers. There is broad agreement among student ministers that quality adult volunteers are critical to their student ministries; however, very few student ministers meet with their adult volunteers to disciple them and equip them for ministry to teenagers. According to Ben Trueblood of Lifeway Students, only 36 percent of leaders coach or equip their adult volunteers every few months, and 35 percent of leaders coach or equip them once a year or never. So, 71 percent of student ministers offer little or no equipping and discipleship to their adult volunteers.[11] Break this negative trend by meeting with your adult volunteers regularly to disciple them, inform them, and equip them to minister more effectively.

5. **Encourage leader input.** Involve volunteer leaders in the formulation and implementation of the student ministry strategy. Adult leaders can often offer much innovation, life experience, passion for the gospel, love for students, and spiritual maturity. Their input in the planning and exercise of the student ministry is invaluable. Involving them in as much of the student ministry's leadership processes as possible reflects a biblical understanding of the body of Christ, encourages every part of that body to function, and increases these leaders' sense of ownership and belonging to the student ministry.

---

[11] Ben Trueblood, *Within Reach: The Power of Small Changes in Keeping Students Connected* (Nashville: Lifeway, 2018), 23.

6. **Encourage leaders regularly.** Encourage your adult volunteers. Send them notes thanking them for their ministry to the students. Ask them how you can pray for them and let them know when you actually pray for their requests. Celebrate when they make progress or reach a spiritual milestone in discipling a student. Every couple of months or so, treat all of your student volunteers to a special appreciation dinner. Ask your adult leaders how you can help them serve the students. All of these steps will boost their morale and let them know you care for and appreciate them. Ministry can often be discouraging for leaders, so your work of constant, genuine encouragement is crucial.

7. **Model servant leadership.** Finally, student ministers must display servant leadership to their adult volunteers. They should never ask a volunteer to do something that they are not willing to do themselves. Modeling servant leadership will create an ethos among the adult volunteers where they are willing to serve sacrificially and with humility. Our adults will emulate the type of leadership we show them, good or bad.

Taking the steps mentioned above will help student ministers to do the essential work of recruiting adult volunteers who are spiritually mature and have hearts to serve students. By doing that, their ministry will benefit immensely.

The Student Ministry Team: Parents and the Family

Students in our student ministries come from varied family backgrounds. Some students live in homes with a mom and dad active in the church and concerned about their child's spiritual development and discipleship. Other teenagers grow up in homes where neither parent expresses concern about their spiritual well-being or that of their children. Single parents raise some of the students in our student ministries. Grandparents or legal guardians raise others.

Whatever the context, students spend the most time interacting with the people with whom they live. Student ministers might see students once or twice a week for a few hours. The people with whom they live see them up to twenty-four hours a day, seven days a week, and thus possess the most potential to influence the lives of teenagers. So how are they doing regarding helping students to grow spiritually?

How Are Parents Discipling Their Children?

Even parents who profess faith in Christ Jesus and are active in the church are not doing well discipling their students. Family ministry advocate and academician Timothy Paul Jones reveals some shocking statistics regarding parents in the church and their families:

- More than half of parents said that their families never or rarely engaged in any sort of family devotional time. Of the minority that did practice some sort of family devotions, one-fourth admitted that these devotional times were sporadic.
- Approximately 40 percent of parents never, rarely, or only occasionally discussed spiritual matters with their children.
- Nearly one-fourth of parents never or rarely prayed with their children; another one-fourth only prayed with their children occasionally. . . .
- More than one-third of parents with school-aged children had never engaged in any form of family devotional or worship times at any time in the past couple of months. For an

additional three out of ten parents, such practices occurred once a month or less.

- Among two-thirds of fathers and mothers, biblical discussions or readings with their children happened less than once each week.

- One in five parents never read, studied, or discussed God's Word with their children.[12]

When one considers that these statistics relate to families who are active in the church, it goes without saying that parents outside of the faith are not discipling their students.

How Often Are Student Ministries Helping Parents?

Before we pick up stones to throw at these parents, we need to see how student pastors are supporting parents in the church. What are student ministers doing to invest in parents and help them to disciple their students? In a recent study, Lifeway Students reports:

Seventy-two percent of student ministers say they spend an hour or less each week investing in the parents of those in their ministries (including 23 percent who don't spend any time with parents). Fifty-nine percent say they have not discipled or trained parents as a group. Sixty-seven percent of them say they invest in individual parents every few months or less (including 28 percent who say they rarely or never do).[13]

---

[12] Timothy Paul Jones, *Family Ministry Field Guide: How Your Church Can Equip Parents to Make Disciples* (Indianapolis: Wesleyan, 2011), 27–29.

[13] Trueblood, *Within Reach*, 40.

These student ministers who lack interaction with parents are missing an opportunity to influence the most influential people in the lives of their students.

How Youth Ministries Can Support Parents

There are several possible reasons that student pastors are avoiding their students' parents and legal guardians. Young student ministers are sometimes intimidated by parents because they are self-conscious of their youth. They might be so engaged ministering to the students that they feel there is no time to invest in parents. Having never raised teenagers, young student ministers might feel inadequate to equip parents, so they do not engage them. Whatever the reason, student ministry leaders must engage and support parents and include them as an essential part of the student ministry team.

Here are some steps student ministers can take to interact with parents to support, encourage, and equip them in student ministry:

1. **Engage parents in conversation.** It seems it should go without saying, but student pastors need to have conversations with parents. We will never get to know the parents if we do not communicate with them. They also will not grant us trust if they do not know us. Engaging parents will take intentionality on the part of the student minister. One excellent opportunity for conversing with parents is when they drop off or pick up their students from the church. This approach is especially useful for getting to know parents who are not part of the church but allow their students to participate in the student ministry. These interactions with parents will build trust and understanding between them and the student minister.

2. **Ask parents how you can pray for them.** Parents deal with a great deal of stress. Raising teenagers is hard work. When talking with parents, ask them what prayer needs they have—they might even tell you or at least hint at them without being asked. You will learn about their lives and communicate your care for them. When they tell you their requests, pray with them at that moment. In doing so, you communicate your sincerity in offering to pray for them.

3. **Keep family finances in mind when planning student ministry events.** Families often face financial stressors. Be mindful of family budgets in planning your calendar. Offer students opportunities to raise funds to pay for summer camp or other higher-cost student events. Plan student fellowships that require no payment from the students. By being mindful of the families' budgets, you support your students' parents. They will appreciate it.

4. **Offer equipping summits for parents.** Provide parents an opportunity to attend a weekend where they learn about youth culture, pressures facing teens, adolescent developmental stages, how to disciple their students, and other topics related to parenting teenagers. These summits are excellent opportunities to collaborate with adult ministry staff in ministering to parents. They can also help the church reach unchurched parents who want to learn more about raising teenagers. Offering these summits also shows parents that student ministry leaders support them and care about their students.

5. **Provide discipleship resources to parents for discipling their students.** Student ministers can create or purchase discipleship material or devotionals that they give to parents for discipling their students. They might connect these

devotionals to what they are teaching the students in small groups or during a midweek service. Aligning what the parents use to disciple their teenagers with what they are learning in the student ministry reinforces these biblical truths in the students' lives and minds.

6. **Connect parents with discipleship groups in the church.** Help parents find a small group in which they can study the Bible and grow in Christ. Coordinate with the adult ministry leaders to help these parents connect with other parents in the church. Communicate with adult ministry staff regarding unchurched parents to whom small group members can reach out and invite. Perhaps through such coordinated ministry, adult small groups can lead unbelieving parents to Christ and equip believing parents to disciple their students.

7. **Invite parents to participate in the student ministry.** Ask parents to serve in the student ministry. Give them an open invitation to attend youth events. Have them serve as chaperones and counselors on trips and at summer camp. Involving parents in the student ministry helps them see what God is doing with the students and increases the number of adult volunteers serving on the student ministry team.

8. **Communicate, communicate, communicate.** Use technology to communicate with parents on multiple platforms. Inform them regarding the student calendar for the year, month, and week. Refer frequently to the mission, core values, and strategy of the student ministry so that parents know why it exists. Communicate with parents regarding the growth that you see in their students.

These suggestions are just a few ways for student ministers to engage parents and involve them in the church's student ministry. As you read them, come up with your ideas. Talk to your team and church staff about how to reach and support parents of teenagers in your church and community and what you could do to improve. Parents are essential to the spiritual maturity and health of students. Make sure that they feel like they are an essential part of your student ministry team.

The Student Ministry Team: Student Leaders

Student leaders are teenagers who are growing in their relationship with Christ and have been selected by the student ministry leaders to serve alongside the student minister, adult volunteers, and parents. Student leaders can be instrumental in leading their peers to Christ and discipling them in the faith. Evangelistic student leaders can also have a transformative impact on the entire congregation. Youth evangelist Greg Stier writes, "Passionate evangelism burning in the hearts of on-fire teens can set a whole congregation ablaze."[14]

Practical Steps to Developing Student Leaders

Students do not develop this passion for sharing the gospel and discipling their peers overnight. Student ministers, adult leaders, and parents must work to develop student leaders. Here are a few steps that student ministry leadership teams can take to develop spiritually mature student leaders who have a burden for Scripture, the gospel, their peers, their church, and the advancement of the kingdom of Christ:

1. **Teach student leaders how to interpret Scripture.** Student leaders must be grounded in the Word of God. They need

---

[14] Greg Stier, *Outbreak: Creating a Contagious Youth Ministry through Viral Evangelism* (Chicago: Moody, 2002), 63.

skills with which to study the Word of God and apply it to their lives. Student ministers and adult leaders must teach student leaders the necessary interpretive skills to study the Bible. This grounding in the Word will help grow leaders who have a firm foundation in faith.[15]

2. **Teach student leaders about the spiritual disciplines.** Help student leaders to develop the disciplines of daily Bible reading, prayer, and journaling. Teach them the relationship between spiritual disciplines and spiritual growth and maturity. Model the disciplines for the students to observe. Encourage the student to share what they learn about the disciplines with their peers. Student ministers might also allow student leaders to mentor younger students in the spiritual disciplines through small groups or mentorship relationships.

3. **Help student leaders discover their spiritual gifts and implement them in ministry.** Read through the New Testament passages that address the gifts (Rom 12:3–8; 1 Cor 12; Eph 4:11–13). Help students understand the meaning of these gifts within the context of these passages. Offer students the opportunity to serve alongside an adult in the congregation or the student ministry in a capacity that aligns with their gifts. Much like the adult volunteer process, the student leader will shadow the adult and watch them serve in ministry. Then, the student leader will serve while the adult observes and gives feedback. Involving

---

[15] For an excellent resource for teaching student leaders basic hermeneutical skills, see Matt Rogers and Donny Mathis, *Seven Arrows: Aiming Bible Readers in the Right Direction* (Spring Hill, TN: Rainer Publishing, 2017).

student leaders in ministry, in the church and the student ministry, ministers to the church and encourages other teenagers to utilize their gifts in ministry in the congregation and student ministry.

4. **Demonstrate to student leaders how to have gospel conversations.** The student minister should arrange opportunities for student leaders to accompany adults as they have gospel conversations with people in the community. As student leaders see these adults doing evangelism, they are more likely to share the gospel with their peers. Their peers are also more likely to share the gospel after observing their example.

5. **Involve student leaders in the student ministry planning process.** Invite student leaders to meet with the student ministry team as it plans the church's student ministry. Student leaders can observe and give input on planning the annual calendar for the student ministry. They can also help plan and lead student ministry events. Involve student leaders in weekly and monthly meetings of the student ministry team. Allowing student leaders to participate in this planning process helps them understand the biblical purposes behind various aspects of the student ministry and grants them a sense of investment in its leadership.

Student ministers who implement the above suggestions will disciple student leaders who assist the student ministry team in accomplishing the student ministry's mission and strategy. They will teach student leaders how to evangelize and disciple their peers. The above tips help develop leaders in the student ministry who continue to lead as adults in the church after graduating from high school.

Conclusion

Student ministers cannot navigate the journey of student ministry alone. God intends for churches to function as bodies made up of many parts as members exercise their spiritual gifts in ministry. Effective student ministry does not disciple students alone but works with various teams God has given them. Like whitewater rafting, student ministry is a team sport and cannot be done alone. Working alongside the teams God has supplied will help student ministers to navigate student ministry well.

Adolescent Development

• PAUL KELLY •

If you are going to navigate student ministry successfully, you need to know where you are going. What are you hoping to accomplish in the lives of the teenagers?

Effective navigation also requires a starting point. Directions to DisneyLand would not actually be all that helpful to me if my GPS were set to start in, let's say, Tacoma, Washington, instead of Ontario, California, where I live.

So, what is our starting point in student ministry?

Theological starting points are essential. The Bible provides important beginnings from which all church ministries must start: a clear description of the gospel, guidance in biblical discipleship, an understanding of the nature of humanity, and the need people have for God. But are there any starting points that are unique to student ministry? What makes student ministry unique, to put it simply, is that youth ministers are ministering with youth. Profound, I know.

Adolescence: A Time of Opportunity

Whether they are in Tacoma, Tallahassee, or Tokyo, young people experience a series of physical changes associated with puberty. The timing of puberty varies from culture to culture and from individual to individual, but the kind of changes young people experience are quite similar. These physical changes, over the course of several years, transition a young person from the body of a child into the body of an adult. Their size and shape change dramatically. They develop the ability to have offspring. Expansion in the abilities of the brain leads to changes in the way young people think, the way they interact socially, and the way they experience emotions. This is a significant time marked by rapid growth and profound change.

This period of transition from childhood to adulthood (often referred to as adolescence) can be a time not only of physical change but also spiritual change. Adolescence presents a crucial time for spiritual investment. In this time, adolescents develop beliefs about God, the church, and themselves that often carry into their adult life. But if you are going to be effective in guiding them during this pivotal time of spiritual development, it will help to think deeply about the changes adolescents experience. Knowing where they're at will equip you to know how to guide them forward.

In a sense, every youth leader knows something about adolescence. After all, we were all once teenagers. We recall the exhilarating experience of seeing ourselves becoming stronger, faster, deeper, and more passionate. We also remember moments of embarrassment and heartbreak, fear of not measuring up to our peers, or anxiety about all the changes we were experiencing. But our memories (thankfully) fade as we get older. Most of us seem to forget how painful it is to have your first love break your heart, or how embarrassing it is when your body seems to be behind others your age in its development, or how your legs ached at times because they were growing so fast.

So, as you prepare to navigate student ministry, we are going to dip back into the experience of adolescence. We are going to revisit some of the changes young people are experiencing and discuss how those changes should affect student ministry. This will help us calibrate our GPS as we prepare for the student ministry superhighway.

Adolescence: A Time of Change

Allen Jackson, my doctoral chair at New Orleans Seminary, often tells his classes, "More physical changes take place in adolescence than at any other time in the life of a human, except in the first eighteen months."[1] Adolescence is a time of intense change. Once the body develops an appropriate level of body fat, the process of puberty begins.[2]

Physical Changes in Puberty

The hypothalamus gland begins a cascading series of hormonal changes in the body. For girls, the ovaries increase their production of the female hormone estradiol by about eight times more than before puberty. For boys, the testes begin to produce about twenty times the

---

[1] Allen Jackson and Dwayne Ulmer, *Introducing the 21st Century Teenager* (Nashville: Lifeway Press, 2001), 40. Jackson attributes this statement to his mentor in youth ministry, Jim Minton.

[2] Jeffrey Jensen Arnett, *Human Development: A Cultural Approach*, 2nd ed. (Boston: Pearson, 2016), 350. (Children who are undernourished tend to begin puberty later than those who are well-nourished.)

level of the male hormone testosterone.[3] This infusion of hormones initiates development of primary and secondary sexual characteristics in the bodies of both sexes. By "primary sexual characteristics," we mean those organs necessary for reproduction: the ovaries, uterus, and vagina for girls; the penis, scrotum, and testes for boys.[4] Girls begin to produce ova (eggs), and boys begin to produce sperm. By "secondary sexual characteristics," we refer to changing characteristics that are not directly related to reproduction but signify sexual maturity. For example, girls experience breast development, boys experience a change in their voice and the growth of facial hair, and both sexes begin to grow hair in the armpits and genital area.

The timing of puberty varies. On average, girls begin to develop about two years earlier than boys. Beyond that, there can be about a two-year difference in the beginning of puberty between an early-developing and a late-developing young person. Youth in developed countries tend to begin puberty earlier than those in developing countries; this is likely due to nutritional issues.

Girls show the first signs of puberty with breasts budding. This happens at about ten years old in developed countries, though the range for individuals can be from about eight to thirteen. Menarche (the first menstrual period) is often seen as the beginning of adolescence for girls. In North America, girls normally experience menarche at about age twelve and a half, though they can reach menarche as early as about ten years or as late as about sixteen.

The first sign of puberty for boys is an enlargement of the testes at about age eleven and a half, but a clear sign of entrance into adolescence is not as easy to define for boys. Some have suggested

---

[3] Arnett, 351.

[4] Laura E. Berk, *Exploring Lifespan Development*, 2nd ed. (Boston: Allyn & Bacon, 2010), 286.

spermarche (the first ejaculation of semen), which occurs at around age thirteen and a half.[5]

Change in size is another sign of beginning puberty. For girls, significant growth in size begins around age ten, and they reach their adult height by about age thirteen. Boys typically begin substantial growth around twelve and a half and reach adult height by about age fifteen and a half.

Changes in the Brain

As the body develops and changes, the brain is also experiencing rapid development. Just before a child reaches puberty, the brain begins a rapid development of new synapses. Synapses are "the gaps between neurons, across which chemical messages are sent."[6] The synapses provide for the electrochemical connection that allows the processing of information.[7] By the time a young person reaches puberty, his or her brain has developed its adult size. As puberty begins, the brain begins rapid synaptic pruning, actually culling large numbers of synapses that are not being used. While it might seem that this pruning would retard brain development, the opposite is actually the case. The brain prunes those connections that are less productive, providing the opportunity for the best synapses to operate in optimal ways. Thought processes improve significantly.

In addition, the process of myelination greatly increases during adolescence. Myelin functions as a lubricant that speeds up thought processes. As Wolfe says, "During the teenage years, then, not only

---

[5] Berk, 286.

[6] Berk, G-10.

[7] Patricia Wolfe, *Brain Matters: Translating Research into Classroom Practice*, 2nd ed. (Alexandria, VA: ASCD, 2010), 229.

does the number of connections change, but the speed of those connections becomes faster."[8]

Synaptic pruning as well as myelination create significant changes in the adolescent brain, particularly in the frontal lobes of the cerebral cortex, the area of the brain known as "the governor of thought and action."[9] Changes in the brain "improve processing speed, attention, memory, planning, capacity to integrate information, and self-regulation."[10] As a result, the student's overall ability to think critically increases dramatically.

However, the emotion centers of the adolescent brain (in the amygdala) develop faster than the prefrontal cortex. This is true of both synaptic pruning and myelination. While the amygdala tends to control reaction, the prefrontal cortex controls reflection. In addition, the new infusion of sex hormones are particularly active in the emotion centers of the brain, leading adolescents to their appetite for thrills.[11]

The brain development in adolescents leads to greater ability in thought processing, but these skills take time to develop. Recent studies demonstrate that the brain is not fully mature until early adulthood. Early adolescents may struggle with reflective thought, leading to emotional decision-making. Their decisions might seem more reactive than thoughtful.

Teenagers, of course, are aware that their bodies are changing. They sense that they are thinking differently than they did a few years before. They are choosing to relate to their family and their friends in different ways. All of this leads them to experience disequilibrium;

---

[8] Wolfe, 84.

[9] Berk, *Exploring Lifespan Development*, 287.

[10] Berk, 287.

[11] Wolfe, *Brain Matters*, 83.

that disequilibrium leads most adolescents to moments of discomfort and anxiety.

Adolescents are actively involved in defining what these changes mean and moderating the effect they will have on their lives. Of course, they can't determine how fast or how much they grow. Girls have little control over the extent to which their bodies are taking on a more womanly shape, and boys cannot change how fast their beards appear. But they do have some control over the way they navigate the changes of adolescence. Some teenagers begin to push away from parents and aggressively engage with peers. Others will find comfort with their family and avoid the major social upheavals often associated with adolescents. Some young people will increase their work in faith development while others flee from the faith of their families. The point is, adolescence is not a passive experience.

The Big Question: Who Am I?

Erik Erikson suggested that the primary task of the adolescent years is to develop a healthy sense of identity. According to Erikson, "Not until adolescence does the individual develop the prerequisites in physiological growth, mental maturation, and social responsibility to experience and pass through the crisis of identity."[12] Without the physical development, sexual maturity, and brain development already described, young people are not prepared to do the reflection necessary to develop a sense of who they are and how they fit into society. Because the development of identity was so core to Erikson's perception of adolescence, he defines the "identity crisis" as the work of adolescence, or, in his words, "the psychosocial aspect of

---

[12] Erik H. Erikson, *Identity: Youth and Crisis* (New York: W. W. Norton, 1968), 91.

adolescing."[13] Erikson claims that identity development is multifaceted, including the development of sexual identity, vocational identity, and social identity, to name a few. Teenagers are determining their fit for their world.

The process of identity development is two-directional; it involves both discovery and construction. In discovery, adolescents are often trying to learn about who they are—personality, temperament, gifts, talents, and so forth. The process of discovery involves both experimentation and feedback from family, friends, and even the culture at large. Middle school students are a lot of fun to be around because they are constantly engaging in what a friend of mine calls "trying on hats." This week they want to be a serious student, next week a jock, and the week after that a poet. They keep trying on different roles to see what seems to fit them best. Adolescents are also constructing their identity. They are making decisions about what they will value, with whom they will develop deep relationships (and who they will avoid), and how they will choose to present themselves. In this process of discovery and construction, our students are asking and answering the question, "Who am I?"

Years ago, Susan was in my youth group. She was a quiet girl who lived near the church. She had a difficult family situation and found a home with our church family. I never thought much about Susan's wardrobe, but she wore black almost exclusively. This seemed to be a matter of personal preference and didn't have much meaning to her beyond that. However, one night she showed up at a youth discipleship group with a question: "Is there something wrong with the way I dress?" she asked. "Why do you ask?" was my response.

Susan told a story about a conversation with one of her teachers at school that day. The teacher brazenly told her, "I know you are

---

[13] Erikson, 91.

using drugs." She was taken back by that and tried to explain that she was a Christian kid; drugs were not something she would even consider. The teacher's response was what prompted her question to me: "I can tell you are using drugs," he said, "by the way you dress." This feedback startled her. Again she asked, "Do people think bad things about me because of the way I dress?"

What I wanted to say to Susan was, "That teacher is a fool. If he would take the time to get to know you instead of making snap judgments, he would not have said that." But, instead, probably at the prompting of the Holy Spirit, I said, "I would not have thought that, but apparently your teacher does." She said, "Should I change the way I dress?" I just said, "I don't know."

Susan pondered that question for a day or two. Ultimately, she decided she did not want to be known as "the girl in black." Little by little, she started adding a pink scarf or a yellow sweater to her closet. While her clothing was only a minor expression of her sense of identity, her choices about how she presented herself to her world indicated a lot about the person she was becoming. While the feedback of the teacher played an important role in this situation, Susan was making choices that helped her to actively construct her identity.

James Marcia said that an adolescent must come to a sense of personal commitment in order to achieve identity.[14] However, he argued that an unchallenged commitment does not lead to a clearly defined identity. A young person must actively choose between multiple alternatives in order to achieve identity, something Erikson called an identity crisis.

[14] James E. Marcia, "Ego Identity Status: Relationship to Change in Self-Esteem, 'General Maladjustment,' and Authoritarianism," *Journal of Personality* 35, no. 1 (March 1967): 119.

Marcia posited four identity statuses that adolescents might exhibit at different times during their experience of adolescence.

1. **Identity diffusion.** An adolescent is not actively engaged in crisis nor has he made any commitment to his identity. Identity issues are simply not being addressed.

2. **Identity foreclosure.** An adolescent has made an identity commitment but has not wrestled with the various choices. For example, an adolescent may have decided she wants to become a doctor like her father. While this would be a worthy goal, the identity commitment may be a reflection of the father's desires; the foreclosed adolescent has not wrestled with the options available to her or her aptitude for medicine.

3. **Identity moratorium.** The adolescent is actively involved in wrestling with the issues of her identity, but she has not made any commitment to who she will be. She may actually become paralyzed by the choices involved.

4. **Identity achieved.** The adolescent has wrestled through the crises related to identity and has committed to whom he will be.

Jeffrey Jensen Arnett argues that the issues of identity development are currently more a focus for persons in their early to mid-twenties, a period of life increasingly being referred to as emerging adulthood. An increase of identity choices, longer periods of education for many, and delayed commitments to marriage and family might lead to a later establishment of adult identity. Arnett seems to believe that identity is an issue now accomplished in the twenties and later rather than in adolescence. While Arnett might be correct in the delay of identity development, Argue, Roose, and Greenway have suggested that adolescents are still dealing with at least three key issues. They must answer three key questions related to identity, belonging, and purpose.[15] Who am I? Where do I belong? What difference do I make? These questions are core issues for adolescents.

Many reasons exist for doing student ministry, but few are more important than helping students find their identity in Christ. Teenagers are experiencing cognitive, social, sexual, or emotional development to do the work of determining what kind of person they will be as an adult. Whether a young person approaches puberty with a strong background in faith or with no faith at all, adolescence is the time when an understanding of the love, forgiveness, and empowerment of the Savior needs to become the driving determiner of their sense of who they are.

Family, Friends, and Everybody Else

The changes adolescents experience in body and in cognition affect the way they think about themselves, but these changes also affect the way they relate to other people. Relationships with friends become much more important to adolescents, but they also place great value in their relationships with their families. As Balswick, King, and Reimer suggest, "To an adolescent, relationships are not just something, they are everything."[16]

---

[15] Steve C. Argue, Caleb W. Roose, and Tyler S. Greenway, "Identity, Belonging, and Purpose as Lenses for Empathizing with Adolescents," *Journal of Youth Ministry*, 18 no. 1 (Spring 2020): 74.

[16] Jack O. Balswick, Pamela Ebstyne King, and Kevin S. Reimer, *The Reciprocating Self: Human Development in Theological Perspective* (Downers Grove, IL: IVP Academic, 2005), 180.

Changing Family Dynamic

In the past many believed that a healthy transition for adolescents required them to have a stormy relationship with their families. The stereotypical adolescent is pictured in his room with the door locked, loud music blazing, and Cheetos covering his bed. But the average teenager views her family as valuable, and the family structure as a place where she is genuinely loved and encouraged by people who believe in her. In fact, most adolescents see the relationships with their parents as their most important relationships. Adolescents are most likely to seek out their parents when they want to talk about school, career goals, or even their hopes and plans for the future. They are most influenced by their parents in their faith and faith practices.

Parents play a large role in shaping the lives of their adolescents. Of course, the life outcomes depend, to some extent, on the styles of parenting. Arnett suggests two components to parenting style that are important: demandingness and responsiveness.[17] Demandingness refers to the extent to which parents prescribe specific behaviors and insist that their adolescent children comply. Responsiveness refers to the extent to which parents engage warmly and with sensitivity to the emotional needs of their adolescent children.

A parenting style that is highly demanding and also highly responsive is referred to as authoritative. Authoritative parents do not hesitate to set limits with their children, but they do this in the context of a warm relationship. Authoritative parents often provide explanations for their restrictions so that the teenager doesn't feel like his parents are providing arbitrary rules. This style of parenting tends to develop qualities in adolescents such as independence, creativity, self-assurance, and social skill.

---

[17] Arnett, Jeffrey Jensen, *Adolescence and Emerging Adulthood: A Cultural Approach*, 6th ed. (Boston: Pearson, 2017), 182.

A parenting style that is highly demanding but low in respon-siveness is referred to as authoritarian. Authoritarian parents set rules and insist that they are followed, but they do this in a context of a cold or aloof relationship. Such parenting often produces young people who are dependent, passive, and conforming.

A parenting style that is low in demands but highly responsive is referred to as permissive. Permissive parents show much love and concern for their adolescent children but do little to set limits or curb behavior. This parenting style tends to produce adolescents who are irresponsible, conforming, and immature.

Finally, a parenting style that is low in both demands and respon-siveness is said to be disengaged. Disengaged parents are largely absent from the life of the adolescent. This style of parenting tends to produce impulsiveness and delinquency and is highly correlated with early sexual involvement and substance use.

Much of the current research related to parenting styles and ado-lescents has been conducted with majority-ethnic families in Western cultures. However, for many cultures outside of the West, parenting styles do not easily fit any of these models. Parents in these cultures tend to have high expectations of compliance from their adolescent children because of the respect in the culture for the role of parent. They are less likely to explain their decisions to their children and not likely to see parental directives as negotiable. While the respon-siveness of these parents may not have the warmth of the responsive-ness in Western parents, the level of family cohesion in many more traditional families may be much stronger. Diana Baumrind suggests that this style of parenting cannot easily be described by any of the previous categories and suggests a new category of parenting: tradi-tional parenting style.[18]

---

[18] Arnett, 187.

Conflict in the home usually increases during adolescence. Disagreement between parents and teens tends to increase dramatically during early adolescence but is normally greatly moderated by the time they reach sixteen or seventeen years of age. While conflicts are frequent, most youth report that they're usually about minor issues (e.g., activities, curfew, clothing), and cause minor disruption in the relational warmth between them and their parents. Teenagers from more traditional cultures are less likely to engage in conflict with parents than those in the West. They might experience the same internal disagreement with their parents but may bend to their cultural values for respect of parental authority.

Teenagers report that the most frequent source of fighting in the family is with siblings. Arnett identifies five possible styles of sibling relationships:

1. **The caregiver.** One sibling takes on the care or protection of another. Arnett suggests that this is the most common style in traditional cultures.
2. **The buddy.** Siblings relate to each other as they would friends.
3. **The critical relationship.** Siblings are involved in a great deal of teasing and conflict. Arnett suggests that American teenagers are most likely to experience this style of sibling relationship.
4. **The rival.** Siblings are constantly competing with each other.
5. **The casual relationship.** Siblings interact little with each other and tend to ignore one another.[19]

Western adolescents spend significantly less time with their families than they did as preteens. In fact, they spend progressively less time with their families as they get older. While most teenagers

---

[19] Arnett, 177–79.

feel warmly about their families, time with friends, school activities, part-time jobs, and other interests tend to crowd out time with their families. To some extent, this is true for adolescents in traditional cultures as well. While those youth are likely to spend much greater amounts of time with their families, the time they spend away from family is much greater than in childhood or adult life. This is more true for boys than for girls.

Changing Role of Friends

As a young teenager, Cameron was close to his parents but struggled with his own sense of significance. He describes his early teen years as being characterized as lonely and depressing. He tells the story of meeting another teenager about his age, Timothy. He didn't really know Timothy, but he invited Cameron to attend his birthday party. Though Cameron was hesitant to attend a party at which he didn't really know anyone, Timothy continued to encourage him. For Cameron, the party became an important moment in which he felt he had a friend he could truly trust. Several years later, Cameron's friend group still includes Timothy and some of the other teenagers he met at the party. He sees the friend group, especially Timothy, as highly important to him.

Though parents have great influence in the lives of adolescents, their friendships become significantly more important to them as well. Like Cameron, most adolescents greatly value their friendships. They tend to "attach great importance to the activities they do with their friends."[20] Arnett says, "Friends become the source of adolescents' happiest experiences, the people with whom they feel most comfortable, and the persons they feel they can talk to most

---

[20] Balswick, King, and Reimer, *The Reciprocating Self*, 174.

openly."[21] Adolescents use their friendships to test their own value outside of their family and find a group where they're accepted.

While the adolescents' friends might sometimes be a source of conflict with parents, Atkinson, Barnett, and Severe say "most adolescents choose friends who have values and expectations similar to those of their parents."[22] Adolescents tend to choose friends who are most like them in terms of age, ethnicity, interests, and values. Most of the friends of younger adolescents tend to be the same sex; however, as they get older, their friendship groups tend to include more opposite sex friends as well.

Arnett suggests that "the most important feature of adolescent friendship is intimacy."[23] While intimacy tends to be more valuable for girls, all adolescents desire friends they can trust. They desire friends with whom they can be open and honest, with whom they can be their genuine selves. Burns agrees that adolescents "tend to want to hang out with their closest group of friends in what I call 'friendship clusters.'"[24] He suggests that parents try to provide as many opportunities as possible for friends to gather together in their homes or at church.

Romantic Relationships

Romantic relationships take on importance for adolescence. Adolescents all over the world describe experiences of falling in

---

[21] Arnett, *Human Development*, 390.

[22] Harley T. Atkinson, W. Lee Barnett, and Mike Severe, *Ministry with Youth in Crisis*, rev. ed. (Eugene, OR: Cascade Books, 2016), 149.

[23] Arnett, *Human Development*, 391.

[24] Jim Burns, *Understanding Your Teen* (Downers Grove, IL: IVP Books, 2017), 21.

love.[25] Of course, that experience is different depending on the cultural context. Youth of European, African, or Latino background might begin a romantic relationship at twelve years of age or younger. Asian adolescents tend to begin romantic relationships much later.[26] While younger adolescents might develop romantic relationships, their reasons for those relationships are different than those of older adolescents. Younger adolescents tend to see having a boyfriend or girlfriend as offering them increased social status. Older adolescents tend to develop romantic relationships for the intimacy, companionship, and affection they experience with their partner.

Adolescents are likely more influenced by cultural norms in romantic pursuits as they are by physical development. In Western cultures, the traditional scripts for romantic relationships tend to be followed by boys and girls even though much has changed in male and female roles. Boys tend to be proactive, offering invitations to a girl and initiating physical activity. Girls tend to be more reactive in their roles.[27]

Sexual intercourse in adolescent romantic relationships is much more likely as adolescents get older. Only about 3 percent of Anglo adolescents have had sexual intercourse by age thirteen. (The numbers are higher for Latinos, about 7 percent, and African Americans, about 15 percent.) By the time adolescents reach college, about 80 percent of them have engaged in sexual intercourse.[28] Sexual intercourse largely occurs in romantic relationships for adolescents.

---

[25] Arnett, *Adolescence and Emerging Adulthood*, 247.
[26] Arnett, 242.
[27] Arnett, 242–43.
[28] Arnett, 255.

Cliques and Crowds

Peers are important to teenagers in a variety of ways. The literature on adolescence and peer interaction identifies two groups of
peers worth our consideration: cliques and crowds. Arnett describes
cliques as "small groups of friends who know each other well, do
things together, and form a regular social group."[29] Adolescents may
be a part of one clique or several. For example, a teenager might hang
out with a group of friends from the basketball team at school and
a different group of friends at church. Balswick, King, and Reimer
suggest that social acceptance is the major function of these cliques
and because of that, the clique members tend to be consistent.[30]
Cliques build norms for the activities members enjoy, the way they
dress, and the kind of language they use. Adolescents develop a sense
of security by belonging to a clique, especially in early adolescence.

As we navigate student ministry, we often see cliques as a problem in our youth groups. They certainly can pose problems when
teenagers feel unaccepted or not included. However, trying to eliminate the cliques from the youth group is unlikely to be productive
and might actually create more problems with feelings of insecurity
and isolation than it solves. As we will address later, a better solution
is to utilize activities that build stronger friendships between youth
from different cliques.

Adolescents also tend to identify with a crowd. While cliques
are small groups of friends, crowds are larger groups of adolescents
that see themselves as belonging to the same group of youth. Arnett
describes the function of crowds as "helping adolescents to locate
themselves and others within the secondary school social structure.

---

[29] Arnett, 391.
[30] Balswick, King, and Reimer, *The Reciprocating Self*, 174.

In other words, crowds help adolescents to define their own identities and the identities of others."[31] Teenagers in a crowd may not see the specific members of their crowd as friends, but they see themselves as belonging to the same large group.

Atkinson, Barnett, and Severe suggest that the peer group—friends, cliques, and crowds—plays an important role in the development of adolescents. They suggest three key functions:

> First, they operate as a mechanism whereby dependence on parental support and guidance is gradually loosened. Second, the adolescent period is seen as one in which interpersonal skills necessary in adulthood are learned through peer relationships. Third, peer groups offer emotional support at a time when young people are often unsure of themselves, questioning how they fit into the scheme of things.[32]

The peer group provides some valuable opportunities for adolescents as they develop. While student ministry can exist without building an alternative peer group, a student ministry that doesn't develop a close-knit group might sacrifice an ability to best shape adolescents into Christian youth. Finding a peer group that accepts them is incredibly important to most adolescents. It is even more important for them to find peers who become trusted friends.

Adolescent Development and Youth Ministry

As we have seen, adolescence is a time of dramatic changes in body, mind, and relationships. Understanding what is happening with adolescents should give direction to our ministry priorities and practices.

---

[31] Arnett, *Human Development*, 392.

[32] Atkinson, Barnett, and Severe, *Ministry with Youth in Crisis*, 131.

Here are a few "street signs" that might prompt your thinking for making application of the changes we have examined to the practice of ministry with adolescents.

Sexual Maturity and Faith

Sexual maturity is one of the major issues that influences identity and faith in adolescence. Developing a sexual identity is an important aspect of the self. This is also one of the issues that gives parents of adolescents the most sleepless nights.

Since the middle of the nineteenth century, the age of puberty has been arriving earlier in society—about three months earlier every ten years. So 150 years ago, teenagers hit puberty around age fifteen or sixteen. now they reach puberty by ten to twelve. This trend is called the secular trend.

G. Stanley Hall has been called the father of adolescence owing to his release of a two-volume set of texts called *Adolescence* (1904). His writing influenced how Western culture sees the teenage years. However, in his books he was describing a relatively short time of life. Puberty hit later in a young person's life, and the assumption of adulthood (occupation, marriage, and so forth) occurred much earlier.

The age of marriage has fluctuated wildly between eras of human history and between cultures; however, for much of human history, the time from sexual maturation until marriage was two to four years (say, from fifteen to eighteen years of age). Now, the time between sexual maturation and marriage is likely to be seventeen years (at current averages, from twelve to twenty-nine years of age for boys).

The cultural response to this has been to attempt to unhinge sexual expression from marriage. This is problematic for a number of reasons, the clearest being that it violates God's intention for a one-man, one-woman lifelong relationship. In addition, it is important to consider that although young adolescents might be physically capable of procreation, they are not cognitively ready for the realities of sexual expression. While the secular trend indicates that students mature sexually much earlier and also achieve greater physical size and more gender-divergent shape at an earlier age, they do not seem to develop cognitive ability any earlier. In other words, twelve-year-olds might look like fifteen-year-olds of 150 years ago, but they still think like twelve-year-olds from 150 years ago.

Sexual development is related to the physical, social, emotional, and cognitive development of adolescents. Because sexual development is so integral to the adolescent experience, it has much to do with the spiritual development of teenagers as well. And our response needs to be more than a "true love waits" message. Sexual feelings are new for younger adolescents. Much junior high humor centers on sex. This is probably because of the sense of discomfort young people feel about their own emerging sexual feelings and thoughts. Regardless of how much conversation adolescents had with their parents about sexuality as children, those conversations were all academic. After youth reach puberty, their understanding of sexuality becomes more experiential. Recent studies indicate that about 20 percent of twelve- to fourteen-year-olds have had sexual intercourse. Teenagers see hundreds of sexual images each week on television, on the internet, in magazines, in movies, and in video games—enough that they tend to become desensitized to them. Sexual curiosity leaves young adolescent males vulnerable to an attraction to (and perhaps an addiction to) pornography, especially given the easy access available on the internet. Masturbation can become habitual for young adolescents.

By high school, adolescents might be less likely to joke about sex, but their expressions of sexuality are increasingly unhealthy. About 70 percent of high school graduates have had sexual intercourse.

About half of high school students have engaged in oral sex. Use of pornography is rampant, especially among young males.

Some teenagers self-identify as homosexual. This is reinforced by social changes in the cultural view of homosexuality. Movies, television, and music all attempt to present teenagers who self-identify as homosexuals as heroes. These messages can be difficult for students to navigate as they try to construct their identity related to their sexuality.

Goals for the student ministry need to connect closely with parents. Goals should probably include issues such as the following:

- Help teenagers understand the biblical teachings regarding sexuality and sexual identity.
- Guide teenagers to discover who they are as sexual beings in Christ.
- Show teenagers how to decode and evaluate cultural messages related to sex and sexuality.
- Discuss the sexual landscape of adolescents with parents.
- Lead parents to determine ways to guide their teenagers toward biblical sexuality.
- Create an environment to allow parents to address the sexual issues and concerns of their teenagers.
- Provide training to parents for addressing specific sexual issues that might affect their teenagers, such as pornography, oral sex, and homosexuality.

Critical Thinking and Spiritual Growth

Some teenagers seem to question everything. How do you know the Bible is true? If you steal from a store and no one gets hurt, why is that wrong? How could Jesus have existed eternally if he was born of Mary?

Some parents are anxious to get their preteens into the youth group because their children are "so mature." And they seem to be. They voice prayers at the end of Sunday school, answer questions the teacher asks, and invite their non-Christian friends to church hoping they will discover God. The problem is that when these "mature" children arrive at their teenage years, they might not even want to go to church. All the things that seemed like such solid values in their life were unquestioned, but as they develop the cognitive skills of a teenager, everything gets questioned.

The changes in the adolescent brain may have more to do with the emerging spirituality of teenagers than we might think. Teenagers develop the ability to think logically. They are more capable of hypothetical thought, considering possibilities rather than simply understanding what is true. They are capable of metacognition—that is, the ability to reflect on their own thinking and learning. For the first time in their lives, they are developing the skills to think about how they think about things. Questions such as "Why did you do it?" have little meaning for younger children. Parents deserve the "I dunno" answer they get. But teenagers can reflect on how they came to a decision. Adolescents have the ability to be more self-reflective and more self-evaluative. Sometimes they are so self-reflective and self-evaluative that they give almost no attention to other people. Adolescents tend to feel like they are always "on stage." Because they are always thinking about themselves, they assume everyone around them is thinking about them, too. But they are also better able to empathize with another person (though children can begin to express empathy at a very early age).

All these skills are developing and are not instantaneously active. Two issues determine how adolescents develop intellectually. First, different areas of the adolescent brain are changing rapidly; however, as we discussed, all areas of the brain do not develop at the same rate.

Areas of the brain that control emotional response tend to develop earlier, hence early adolescents' hunger for excitement and a propensity to make decisions based more on feeling instead of thought. The part of the brain that controls high-level reasoning tends to develop later and might actually not fully develop until their early twenties. Part of the development of adult thinking and reasoning skills, then, is biological.

There is also evidence that the adolescent brain develops the ability to do higher-level thinking through practice. Researcher Ronald Dahl writes:

> A strong body of work suggests that most measures of cognitive development correlate with age and experience—not sexual maturation. Measures of planning, logic, reasoning ability, inhibitory control, problem solving and understanding consequences are probably not puberty-linked."[33]

Higher-level reasoning in adolescents, then, does not merely occur as a natural function of biology. Rather, adolescents develop cognitive skills by applying reasoning to their life experiences. Dahl insists that adolescents need parents, teachers, and mentors who will help them develop the skills needed for adult life.[34] Adolescents develop their reasoning and thinking skills with stimulation and practice.

Adolescents' new ways of thinking open up myriads of new ways for young people to consider their faith in God. These changes

---

[33] Ronald E. Dahl, "Adolescent Brain Development: A Period of Vulnerabilities and Opportunities. Keynote Address," *Annals of New York Academy of Sciences* (July 2004), 18, https://www.researchgate.net/publication/8457353_Adolescent_Brain_Development_A_Period_of_Vulnerabilities_and_Opportunities_Keynote_Address.

[34] Dahl, 20.

should mean a change in how to teach teenagers. Teaching and training with adolescents should consider the following principles:

- Do not simply tell teenagers the answers. Give them guidance to discover answers for themselves. The older the teenager, the better at this he or she will be, but even young
  teenagers should wrestle with more complex spiritual issues.
- Give teenagers opportunities to reflect personally on their
  lives as they confront truths of the faith.
- Guide teenagers to practice articulating their faith. Youth
  ministry events that speak to teenagers but do not allow them
  opportunities to speak back or speak to each other are probably limiting the help they give teenagers to learn and grow.
- Scratch the "excitement-hunger" of teenagers, especially
  young teenagers. If learning seems boring, they might have
  difficulty connecting with new ideas.
- Use experiential learning with younger teenagers. They often
  struggle to put complex ideas into words. Effective teaching gives them concrete experiences that show them (instead
  of telling them about) complex ideas. Good teaching also
  exercises patience with younger teens and doesn't rush past
  important moments of wrestling.
- Engage youth with problem-solving and decision-making
  practices. Rich Bible study will ask teenagers to do both.

Peer Groups and Youth Ministry

American teenagers spend much of their time with peers almost
exactly their age (i.e., within a few months). If recent studies about
the amount of time teenagers spend in meaningful conversation
with their fathers and mothers are reliable, then most of the real

conversations American teenagers have are with their peers. A student's peer group (both their clique and their crowd) greatly influences what they do, what they wear, what language they use, and what they think about certain things. Finding a crowd to belong to (freaks, geeks, jocks, skaters, etc.) gives them a place to belong and a sense of protection from the harsh adolescent pecking order.

Despite the potential landmines, the peer group does tend to perform some important developmental functions. Peers provide a sounding board for teenagers to begin to explore their view of the world. As children, their view of the world was simply the view they learned from their parents. Whatever parents told them was generally what they believed. Ten-year-olds might discuss an issue such as abortion, but, except in very unusual circumstances, the view of each child would be the view of his or her parents. And if they want to refine their view after the discussion, they would return to their parents for direction. Teenagers begin to have an ability to weigh and evaluate the view of the world their parents have given them, though research indicates that, in the long run, the values of young people most often reflect the views of their parents. Nevertheless, young people will try on the values of their parents and see how they work outside the family. The peer group becomes a practical place to do that. Peers give teenagers practice in camaraderie, romance, debate, loyalty, and teamwork—all skills they will need for life. They allow teenagers a relatively safe place to ask questions and express doubts and confusion.

Researcher Merton Strommen suggests that one of the primary functions of a student ministry should be to provide a healthy peer group for teenagers.[35] When students are developing social skills,

---

[35] Merton P. Strommen and Richard A. Hardel, *Passing on the Faith*, rev. ed. (Winona, MN: St. Mary's Press, 2008).

a healthy peer group—one that provides warmth, forgiveness, and affirmation of faith—can make a tremendous difference in how teenagers in the group develop. This would seem to suggest important focal points for student ministry:

- Develop a group of teenagers and adults that is characterized by positive interaction, warmth, and forgiveness. Activities that build healthy group dynamics are invaluable.
- Provide social times for students to interact and explore ideas.
- Set Bible study in a warm, caring environment—something developed by both peers and youth leaders.
- Create a unique culture to your youth groups. Things such as inside jokes, shared stories, and accepted ways of doing things all help develop the culture.
- Encourage youth to develop close friends within the youth group and provide opportunities for those friendships to be nurtured.

Conclusion

Adolescents are constantly changing physically, cognitively, relationally, and in countless other ways. As a student minister, these are the people with whom you do student ministry. The transitioning nature of their lives must shape how you teach, what activities you organize, how you build relationships, and how you exert influence on them. Thoughtfully ministering to teens in this chaotic and exciting time of their lives will help build a faith that will carry them through what lies ahead. These are challenging years for ministry, but they're also ripe with unbelievable possibilities.

Student Ministry
and Youth Culture

• KAREN JONES •

A dolescents make up approximately 16 percent of the world's population.[1] In the world's forty-eight least-developed countries, children or adolescents actually make up a majority of the population.[2] In the United States, about 12.9 percent of the country's population are youth, and while they are predicted to represent a smaller portion of the country's population in the future, estimates show that the actual number of adolescents in the United States will

---

[1] UNICEF, "Adolescents Overview," UNICEF, October 2019, https:// data.unicef.org/topic/adolescents/overview/.

[2] Report of the Advisory Committee for the International Youth Year, A/36/215, annex. 2, https://www.un.org/development/desa/dpad2. 2019.

continue to grow, reaching almost 44 million in 2050.[3] These stats offer both opportunities and challenges for the church.

The Challenge of Youth

It's no secret that adults are often hesitant to engage in ministry with teenagers, but have you ever wondered why? Is the reluctance due to negative media coverage of delinquent behaviors or dangerous cultural trends among young people? Is it because adults remember their own difficult passage through the waters of adolescence? Regardless, the criticism of youth and youth culture is not a modern phenomenon. Consider the comments made by Aristotle in the fourth century BC:

> [*They*] Have strong passions, and tend to gratify them indiscriminately. They are changeable and fickle in their desires, which are violent while they last. They are hot-tempered and quick tempered . . . owing to their love of honour they cannot bear being slighted, and are indignant if they imagine themselves unfairly treated. While they love honour, they love victory still more; for youth is eager for superiority over others. They have exalted notions, because they have not yet been humbled by life or learnt its necessary limitations; . . . All their mistakes are in the direction of doing things excessively and vehemently . . . they love too much and hate too

---

[3] *Projected 5-Year Age Groups and Sex Composition: Main Projections Series for the United States, 2017–2060* (Washington, DC: U.S. Census Bureau, Population Division), https://www2.census.gov/programs-surveys/popproj/tables/2017/2017-summary-tables/np2017-t3.xlsx.

much, and the same with everything else. They think they know everything, and are always quite sure about it.[4]

Though the specifics of youth culture continuously change, adults' descriptions of teen problems remain historically consistent.

This negative view of youth in history is recorded not only in secular sources, but Christian sources as well. Note the language in these two excerpts from seventeenth- and eighteenth-century sermons:

> Of all others, young persons are most apt to neglect the fear of God and be unmindful of the Maker through the temptation of sensual pleasures and youthful lusts . . . their age is most inviting to the Devil to bend his chiefest forces against them, rather than against children, or aged persons, the former not being capable of making a choice, and the latter being fix'd and resolv'd in their way; his principal endeavors therefore are levell'd against youth, to draw off their hearts from God and holy things, and to divert their thoughts from the consideration of death and judgment, which would otherwise restrain and check them in pursuit of their lusts.[5]

> Look abroad into the world: consider the generality of our youth in this age, what they are, what manner of lives they lead, how vain, lewd, and debauched the most are in their conversation; how rare it is to find one amongst many that is solid, sober, and religious, that makes real conscience of

---

[4] Aristotle, "Rhetoric" in *The Basic Works of Aristotle*, ed. Richard McKeon (New York: Random House, 1941), 1403–4.

[5] John Shower, *An Exhortation to Youth to Prepare for Judgment: A Sermon Occasion'd by the Late Repentance and Funeral of a Young Man, Deceased September 29* (J.G., 1681), 12–14.

avoiding all known sin, and of performing holy duties, or of exercising himself to godliness, as becomes his Christian profession. Nay, do not many of them walk, act, and talk more like atheists, or infidels, than Christians.[6]

No matter one's faith or the time in which they lived, adults have always found youth a challenging and difficult group with which to work.

So how can one push through the difficulties and reach youth with the gospel? Among the many good answers, this chapter will focus on one: by studying the culture in which youth live.

The Importance of Understanding Youth Culture

Understanding how youth culture is created, defined, and identified will help adults seeking to effectively minister to teens. As with any missionary endeavor, if there is any hope of reaching young people with the truth of the gospel, it is imperative to understand and penetrate their surrounding culture. The evangelistic and discipleship goals of student ministry will be realized in proportion to the success of the youth leader in ministering thoughtfully within the context their youth's culture.

What Is Culture?

All human behavior occurs within a culture that is a socially defined context. Culture isn't easily identified or recognized from the inside. It is the total context of the life one is living, similar to the water in

---

[6] See C. John Sommerville, "Breaking the Icon: The First Real Children in English Books," *History of Education Quarterly* 21, no. 1 (1981): 51–75, https://doi.org/10.2307/368004.

a fishbowl for a fish. It isn't contemplated; it just is. Defining culture isn't simple, as more than a hundred definitions exist for the word. The English word *culture* is derived from the Latin *cultura* or *cultus*, which means "care." Many other English words have the same origin, such as "cult." Cult refers to a religious organization, typically with a strong leader who asserts power over a group in order to shape their behavior or brainwash them.[7] Culture is similar in that it is a powerful shaper of behavior for those within its sphere of influence. Especially for teens, aspects of culture have completely captivated their loyalty.

Culture is probably best understood in terms of how a group determines what is or isn't appropriate. These standards change depending on where one is located, either geographically or historically. Consider how standards of dress for worship, funerals, and weddings have changed in the last several decades. Styles of dress and music represent categories anthropologists use to explain culture. They are some of the unique ways a group of people defines itself, the distinctive characteristics of a group's way of life. Other cultural characteristics include dress, customs, beliefs, values, leisure and entertainment, and artistic expression. The characteristics of any given culture reveal much of its sensibilities and sense of normalcy.

In addition to cultural standards, there is always more than one culture at play for any individual such as nation, region, community, or family. Think about how people in various regions of the country interact with strangers, their sense of hospitality, or the foods they prefer. What about the various words they use to describe things? Though many people might share a common national culture (e.g., American), the other cultures to which they belong (e.g., Southern,

---

[7] Arthur Asa Berger, "The Meanings of Culture," *M/C: A Journal of Media and Culture* 3, no. 2 (2000): https://doi.org/10.5204/mcj.1833.

East Coast, Midwest) create a wide diversity in the ways they think, speak, and act.

Any one specific culture often has multiple layers within it. The idea of a Christian culture is a good example. Popular entertainment or gathering spots for youth in a particular community might differ from other regions in the state, but even within that community there are probably different acceptable standards for Christian youth than non-Christian young people. This can even differ from church to church or denomination to denomination. These standards of acceptable behavior represent various cultures. Neighborhoods have their own unique cultures, as do schools and even corporations. Employees are trained on the nonnegotiables of their various corporate cultures. Each family also has a unique cultural structure, and it is in the family where culture is first experienced, and that unique culture typically has the greatest power and influence in a person's life.

What Is Youth Culture?

Adolescence is the stage of the life when the power of the family culture often takes a backseat to development. Youth are thinking differently, making their own decisions, trying to figure out who they are apart from their parents, desperate for friends and to identify with a peer group, trying on new roles, and discovering their own moral and spiritual beliefs. This draws them into a separate cultural reality.

Teenagers' developmental changes plunge them into a separate sea of youth culture, but they wade into those waters at varying degrees. "Youth culture" is an umbrella term, and characteristics of a universal youth culture will always be nuanced or amplified within specific contexts. For example, if you have participated in a national youth gathering, you will have noticed marked differences in the youth groups represented. Each group represents a unique culture. A helpful description of youth culture is this:

> the specific society of teens and young adolescents, that frequently is inclusive of types of clothing, talk, music, and actions which are reasonfully at variance to those of the dominant society.[8]

Even though parents and churches are highly influential with respect to cultural norms, at some point in time the vast majority of youth do begin to resemble one another culturally, and often in a way that is "at variance to those of the dominant society." This happens on a global scale. While culture begins in families and is shaped by the surrounding community, technology has united young people worldwide and advanced many aspects of youth culture on a global scale.

Within the broader, universally recognized youth culture there are also dozens of youth subcultures. Subcultures are identified by their unique characteristics in certain categories such as language, behaviors, fashion, ideas, beliefs, worldview, music, or art. As an example, art refers to the creative works produced by a particular subculture, including both visual (e.g., anime or manga) and performing arts like dance or music (e.g., popping, grinding, krumping). These are generally unique to youth culture but don't describe mainstream youth activities. They are characteristic of various youth subcultures. Another example is fashion, which might be the most important aspect of some subcultures and may even relate to an artform such as music or theatrical activities. Cosplay is a good example of this relationship. It provides a way for individuals to identify themselves as distinct yet also as members of a particular group. It can include

---

[8] N. Pam M.S., "Youth Culture," in PsychologyDictionary.org, April 29, 2013, https://psychologydictionary.org/youth-culture/.

not only clothing, but footwear, jewelry, hairstyles, or body art. The behaviors might also include social and individual activities, events, traditions, and ways of relating to one another that make the subculture distinct from the larger, surrounding culture.

How Do Youth Acquire Culture?

How do people actually acquire their various cultural values and norms? It happens in one of two ways: enculturation or assimilation. Enculturation is how people are raised, how they grow up. It is the learning a child accepts without questioning, the way someone acquires a cultural heritage. It is when culture is put into someone. Assimilation is when people learn to fit in with a culture that is different than that of their heritage. It is when someone puts themselves into culture. To explain it simply, teens in your youth group have been raised in families and neighborhoods. Some of them have been brought up in the church. They have been enculturated in those areas of their lives. When they enter school for the first time, they must assimilate to the school culture. If participation in a church isn't part of their upbringing, they must assimilate into that culture when they become part of your youth group. If they move or change schools or churches, their family configuration changes, or they begin a job, they must assimilate into a new culture. Each person's unique cultural sensibilities are acquired through both the enculturation they've been taught and assimilation they've sought.

How Should We Minister to People in a Different Culture?

In all interpersonal interactions, people must consider both their personal and their shared cultures. A person's own culture sets the standard by which he or she makes judgments about others and all new situations and ideas. That judgment is made on the basis of his or her own values and ways of life acquired through the culture. This is known as "ethnocentrism," looking at others and making judgments based on one's own cultural standards.

Ethnocentrism is probably the leading causes of intergenerational clashes and the negative feelings adults have for youth culture. These conflicts occur when the standards and priorities of one culture are different than those of another culture and when moral force is attributed to a specific priority in a culture. The cultural priorities and practices of adults and youth differ, and conflicts will arise when either group considers its own practice better or more just. Recognizing that culture is always changing, it is easy to understand that these generational clashes are inevitable.

It is imperative that youth workers view teen behaviors through the lens of development and culture, and that personal judgments are minimized. There is a place for judgment from a biblical perspective on morality and righteous living so that spiritual formation is fostered in the lives of young people, but it isn't always easy to separate cultural preference from biblical truth. Concerns about such things as music and fashion might be legitimate if they violate Christian teachings on morality and purity, but all too often adults instigate arguments over aspects of youth culture that only serve to alienate young people.

Adults who want to minister effectively to youth must understand youth culture. To do this, it is crucial to approach youth culture as an outside researcher seeking to understand the world as youth do. Though adults can observe the language, dress, customs, and artistic expressions, it is important to remember they are not part of that distinct group of people and often won't interpret the meaning of those elements as a teen does.

Though youth workers should study youth culture to understand the students to whom they minister, youth workers should be careful to not enter the culture to become an insider. It is helpful for youth workers to understand the cultural language of teens, but trying to make the language one's own isn't advised. They would sound ridiculous for one thing, but more importantly youth need adults who look and sound and relate as adults. They need to know that someone is out there who can protect and advise and listen to them, adults who love them and give them space. What they don't need are adults trying to act like teenagers. When teens wade too far into the cultural sea they want someone on shore to be able to rescue them, not someone who is being swept away in the same currents.

Jeff Keuss makes the case that we must seek to understand young people as those who are blurring the boundaries of identity and culture. To understand this concept, adults must move between and beyond their differing interpretations of meaning and acknowledge that there is a lot going on beneath the observable surface of the lives of young people, things that adults just don't experience. Keuss calls adults to work with youth as "sacredly mobile adolescents."[9] They are sacred because they are created in the image and likeness of God. Adolescents are in a particular stage of development, and they are mobile because they are deepening and forging their identities. Their musical choices, for instance, could be interpreted as a reflection of their spiritual longing and celebration. These might very well be their attempts to break free from a cycle of meaninglessness, or they might even be quests for new beginnings and meaning. Sometimes their musical choices are the ways in which they connect with a larger community beyond themselves.[10] If

---

[9] Jeff Keuss, *Blur: A New Paradigm for Understanding Youth Culture* (Grand Rapids, MI: Zondervan, 2014), [*].

[10] Keuss.

adults allow themselves to be simply offended or annoyed by the musical preferences of youth, they'll miss the opportunity to learn what the music itself teaches them about the youth they love.

Culturally sensitive student ministry is also strengthened when adults take a step back to remember their own adolescent journey. Youth culture, superficially dominated by musical tastes, slang, fashion, and objectionable hairstyles, is simply part of growing up. Sociologists have documented these little rebellions since the nineteenth century when, as author Jon Savage describes, the notion of youth as a completely separate rebellious stage of life began.[11]

How Student Ministries Can Engage the Surrounding Culture

Youth workers hold their own philosophies about how to approach youth and culture, and these philosophies are reflected in the ways their ministries are structured. These philosophies are seldom articulated but are certainly operant and can be recognized by observing what takes place within the structure of a ministry. They shape the culture of a church's student ministry, from its programming to the ways in which adults and youth interact. Merton Strommen and Richard Hardel explain why cultural views are significant in student ministry:

> [Culture] is a way of living that has become normative for a group of human beings. Culture includes music, art, media, and intellectual stimuli that contain and communicate norms and values. But a culture whose basic norms and values are

---

[11] See Jon Savage, *Teenage: The Prehistory of Youth Culture: 1875–1945* (New York: Penguin Group, 2008.)

life-enriching and are a source of enjoyment and blessing can be misrepresented and eroded by the media that communicate them. Media that encourage self-gratification, individualism, antiauthoritarianism, and the like are powerful shapers of the attitudes and values not only of young people but also of families, communities, and the culture itself.[12]

A helpful way to think about youth leaders' philosophical approaches to culture within the context of ministry is to consider the five views proposed by Richard Niebuhr in his book, *Christ and Culture*. The five approaches are titled Christ of Culture, Christ Against Culture, Christ Above Culture, Christ and Culture in Paradox, and Christ the Transformer of Culture. The Christ of Culture view tends to accept cultural expressions as a whole, uncritical and celebrated as a good thing. Christ Against Culture views cultural forms outside the church with suspicion and corrupted by sin. They should be avoided as much as possible. Another view is Christ Above Culture, where cultural forms are viewed as basically good, but in need of perfection by the work of the church, with Christ supreme over both. The reality of the future suggests that Christ will ultimately redeem all human culture. The fourth view is Christ and Culture in Paradox, where human culture is viewed as a good creation that's been tainted by sin. There is tension in the Christian's relationship to culture, embracing and rejecting certain aspects of it. The final view is Christ the Transformer of Culture, which recognizes human culture as initially good and subsequently corrupted by the fall, but since Christ is redeeming all of creation, the Christian can and should be working to transform culture for

---

[12] Strommen and Hardel, *Passing on the Faith*, 257 (see chap. 6, n. 35).

God's glory.[13] More or less, each student ministry will fall into one of these five categories in how they relate to and engage the wider culture around them.

Earlier in the chapter, water in a fishbowl was used to explain both the presence of culture and why it is often overlooked. Just as a fish cannot help but live in water, so every person cannot help but live within a cultural sphere. Even a hermit living alone in an isolated part of the world has established a culture, a way of doing life complete with fashion and philosophies and values. Culture is an inescapable part of human existence. Too much reliance on or indulgence in various cultural forms, however, can be detrimental to one's existence. Some aspects of culture are polluted and can be threatening to physical, emotional, social, or spiritual aspects of life. There are various cultural expressions that have corrupted life and are harmful, even consumed in small quantities. These represent the dangers that frighten adults when they think about youth culture. Remember that there is nothing inherently evil about youth culture. It is a natural part of development and identity discovery, but there are expressions of youth culture that can be harmful. The wise adult will practice discernment, protecting teens from that which endangers them and tolerating those behaviors that are merely annoying.

It is imperative that adults understand youth culture as the outcome of a process young people go through as they seek a community that's distinct from what they've experienced as children. It is a period rich in self-expression and the negotiation of social boundaries. What makes adolescents and youth culture unique at this period in history is that there are open communication platforms at their

---

[13] Richard H. Niebuhr, *Christ and Culture* (San Francisco: Harper & Row, 1951).

fingertips that allow them to connect on a global scale with people going through the same biological, psychological, and social changes. Instead of merely creating a group identity in their schools or at the mall, they have the potential to do it through social networks and in networked computer games.

It isn't important to know all the facts presented in all the research on teens and youth culture. For one thing, the statistics and trends are always changing. That's the key characteristic of youth culture; it is never static. There are also countless individuals and groups doing the work of researching teenagers and youth culture for you. Walt Mueller's Center for Parent/Youth Understanding (CYPU) is one example. As a Christian resource that collects information from a number of other sources, it can be of particular help and interest to student ministers. Youth workers are probably familiar with Barna, Lifeway, Pew Research, and Gallup, organizations that often engage in important youth research. It can be valuable to familiarize yourself with companies that research teens for commercial purposes as well. There are market research companies that focus on teens' attitudes, values, lifestyles, consumer behaviors, and trends. They typically serve advertising/marketing agencies that work with various industries (e.g., food, entertainment, retail). These companies spend millions of dollars to study teen culture, and the information they obtain can often be valuable for those wanting to reach the same demographic with the gospel of Jesus.

Teenagers have always been important to brands because they tend to be early adopters and because, traditionally, their brand preferences aren't yet firmly defined. One unique difference between today's teenagers and past generations is that they're not listening to what the media and older generations are telling them is cool. According to Mark Green, "Oliver Pangborn, senior youth insights consultant at the market research firm The Futures Company, said,

'Teenagers have now become the gatekeepers to modern trends. With the internet and social media, teenagers have more access to that information than ever before.'"[14] Teens also influence a significant amount of the purchases made in their families, especially in the area of technology. The challenge with this generation of teens becoming the new gatekeepers is that they're less loyal to brands and businesses than the generations that came before them. They've grown up in a time when the next greatest thing is always available months after they've purchased the last greatest thing. They're more loyal to the best product than a particular brand, and they're also more interested in value than past generations. These preferences impact not only technology but also fashion. While expensive pairs of destroyed jeans flew off the shelves of popular youth retailers in the past, many of these chains are in decline and thrift stores and clothing-exchange boutiques have taken the lead as the shopping destinations of choice.

Media and technology often rise to the top of our cultural concerns list, and they are arguably the primary means by which today's youth culture is shaped and transmitted. Adults are concerned about what teens are seeing and hearing; they are bothered by the amount of time they spend online; they worry about who they are meeting and what they are sharing; and they wonder why they seem to have an incessant need to post and text and chat. How is their identity being shaped? How can they find time to simply be still and meditate on God when their minutes are consumed with technology and there is no downtime?[15]

---

[14] Mark Green, "How Data Science Connects Brands to Teens," Dataversity, November 18, 2015, https://www.dataversity.net/how-data-science-connects-brands-to-teens/.

[15] See Craig Detweiler, *iGods: How Technology Shapes Our Spiritual and Social Lives* (Grand Rapids, MI: Brazos Press, 2013).

All forms of media have always had a phenomenal influence on adolescent development. This concern about youth and media isn't new; the forms have just changed, and the amount of time spent in consuming and connecting has increased. There are no longer natural limits that can easily be controlled by adults. It is always on, unlike the test pattern that used to appear on the one television screen in a home.[16]

This idea of screen time is also often associated with unrealistic expectations for life, presenting stereotypes, increasing weight gain, providing a platform for bullying, exposing students to danger, and modeling violent and aggressive behavior. Technology exposes teens to cultural values and norms very different from those with which they were enculturated. Not all researchers share the same opinions on the impact of networked teens, however. Some argue that it puts teens in the center of creating culture and not just consuming it.

Another important and surprising research finding related to technology is that, despite the constant talk about a global network, there is little evidence for a common global youth culture. In fact, most teens use technology to interact with people they already know. Danah Boyd, a researcher at Microsoft, makes the claim that teenagers surround themselves on social media with friends who share their same beliefs and values, thoughts and anxieties. They live in a world where they begin to believe that everyone thinks like they do. They spend less time with people who are different, so rather than a global monolithic youth culture, there are lots of little tight-knit fragments. Boyd argues that ever since the word *teenager* was coined seventy years ago, adults have always defined adolescents by one extreme or another. In her research, she discovered that teens would much rather hang out with their friends in person than online, but they can't.

---

[16] See Detweiler.

They have less freedom to hang out than any previous generation. Many American teenagers have been raised to fear strangers. They attend schools outside of their neighborhoods. They have jobs, or play sports, or take lessons. Social media is the only way some teenagers can experience life, according to Boyd. They go online to have a sense of control. It is a tool they can use to manage their pressures and limitations.[17]

It is important to understand why media usage and technology is such a draw for teens. Many adults think of teens' obsession with technology in terms of the "moth effect," that they are attracted to the light of the screen. This hypothesis is debunked by researchers such as Andrew Zirschky. In his book, *Beyond the Screen: Youth Ministry for the Connected but Alone Generation*, Zirschky provides evidence for his belief that teens' apparent social media addiction is borne out of their desire for true community. The average teen has 3.5 personal digital gadgets and spends an average of 10.5 hours per day in mediated screen time, but they are using social media, he argues, to establish full-time intimate communities that provide always-on relationships. This might explain why text messaging remains their main app as opposed to other social media platforms. It allows them to take their friends with them and provides presence in absence. Why the need for this sense of presence in absence? Unfortunately, teens often feel alone even when they're with teens in a physical setting. Being together doesn't guarantee relationship or acceptance. Even though the majority of teens don't believe that online relationships are as fulfilling as offline relationships, many young people, even in our youth ministries, aren't finding genuine community.[18]

---

[17] Danah Boyd, *It's Complicated: The Social Lives of Networked Teens* (New Haven, CT: Yale University Press, 2014).

[18] Andrew Zirschky, *Beyond the Screen: Youth Ministry for the Connected but Alone Generation* (Nashville: Abingdon, 2015).

This argument for community doesn't account for the hours spent on YouTube or Netflix or Hulu, watching entertainment alone. But keep in mind, when family and other societal structures are strong, cultural forces make much less of an impact on a young person's development. Cultural forms such as media are strongest when other social structures are weak. Perhaps young people aren't being challenged to find purpose or meaning beyond themselves.

Cultural changes in family structures and schedules also shape adolescents in powerful ways. Chap Clark reports on his personal research with adolescents. Instead of focusing on differences he observed, Clark emphasizes the commonalities among the youth population.

Adults tend to view teens in one of two ways, as either doing well or in dire straits. He concludes that teens are really operating out of multiple selves in order to survive. They're friends, athletes, students, and children. They have been largely cut off from adults who have the experience they need to help them navigate into adulthood. They have been abandoned, forced to create their own world that can protect them from the adult community. Not everyone agrees with Clark's work, but he makes some strong arguments supported by his observations and conversations with young people.[19]

Another major change taking place in youth culture is related to teens' search for identity. This is the key task of adolescence, according to Erikson. They experiment and try on roles; they join groups and teams and play instruments; they switch their manner of dress and groups of friends, all in an effort to figure out who they are, what they're good at, and where they fit in the world. This has become more complicated as young people are receiving mixed messages

---

[19] Chap Clark, *Hurt 2.0: Inside the World of Today's Teenagers* (Grand Rapids, MI: Baker Academic, 2011).

about gender identity while the larger adult culture redefines what it means to be human. No longer can teens focus on what it means to be an adult male or female within their culture, but they're often encouraged to take on various hybrid sexual identities. Adolescents are vulnerable at this stage of life. They are discovering what it means to be a sexual being. Their shifting emotions, feelings of self-doubt and insecurity, and desire for acceptance can lead to manipulation by others. Adults can prey on teens and take advantage of them for their own personal or political gain.

This identity confusion can involve devastating consequences. Suicide is the second leading cause of death among the nation's teenagers, and LGBT youth are more likely to both have suicidal thoughts and actually attempt suicide than their heterosexual peers. According to findings of the Youth Risk and Behavior Surveillance System (YRBSS), "among high school students who identified as LGBT, 60.4 percent felt sad and hopeless, 42.8 percent seriously considered suicide, and 38.2 percent planned how they would attempt suicide; 29.4 percent attempted suicide one or more times, and 9.4 percent made a suicide attempt that resulted in an injury, including poisoning or overdose that had to be treated by a medical professional."[20]

Teenagers are prone to emotional swings and susceptible to depression due to hormonal changes related to their physical development. They are also in a time of life when the opinions of others are more important than any other stage of the lifespan, and they are not making the most rational of decisions due to their continuing brain development. While they are capable of logical reasoning and abstract thought, much of the time they are still operating on emotion more than reason.

---

[20] R. Aranmolate, D R. Bogan, T. Hoard, and A. R. Mawson, "Suicide Risk Factors among LGBTQ Youth: Review," *JSM Schizophria* 2, no. 2 (2017): 1011.

A study of youth culture could explore a variety of topics and issues, but due to the ever-changing nature of youth culture, it is more important to become a student of culture than a consumer of statistics. More specifically, youth workers must begin seeking to understand their own local youth cultures if they are going to be effective ministers. Read the available published research, but also take time to enter the world inhabited by your youth. Observe, ask questions, and listen. Look for clues in understanding your local youth culture. What are the markers of maturity and autonomy for young people? What do they believe about God and spirituality? How do teens identify as members of a subculture? What is the glue that holds their groups together? How do teens in my community deal with their pain or fear? What movies do they watch and what music do they listen to that brings them together or inspires them to create? What does their media consumption say about them that adults have not taken the time to understand? What are their ideas about how the world should operate? What brings them joy, moves them to tears, or causes them to laugh? As you observe what's going on, ask yourself what it means. What are they looking for and have they found it?

Conclusion

As you relate to teenagers and youth culture, make every effort to imitate Christ and his relationship to culture. The incarnation represents, in many ways, a cross-cultural ministry. Jesus Christ, fully God, entered the world as a helpless baby, fully man. To be a youth worker is to be a cross-cultural minister. It requires taking on the posture of a learner, exercising humility, refraining from judgment, and leaning in to listen with love.

Student Ministry
and the Family

• TIMOTHY PAUL JONES •

What does student ministry have to do with the family? Throughout my early years as a student minister, my answer to this question was, "As little as possible."

As far as I was concerned, my best ministry happened when I ignored the family and connected directly with the students. All the fastest-growing youth ministries around me seemed to be bypassing the family, so I did, too. I pursued this pattern pragmatically because my goal was to gather as many students as possible. I even had a couple of Bible verses that supported this tactic. Hadn't Jesus said that his true family was anyone who followed his Father's will (Matt 12:50)? Jesus had even commanded his disciples to disregard their parents, if their parents stood in the way of following him (Matt 8:21–22;

10:35–37)! That's what I convinced myself I was doing as I gathered teenagers and challenged them to be faithful to Jesus, which mostly meant going to youth group activities and vowing not to have sex until they were married.

During those years, I did succeed in gathering a growing group of middle schoolers and high schoolers who, for the most part, showed up at youth group and didn't have sex. All the while, I intended to disciple these crowds of students as well. And yet, attracting them, entertaining them, and building connections with them required so much energy that little time was left in my calendar for comprehensive discipleship.

I spent about three years pursuing this approach. The result was frustration and eventually burnout. It took several years and a transition in my role before I began to recognize that bypassing the family hadn't been the best strategy for ministry. More importantly, it wasn't biblical. I didn't know it at the time, but the pattern I had pursued as a young student minister was part of a problem that had been seething beneath the surface of student ministry for several decades. In fact, one student minister had already provided a picturesque title for the problem in the late 1980s. He called it "the one-eared Mickey Mouse."[1]

Youth Ministry and the Family:
Separate Ships Sailing in the Same Direction

Imagine the simplest possible sketch of Mickey Mouse, with a large central circle representing his head and two round ears that barely touch the larger circle. Now, erase one of the renowned rodent's ears

---

[1] Stuart Cummings-Bond, "The One-Eared Mickey Mouse," *Youth-worker* (Fall 1989): 76.

so that you end up with a one-eared Mickey Mouse. That's how a student minister named Stuart Cummings-Bond depicted the relationship between his ministry and the rest of his congregation in 1989. The head of the cartoon mouse stood for the church as a whole, and the single ear represented his student ministry. Like the ear of the mouse on Walt Disney's drawing board, his ministry to students was barely connected to the rest of the body. The student ministry and the larger congregation were technically linked together. Yet the two ministries functioned independently, with each one pursuing its own separate purposes and passions. Conceived in the late nineteenth century and professionalized at the height of the baby boom, this ministry model seemed like an attractive option for many churches in the late twentieth century.[2]

Here's another less macabre analogy that probably fits the theme of this book a bit better than a mutilated mouse: Imagine two ships, both sailing near each other and headed in a similar direction. One of the vessels is a bit smaller, and the occupants are younger and louder. The larger vessel is packed with passengers who are older and calmer, but many of them have younger children clustered around them as well. Once in a while, the captains of the two ships shout instructions at each other. Sometimes, someone might even dare to cast a rope from one ship to the other, and a few mariners and passengers slide across the space between them. For the most part, however, the two watercraft remain on courses that are parallel but separate.

---

[2] For more on the history of this approach to youth ministry, see Timothy Paul Jones, "Models of Family Ministry," in *A Theology for Family Ministries*, ed. Michael Anthony and Michelle Anthony (Nashville: B&H, 2011); and W. R. Steenburg, "Growing Gaps from Generation to Generation," in *Trained in the Fear of God*, ed. Randy Stinson and Timothy Paul Jones (Grand Rapids, MI: Kregel, 2011).

The smaller ship in this maritime analogy represents the church's student ministry; the larger vessel is the rest of the church, where parents and other family members find fellowship. In some congregations, the number of ships isn't limited to two; there may be an entire flotilla of vessels sailing the seas together. Children's ministries, singles groups, and senior adult programs might all be plotting their own paths across the sea in their own ships. The primary focus of this particular book is, however, ministry to teenagers. As such, the only ship that I'll be tracking is the one with the words "Youth Ministry" emblazoned on the bow.

The purpose of this chapter is to consider one simple question: What would the relationship between student ministry and the family look like if churches began navigating according to a theological map of the seas instead of pursuing a pragmatic cartography? To help us make this transition in our thinking, let's first take a careful look at the family from a biblical point of view.

A Biblical Theology of the Family

For those who receive the Scriptures as their ultimate written authority, the human family must be defined as a community formed by a lifelong covenant between one woman and one man (Matt 19:4–9).[3] In keeping with the divine design, this community may also include the blessing of adopted and biological children (Gen 1:26–28). The lives of these family members are embedded in larger communities

---

[3] Although polygamy was practiced in biblical times, the singular nouns in Gen 2:24 suggest that monogamy was God's design from the beginning. See David W. Jones and Andreas J. Köstenberger, *God, Marriage, and Family*, 2nd ed. (Wheaton, IL: Crossway, 2010), loc. 546 of [*], Kindle; and Charles M. Sell, *Family Ministry*, 2nd ed. (Grand Rapids: Zondervan, 1995), 76.

and inextricably linked with grandparents and in-laws as well as more distant family members.

Neither marriage nor family is a purely human construction. Marriage is "rooted in God's creative act of making humanity in his image as male and female."[4] The family, too, is God's idea. It was God himself who formed the primal family by bringing Adam and Eve together and commanding them to multiply. As such, the family can never be rightly understood until the family is seen in the context of God's plan.

According to the Scriptures, at the center of God's plan stands a singular act: In Jesus Christ, God personally intersected human history and redeemed humanity at a particular time in a particular place. Yet this central act of redemption does not stand alone in the story of God. It is one part of a metanarrative that includes God's good creation and humanity's rebellion on the one hand and the consummation of God's kingdom on the other. This fourfold storyline of (1) creation, (2) fall, (3) redemption, and (4) new creation summarizes the most essential points in an age-old plotline that Christians have embraced ever since Jesus ascended and sent his Spirit to dwell in his followers' lives.[5]

When the family is examined in the context of this metanarrative, it becomes clear that God has always intended the family to serve as a divinely ordained means for the fulfillment of his purposes. This reality should shape the ways that the family and student ministry

---

[4] Jones and Köstenberger, *God, Marriage, and Family*, loc. 351 of [*].

[5] Although this metanarrative may be found implicitly in the New Testament and in the apostolic fathers, the fourfold form that has become familiar in biblical theology seems to be rooted in the states of humanity formulated by Augustine of Hippo, particularly in *Enchiridion de Fide*: "Harum quattuor differentiarum prima est ante legem, secunda sub lege, tertia sub gratia, quarta in pace plena atque perfecta" (31 [118]).

relate. With this in mind, let's develop a biblical theology of the family by looking at the family from the perspective of each movement in God's plan for humanity. Then, throughout the remainder of the chapter, we'll unpack the implications of these theological truths for the practice of student ministry.

Creation: Family before the Fall

Before humanity's fall into sin, God formed the human family so that images of himself would be multiplied throughout the cosmos (Gen 1:28). Neither family roles nor gender roles constitute the essence of creation in God's image.[6] At the same time, genderless humanity is an impossibility.[7] In God's design, gender is binary and fixed, and the complementarity of male and female forms the foundation for the multiplication of God's image through families. "When we are ordered to 'be fruitful,'" Protestant reformer Pietro Vermigli pointed out, "it is with the understanding that we should beget such images of God as we have been made to be."[8] Because every human being is formed in God's image, parents and student ministers should view every child and student as a gift from God, stamped with evidence of the Creator's good design.

---

[6] Peter J. Gentry and Stephen J. Wellum, *Kingdom through Covenant* (Wheaton, IL: Crossway, 2012), 189.

[7] "There can be no question of an 'essence of man' apart from existence as two sexes. . . . There can only be anything like humanity and human relations where the human species exists as twos. . . . Every deliberate detachment of male from female, can endanger the very existence of humanity as determined by creation." C. Westermann, *Genesis 1–11*, trans. J. Scullion (Minneapolis: Augsburg, 1984), 160.

[8] Pietro Martire Vermigli, *In Primum Librum Mosis* (Zurich: Christophorus Proschoverus, 1579), 7:v.

Fall: The Family Fractured by Sin

After humanity's choice to rebel against God, sin spread like a pandemic and infected every aspect of God's creation, including the family. Nevertheless, the family remained part of God's good plan. According to God's word of judgment spoken to the satanic serpent, the family would be the means by which God would bring a Savior into the world to shatter the dominion of sin (Gen 3:15). For more than a millennium, God preserved the descendants of Abraham, Isaac, and Jacob so that he could provide the world with a messiah; the children of Israel throughout this epoch of history bore and raised children with this messianic hope in mind.[9]

The family was, however, something more than a means by which God planned to bring a messiah into the world. In God's good design, families also functioned as a context for preserving the message of God's mighty deeds (see, e.g., Exod 12:25–28; Deut 6:6–7; 11:1–12; Ps 78:1–7). Even in the Old Testament, parents were to be "involved in the teaching of the children. The teaching [was] to be done 'diligently' [Deut 6:7a], which . . . has the idea of repeating. This is not an occasional thing that parents do; it is a regular part of the life of the family."[10]

When parents in Israel diligently taught their children, they told stories (see, e.g., Deut 6:20–25; Ps 78). The framework for these stories was a repeated pattern of humanity's sinfulness followed by God's mighty provision. Through these narratives, parents reminded their children and themselves that they were sinners, entangled not only in their own personal rebellion but also in systems of sin and oppression that began before they were born.

---

[9] James M. Hamilton Jr., *God's Glory in Salvation through Judgment* (Wheaton, IL: Crossway, 2010), 82.

[10] Ajith Fernando, *Deuteronomy: Loving Obedience to a Loving God* (Wheaton, IL: Crossway, 2012), 264–65.

Redemption: Family as a Means and a Sign

After the redemption of the cosmos through the cross of Christ, believing families continued to function as a means and a context for diligently teaching children. "Fathers," Paul urged the church in Ephesus, "don't stir up anger in your children, but bring them up in the training and instruction of the Lord" (Eph 6:4).[11] Elsewhere in Paul's writings, the terms translated "training" and "instruction" in this text described how a pastor admonishes his flock and how God's Word shapes the lives of God's people (see, e.g., 1 Cor 10:11; 2 Tim 3:16; Titus 3:10). Part of what these words in Ephesians reveal is that Paul expected Christian parents to incorporate practices of discipleship into their daily lives at home.

In the New Testament no less than in the Old, the family is a means and a context for discipleship. The Christian household is to function, in some sense, as a microcosm of the larger community of faith. At the same time, the new covenant initiated by the blood of Jesus Christ also revealed a deeper purpose for the family. According to Jesus, his true sisters and brothers were his followers, and his true family was the community of those who pursue his Father's will (Matt 12:48–50; 28:10; Mark 3:33–35; Luke 8:21; John 20:17). In time, these teachings of Jesus led his first followers to recognize human families not only as a means for discipleship but also as a sign that points to a greater family.

---

[11] "The genitive noun κυρίου ["of the Lord"] . . . is subjective, and Paul refers to the training and instruction that the Lord gives to children through the family father." F. Thielman, *Ephesians* (Grand Rapids, MI: Baker, 2010), 402. It is conceivable, though not certain, that πατέρες ("fathers") could in this context refer both to fathers and mothers. See W. Larkin, *Ephesians* (Waco, TX: Baylor University Press, 2009), 147.

From the moment the first family was formed, God's plan and purpose for the family has always been the same: From the beginning, God created the covenant relationship of a husband and wife to signify the greater and more perfect love of a Savior who would give his life to redeem his church and continue to care for her until she's radiant (Eph 5:27–33).[12] In the new covenant, the church becomes our first family (Matt 12:46–50).[13]

Although healthy marriages and families are wonderful gifts, marriage and human families have never been God's ultimate goal. "While remaining the foundational divine institution for humanity, which should be nurtured, cared for, and protected, marriage should not be viewed as an end in itself, but should be subordinated to God's larger salvation purposes."[14] Marriage and earthly families are signs that turn the believer's gaze toward Christ's sacrificial love for the church. "Every family in heaven and on earth"—even families that have not yet trusted Jesus Christ—are signs that point to a reality greater than themselves

---

[12] "As surprising as it might seem, Paul is saying in Eph 5:31 that God instituted marriage 'because' the church is Christ's body. This probably means that the union of husband and wife in 'one flesh' was originally intended to prefigure and to illustrate the union that Christ now has with the church. This is something that could become clear only after Christ had died to create the church in its new, multiethnic form." Thielman, *Ephesians*, 389. For further exegetical rationale for this understanding, see the third option listed in Benjamin L. Merkle, *Exegetical Guide to the Greek New Testament: Ephesians* (Nashville: B&H, 2016), 189.

[13] Jesus's earthly family was, according to Matt 12:46, "outside"—both literally and symbolically—while his disciples were on the inside, hearing and believing his words. "It is this posture of presence and belief, then, that constitutes the new and lasting family that God was constructing in and through Christ." Frederick Dale Bruner, *The Christbook* (Dallas: Word, 1987), 471–74. For the phrase "first family," see Rodney R. Clapp, *Families at the Crossroads* (Downers Grove, IL: InterVarsity Press, 1993).

[14] Jones and Köstenberger, *God, Marriage, and Family*, loc. 951 of [*].

(Eph 3:14–15). This greater reality is the love that binds Christ to the church for which he sacrificed his own life (Eph 5:25–27).

The place of the family in God's plan provides a vital foundation for any biblical theology of student ministry. These truths call us to train students to glimpse the beauty of godly marriages and parenthood, but they also caution us against seeing marriage or parenthood as the ultimate goal. Perhaps more importantly, the centrality of the church in God's plan reminds us that a youth group will always fall short when it comes to providing a family for students whose earthly families have not yet received the gospel.

That's part of what I missed during my early years in student ministry. I tried to create a Christian community for youth that bypassed parents and extended only as far as the students' peers and a few twentysomething volunteers. And yet, the whole church in all its multigenerational messiness was the community that those youth (and I!) needed most. Youth groups may provide a helpful context for students to hear the gospel and to learn how to live the gospel. The community that their souls need will never, however, be found primarily in a youth group; it is located in a local congregation that draws together a diversity of generations.

New Creation: Family Fulfilled

The human family is a means and a sign, but earthly families are not forever (Matt 22:30). Families are a temporary context that hint at a future communion that will be perfect and eternal. In the end, "the intimacy that a human being shares with one other person in marriage is universalized in the joy and love of heaven."[15] The purpose of

---

[15] E. Michael Green, *The Message of Matthew* (Downers Grove, IL: InterVarsity Press, 2000), 235.

the human family will have been fulfilled, and families as we know them on earth will give way to an eternal fellowship. This everlasting community will be comprised of every person who has trusted in Jesus.

What this means practically is that if parents enter God's everlasting bliss alongside their children, they will not do so as parents and children in earthly families. They will enjoy eternity together as blood-bought brothers and sisters in an eternal family. The church that Jesus loves and the souls of the students in our care are the realities that will outlast the rise and fall of all the kingdoms of the earth. These lasting realities should shape every pursuit that we prioritize in student ministry.

Implications for family	GOD'S METANARRATIVE	Implications for child
The earthly family is a means designed by God to reveal his glory.	1. CREATION	Parents should see their children as gifts.
The earthly family is a community distorted by sin and a means by which God promised to send a Savior.	2. FALL AND LAW	Parents should see their children as sinners.
The earthly family is a sign that points to a greater family.	3. REDEMPTION	Parents should participate in their children's discipleship.
Church family is forever, but the earthly family is not.	4. NEW CREATION	Parents should recognize their children are forever.

How a Biblical Theology of the Family Reshapes Youth Ministry

Two theological dynamics emerge from this examination of God's design for the family throughout the biblical metanarrative:

1. The family is a means of discipleship, and parents are responsible to train their children in God's ways.
2. The earthly family is not an end in itself; marriage and earthly families are signs that point to a greater family.

The first of these two dynamics can be summarized by the phrase "family-as-church," because it calls Christian parents to cultivate in their home some of the same practices that happen in the church. "Church-as-family" is how I've chosen to describe the second dynamic; God designed the church to function as a greater family in which all other identities and allegiances are radically relativized.[16] Both of these dynamics can be seen clearly in this definition of family ministry: "Family ministry [is] the process of coordinating the practices of a church so that members develop diverse discipling relationships [that's church-as-family] and so that parents are acknowledged, equipped, and held accountable as primary disciple-makers in their children's lives [that's family-as-church]."[17]

---

[16] The words of Jesus in Matt 12:48–50 "do not dissolve family bonds but rather relativize them." W. D. Davies and Dale C. Allison Jr., *A Critical and Exegetical Commentary on the Gospel According to Saint Matthew*, vol. 2 (Edinburgh: T&T Clark, 1991), 364.

[17] Timothy Paul Jones, *Perspectives on Family Ministry*, 2nd ed. (Nashville: B&H, 2019), 45–48. Mark Cannister has persuasively argued that the church's engagement with youth includes two separate and distinct aspects:

The remainder of this chapter will unpack the implications of each of these two dynamics for student ministry. As you consider each one, it might be tempting to wonder, "Which one is more important for student ministry, church-as-family or family-as church?" Both dynamics are, however, deeply grounded in the meta-narrative of Scripture. As such, asking whether church-as-family or family-as-church is more vital would be like asking a ship's captain, "Which side of the ship's hull do you need most to stay afloat, starboard or port?" Neither side of the ship is disposable, and neither of these dynamics is dispensable. Like a ship that needs both sides to sail safely to its destination, you need both theological dynamics to navigate your student ministry toward practices that are faithful to God's design.

---

youth ministry and Christian education of youth. Youth ministry "grew out of revivalism and is based on missiological theology"; Christian education of youth is "based upon the theology of nurture, especially since the influence of Bushnell and Coe." "Youth ministry," as defined by Cannister, includes some aspects of the dynamic that I have described as church-as-family while family-as-church hints at the familial nurturing component of "Christian education of youth." See Mark Cannister, "Why Christian Education and Youth Ministry Are Different Disciplines," *American Baptist Quarterly* 19 (March 2000): 74.

	Youth ministry does not equip parents to disciple their youth	Family-as-church
Church-as-family	**Church-as-family without family-as-church** Equipping parents to disciple youth? No Intergenerational discipling relationships? Yes	**Church-as-family and family-as-church** Equipping parents to disciple youth? Yes Intergenerational discipling relationships? Yes
Youth ministry does not connect youth with other generations	**Neither church-as-family nor family-as-church** Equipping parents to disciple youth? No Intergenerational discipling relationships? No	**Family-as-church without church-as-family** Equipping parents to disciple youth? Yes Intergenerational discipling relationships? No

What Does Youth Ministry Look Like When Church Is Family?

The goal of the theological dynamic that I have dubbed "church-as-family" is to enable God's people to relate to one another more like a family, recognizing that the family of God constitutes a new humanity in Christ that relativizes commitments to any other family.[18] The dynamic of church-as-family declares implicitly that our

---

[18] For more on the people of God as a new humanity, see Jarvis Williams, *One New Man* (Nashville: B&H, 2010); and David E. Stevens, *God's New Humanity* (Eugene, OR: Wipf & Stock, 2012).

earthly families are not enough.[19] Inasmuch as we are united with Jesus Christ and adopted in him, we need the communion of the people of God more than we need any other kinship.

When church-as-family intersects with student ministry, it produces a passion for proclaiming the gospel to students whose earthly families have not yet turned to Christ. This dynamic does not end, however, with inviting unbelieving students to embrace the gospel and to be enfolded into a church family. When applied to student ministry, the dynamic of church-as-family results in patterns of provision for spiritual orphans.

The biblical author James—a son of Joseph and Mary, whose half-brother Jesus was adopted by Joseph—had this to say about orphans in his letter to first-century Christians: "Pure and undefiled religion before God the Father is this: to look after orphans and widows in their distress and to keep oneself unstained from the world" (Jas 1:27). Although James was speaking primarily about children whose parents were absent or deceased, there are implications here for "spiritual orphans" as well.

What I mean by "spiritual orphans" are youth and children who attend your church but whose parents are not yet receptive to the gospel. As the dynamic of church-as-family takes root in a student ministry, spiritual orphans—teenagers whose parents are far from Jesus Christ—will find their lives intertwined with more mature believers who become their spiritual parents and grandparents. In many churches, the dynamic of church-as-family is applied practically through a families-in-faith ministry. A family-in-faith is simply a faithful family in your church that's connected with one or more specific students or children who attend church without their

---

[19] Joseph Hellerman, *When the Church Was a Family* (Nashville: B&H, 2009), 96.

parents.[20] Families-in-faith engage with these teenagers at church and make themselves available to join their designated youth in church activities in which a parent might typically participate. This is one of many key areas where senior adults can make vital contributions to student ministry.

Challenges to Church-as-Family

So what stands in the way of practicing church-as-family in youth ministries today?

One challenge for church-as-family is the fact that some churches have become so radically segmented that persons from different generations rarely, if ever, interact one another. This isn't because young people are unwilling to build relationships with adults in their churches. According to sociologist Christian Smith, nearly 80 percent of religiously involved teenagers enjoy conversing with adults in their faith communities. Despite this openness among the youth, nearly 40 percent of them have no adult in their faith communities to whom they might turn in times of distress; another 27 percent have only one or two such adults. Among the youth who had no adults in their churches with whom they could converse, 61 percent wished they had such a relationship.[21]

This pattern of separation between the generations stands in stark contrast to the expectations of the New Testament. The apostles John and Paul addressed "children" and "young men" alongside

---

[20] A guide for developing a families-in-faith ministry as part of a church's youth ministry may be found in Timothy Paul Jones, "When Churched Kids Don't Have Churched Parents," in *Recalibrate,* ed. Ron Hunter Jr. (Nashville: Randall House, 2019).

[21] Christian Smith with Melina Lundquist Denton, *Soul Searching* (New York: Oxford University Press, 2005), 60.

parents and elders, apparently expecting these letters to be read in congregations that mingled older and younger believers together (Eph 5:22–6:4; 1 John 2:12–14). In his letter to a young pastor named Titus, Paul specifically called for the formation of mentoring relationships that connected older members with younger believers (Titus 2:1–8). The authors of the New Testament assumed the presence of intergenerational connections that equipped youth to grow in wisdom alongside older generations.

The presence of intergenerational connections doesn't require the dissolution of youth groups or children's ministries. I spend many Sunday evenings interacting with youth and playing guitar in my church's student ministry. There is something to be said for recognizing distinctions in the developmental capabilities of children, youth, and adults. There is much to be said for age-organized small groups and Sunday School classes as well. At the same time, part of the scandal of the cross should be the fact that those who rub shoulders in the shadow of the cross are a family made up of people whom the world would never dream of mingling together (1 Cor 1:23–29; 12:13; Gal 3:28; Eph 2:14; Col 3:11). In a culture that has severed vital ties between the generations, churches must develop intentional plans to bring the generations together.

"What kids need from adults is not just rides, pizza, chaperones, and discipline," journalist Patricia Hersch acknowledged in a study of adolescent culture. "They need the telling of stories, the close ongoing contact so that they can learn and be accepted. If nobody is there to talk to, it is difficult to get the lessons of your own life so that you are adequately prepared to do the next thing."[22] If this is true in the context of social maturity, it is even more true when it comes to an adolescent's growth in the gospel. Youth need relationships filled

---

[22] Patricia Hersch, *A Tribe Apart* (New York: Ballantine, 1999), 364.

with wisdom and acceptance from middle-aged and older adults to develop into mature disciples of Jesus Christ.

Church-as-Family and Youth Ministry

When the theological dynamic of church-as-family reshapes a student ministry, the primary goal is no longer to gather a massive group of peers to engage in activities together. The aim is to orient students toward the joy of Christ and to entwine their lives with the church that Jesus loves. A church that pursues the dynamic of church-as-family will draw youth, children, and adults together in a multicultural and multigenerational family, filled with God's Spirit and formed by God's Word. This weekly family reunion declares to the world that the gospel of Jesus Christ is strong enough to shatter every division that stands between those who have embraced the good news of God's kingdom. In Christ, "the apparently absolute antitheses that divide us are revealed to be relative."[23] The barriers have been broken, and the Spirit of Christ has bonded us together in a way that transcends human understanding (Eph 2:14–15; 4:1–6).

The biblical authors describe the church as a glorious bride that Jesus loves like a husband loves his wife (Eph 5:29–32; Rev 21:1–9). To love the church is to love what Jesus loves. It shouldn't surprise us, then, that youth who learn to love this gritty but glorious community are far more likely to remain connected to the church long after their years in youth group are over.[24] In the words of my friend and family

---

[23] Karl Barth, *The Epistle to the Ephesians,* trans. Ross Wright (Grand Rapids, MI: Baker, 2017), 141.

[24] One of the most significant predictors of whether young people remain in the faith has to do with whether they have developed meaningful intergenerational relationships with other Christians. See Drew Dyck, *Generation Ex-Christian* (Chicago: Moody, 2010), 177–78.

ministry hero Richard Ross, "Teenagers who have little love for the bride will eventually walk away from the groom, but teenagers who spend their time with all the generations in the church tend to stay in church."[25]

What Does Youth Ministry Look Like When the Family Is a Context for Discipleship?

The first theological dynamic—church-as-family—transforms student ministry by moving multigenerational relationships from an option to a necessity. The second dynamic—family-as-church—is a dynamic of nurture in the context of earthly families. This second theological dynamic reshapes student ministry by prioritizing the role of Christian parents as disciple-makers in their children's lives.

The phrase "family-as-church" is not intended to suggest that the earthly family is a church. A church is a covenant community in which the Scriptures are rightly taught by duly appointed elders and the Lord's Supper and baptism are rightly practiced.[26] These ecclesiological markers are not present in an earthly family; as such, the family is not and cannot be a church. The point of "family-as-church" is to underscore the fact that Christian families are called to practice the same habits of discipleship in the home as in the church. The specific aim of family-as-church is to equip parents to become active participants in their children's spiritual formation and education. "Marriage," Dietrich Bonhoeffer rightly observed, "is not only a

---

[25] Personal conversation with Richard Ross at the D6 Conference, Orlando, FL, September 2019.

[26] J. Calvin, *Institutio Christianae Religionis*, 4:1:9. See also the Augsburg Confession, article 7.

matter of producing children but also of educating them to be obedient to Jesus Christ."[27]

The New Testament simultaneously relativizes and reinforces the Old Testament expectation that parents should train their children in God's ways (Deut 6:4–9). The New Testament relativizes family discipleship by providing a way for children from unbelieving families to be discipled by more mature brothers and sisters in their church family. That's how the unmarried apostle Paul ended up as a father in the faith for a young man whose father was not a believer (Acts 16:1–5; 1 Cor 4:17; 1 Tim 1:2, 18; 2 Tim 1:2, 5).[28] This pattern represents a practical application of the first theological dynamic of church-as-family. At the same time, the importance that Paul placed on church-as-family never eclipsed his expectation that Christian parents should pursue family-as-church. The same Paul who was a father in faith to Timothy also commanded believing fathers to train their children in God's ways (Eph 6:4).

Challenges to Family-as-Church

So what stands in the way of the theological dynamic of family-as-church in our practices of student ministry today? Each generation of Christians has struggled in different ways to practice church-as-family, and our current generation is no different. In Western cultural contexts, one reason church-as-family is difficult today is

---

[27] Dietrich Bonhoeffer, *Ethics*, trans. N. Smith (London: SCM, 1955), 183.

[28] Timothy's father was an unbeliever and might have passed away prior to the point when Paul met Timothy in Lystra (Acts 16:1–3). See I. H. Marshall, *The Acts of the Apostles* (Grand Rapids, MI: Eerdmans, 1980), 259–60. If so, Timothy was both spiritually and physically fatherless.

because churches are still dealing with the impact of the Industrial Revolution on families.

Prior to the Industrial Revolution, an individual's residence and workplace were usually in the same location. Whether a family farmed or crafted tools or sold goods, the beds where family members laid their heads at night were typically on the same property where they had worked during the day. In such contexts, parents and children labored alongside one another, and family discipleship could be woven into ordinary patterns of life. The rise of factories turned parents—and fathers in particular—into wage-earners whose spheres of labor shifted away from their homes. And thus, in the Industrial Revolution, "to a large extent the family lost the father."[29] This disengagement of fathers coupled with an increasing perception of religion as feminine seems to have correlated with a decline in family discipleship.[30] For enslaved families in this era, family discipleship was even less possible, due to systemic oppression through enforced illiteracy and intentional separation of family members.[31]

---

[29] Henry Frederick Cope, *Religious Education in the Family* (Chicago: University of Chicago Press, 1915), 20. See also Diana R. Garland, *Family Ministry*, 2nd ed. (Downers Grove, IL: InterVarsity Press, 2012), 32–33.

[30] For nineteenth-century reports of decline in family worship, see James W. Alexander, *Thoughts on Family-Worship* (Philadelphia: Presbyterian Board of Publication, 1847), 2; K. Moody Stuart, *Brownlow North: The Story of His Life and Work* (London: Hodder and Stoughton, 1879), 226; and John Gregory Pike, *A Guide for Young Disciples of the Holy Saviour in Their Way to Immortality*, 3rd ed (London: Richard Baynes, 1831), 233. On the feminization of American religion, see Ann Douglas, *The Feminization of American Culture* (New York: Farrar, Straus, and Giroux, 1977); and Steven J. Keillor, *This Rebellious House* (Downers Grove, IL: InterVarsity Press, 1996), 181–83.

[31] For illiteracy and intentional fragmenting of enslaved African American families, see Damian Alan Pargas, "Disposing of Human Property," *Journal of Family History* 34 (2009): 251–74; Thomas D. Russell, "Articles Sell Best Singly," *Utah Law Review* (1996): 1161–1209; and J. Lichtenberger,

In this way, the Industrial Revolution introduced a spatial separation of children and parents during the workday. Social shifts in the decades after World War II contributed to a cultural separation that extended into every part of life. For the first time, teenagers possessed sufficient spending money to influence the economy. The music and magazines that they purchased were part of a youth culture that repudiated the cultural values of their parents. It was in this context that the one-eared Mickey Mouse emerged as an attempt to reach teenagers while keeping youth culture at arm's-length from the rest of the church.

By the closing decades of the twentieth century, youth groups provided a smorgasbord of activities for churched and unchurched students with little connection to parents beyond an occasional permission slip. If effectiveness is defined as attracting large numbers of youth, this one-eared Mickey Mouse model of ministry worked. During the heyday of the model in the 1980s and 1990s, permissive parenting was viewed positively, and activities with peer groups were perceived as the proper context for teenagers' identity formation. Parents prioritized student ministry because—at least in parents' perceptions—youth groups provided a safe context for peer-driven identity formation.[32] In the process, many parents seem to have disengaged even further from practices of discipleship with their teenagers. According to one comprehensive survey of family discipleship practices, two-thirds of churched parents read or discussed the Bible with their children less than once each week. More

---

"Illiteracy in the United States," *Annals of the American Academy of Political and Social Science* 49 (1913): 177–85.

[32] Andrew Root, *The End of Youth Ministry?* (Grand Rapids, MI: Baker, 2020), chapters 2–6.

than one-third of church-involved parents had never engaged in any form of family devotional or Bible study with their children, while an additional three out of ten households did so once a month or less.[33]

Family-as-Church and Youth Ministry

In the early twenty-first century, an increasing number of student ministry leaders began to glimpse fault lines that revealed the failure of activity-driven models of student ministry.[34] One of these fault lines was a clear pattern of parental disengagement from the discipleship of their children. The result has been a family ministry movement that has brought about a renewed focus on the dynamic of family-as-church in student ministry.[35]

Family-as-church means that student ministry is never merely ministry with youth. Youth ministry must also be parent ministry. If a student's parents are unbelievers, student ministry means building

---

[33] Timothy Paul Jones, *Family Ministry Field Guide* (Indianapolis: WPH, 2011), chapters 1–2, 7–8.

[34] For an analysis of other reasons the activity-driven youth group ministry model has failed, see Root, *The End of Youth Ministry?* Perhaps not coincidentally, the rise of interest in family ministry coincided with a societal shift from permissive parenting to a pattern of parenting that closely but selectively monitors behaviors and risks in an attempt to keep children safe.

[35] Key early texts in this movement included Voddie Baucham Jr., *Family-Driven Faith* (Wheaton, IL: Crossway, 2007); Mark DeVries, *Family-Based Youth Ministry* (Downers Grove, IL: InterVarsity Press, 1994, 2004); Brian Haynes, *Shift* (Loveland, CO: Group, 2009); Richard Ross, *Student Ministry and the Supremacy of Christ* (Bloomington, IN: Crossbooks, 2009); Reggie Joiner, *Think Orange* (Colorado Springs: Cook, 2009); and Timothy Paul Jones, *Perspectives on Family Ministry*, 1st ed. (Nashville: B&H, 2009).

connections with those parents to provide every possible opportunity to share the gospel, so that the student can begin to experience family-as-church. When a student's mother or father is a Christian, the theological dynamic of family-as-church calls student ministers to equip parents with resources and training to disciple their children. Equipping of parents is not an optional add-on in student ministry; it is a biblically grounded priority.

A Theology That Began on a Concrete Floor

I pressed my face against the cold concrete floor in the corner of the new gymnasium. The flooring wouldn't arrive for another couple of weeks, but we were already using the facility for youth events. On the illuminated stage at the other end of the gymnasium, the revival speaker was beginning to move into the final point of his message. In the dark void between the speaker on the stage and me on the floor, there were well over a hundred students. From my point of view, curled in the corner at the back of the gymnasium, I could see the students only as shadows silhouetted against the stage lights. Even as silhouettes, I knew each one of them, and I loved them.

I was a success as a student minister, and I was a failure. Over the past three years, I had succeeded in growing a youth group, but an unending stream of bigger and bigger events had left me exhausted and empty. This youth revival was the final event of the summer, and I had just spent ten out of the past twelve weeks at camps, mission trips, and retreats. I was leading a youth group that was its own community, connected to the congregation by little more than a handful of budget line-items and a few volunteers who also happened to be parents. Most of the students who gathered on Wednesday evening never showed up on Sunday morning—and, my thought at the time was, *Why should they?* After all, the Sunday morning worship music was lifeless and dull; it was nothing like the youth group's worship celebrations that were so energetic that we once left a human-sized hole in the sheetrock.

But now, here I was, alone on the floor in the corner of the gym as the speaker ended his message with a prayer. I forced myself to my feet so that I could stand in front of this group one more time, where my words would throb with forced enthusiasm and energy even as my soul was dying. A couple of weeks later, I met with the church's personnel committee. I resigned from student ministry but not from the church. Instead, I ended up as the pastor of administration and education in the same congregation.

As I reflected on my practices of student ministry over the next couple of years, I slowly recognized that I had been steering the ship in all the wrong directions. The North Star by which I had been navigating as a student minister had been numbers and activities when it should have been the joy of Christ and the fellowship of his people. One of my projects in those years became the development of a theologically grounded model of student ministry. That's when I first recognized the biblical foundations for the dynamics that I now call "family-as-church" and "church-as-family."

And so, this is a theology that, for me, began on a concrete floor.

Without a congregation that was more gracious to me than I deserved, my ministry probably would have ended there. At the time, I didn't think the youth needed other generations, and I saw no value in equipping their parents. And yet, in the end, the church as a whole was precisely what God utilized to mature me as a pastor and as a leader.

Conclusion

I know that it's difficult to pursue family-as-church and church-as-family as a student minister. I also know this: What's even more difficult in the long run is to try to do student ministry without engaging parents or drawing from the wisdom of the congregation or connecting your students with other generations. To navigate toward the right destinations, every student ministry needs family-as-church and church-as-family.

Student Ministry
and Evangelism

• JUSTIN BUCHANAN •

John Harper lived an evangelistic life to his final breaths. Born in Glasgow, Scotland, to Christian parents, he did not place his faith in Jesus Christ until he was fourteen. At seventeen, John was passionate to see people reconciled to God through faith in Jesus, so he began proclaiming the death and resurrection of Jesus on the streets of his village. He eventually planted a church in London. The church grew to more than five hundred as a result of John's evangelistic zeal.

John's reputation caught the attention of the Moody Church in Chicago, Illinois. They invited him to preach, and the meetings had such impact that John was invited to preach again. He accepted and made plans for him and Nana, his six-year-old daughter, to travel across the Atlantic.[1]

The two set sail from Southampton, England, but only a few days into the journey John woke Nana to inform her that their ship, the *Titanic*, had struck an iceberg. He secured Nana on a lifeboat, assuring her that he would board the rescue boat coming and meet her later. That boat never came. The *Titanic* sank quickly, plunging hundreds of passengers and John into the icy waters.

John held onto debris in the water. He maneuvered his way to other passengers treading water to survive. John asked each the same question: "Are you saved?" When he asked a Scotsman, the man replied, "No." Without hesitation, John shared, "Believe on the Lord Jesus Christ and you will be saved." John floated away only to reappear, asking again, "Are you saved?" The Scotsman replied again, "No." John declared again, "Believe on the Lord Jesus Christ and you will be saved."

Moments later, the Scotsman looked on helplessly as John lost his grip and slipped beneath the water's surface. In the icy waters awaiting physical rescue, the Scotsman found spiritual salvation. He believed on Jesus and received new life and relationship with God. Months later, the Scotsman stood in a church service recounting John Harper's witness. He said to the congregation, "I am the last convert of John Harper."[2]

---

[1] Mark Dever, *The Gospel and Personal Evangelism* (Wheaton, IL: Crossway, 2007), 13–14.

[2] Douglas Mize, "As *Titanic* Sank, He Pleaded, 'Believe in the Lord Jesus!'" *Baptist Press*, April 13, 2012, http://www.bpnews.net/37601/as-titanic-sank-he-pleaded-believe-in-the-lord-jesus.

The Critical Work of Missions and Evangelism

We, as ministers of the gospel and shepherds of God's people, must aim to encourage and equip followers of Jesus to advance God's mission through evangelism and missions with the same unrelenting urgency and passion as John Harper did. Successfully navigating student ministry requires the intentional work of raising up and releasing students, their parents, and adult volunteers to live evangelistic lives no matter their location or vocation.[3] The work of evangelism and missions is the primary work of the church. C. S. Lewis explains, "The church exists for nothing else but to draw men into Christ, to make them little Christs. If they are not doing that, all the cathedrals, clergy, missions, sermons, even the Bible itself, are simply a waste of time. God became man for no other purpose."[4] Though churches can engage in many good works, the work of evangelism is something in which they must engage.

The church exists to advance God's mission of making followers through proclaiming the good news and leading individuals to faith in Jesus. Colin Marshall and Tony Payne thus write:

The mandate of disciple-making provides the touchstone for whether our church is engaging in Christ's mission. Are we making genuine disciples of Jesus Christ? Our goal is not to make church members or members of our institution, but genuine disciples of Jesus."[5]

---

[3] See Gene Veith, *God at Work* (Wheaton, IL: Crossway, 2011).

[4] C. S. Lewis, *Mere Christianity* (New York: Macmillian, 1952), 30.

[5] Colin Marshall and Tony Payne, *The Trellis and the Vine* (Newtown: Australia: Matthias Media, 2009), 14.

When God measures our success, individually and corporately, he evaluates it according to our faithfulness to him, his Word, and his mission. We are responsible before God to call, equip, lead, and send out those entrusted to us to carry out the task of advancing the gospel as a critical part in making disciples.

But before we go any further, we have to ask the crucial question, "What exactly is the gospel?"

What Is the Gospel?

The centrality of the gospel and importance of proclaiming the good news can be grasped through the overarching story of Scripture that declares to us God's mission. We must preach and teach the grand story of the whole of Scripture as essential to leading believers to understand God's mission and the importance of sharing the gospel to advance his mission.

The critical role of teaching on God's mission and in leading God's people into his mission is captured by Gary Bredfeldt when he writes, "The most powerful means of leading the people of God is by teaching them the Word of God."[6] The church is a primary "teaching-learning organization."[7] If we desire to lead teenagers and adults to live as colaborers with Christ in his mission, we must teach them from Scripture what is his mission, how his mission advances, the centrality of the gospel to his mission, and the expectation God has for his followers in his mission. Teenagers, parents, and volunteers can capture the grand story of the Bible through the "four major plot movements—creation, fall, redemption, and restoration."[8]

---

[6] Gary Bredfeldt, *Great Teacher, Great Leader* (Chicago: Moody, 2006), 18.

[7] Bredfeldt, 17.

[8] Bruce Ashford, ed., *Theology and Practice of Mission: God, the Church, and the Nations* (Nashville: B&H Academic, 2011), 6.

Creation

Scripture begins with God and his creative work. God made all things and nothing was created without him (Gen 1; John 1:1–3). The crown jewel of God's creation was man and woman, whom he made on the sixth day.[9] God made humanity distinct from everything else. We bear the image of God, reflecting his likeness on the earth as no other part of creation was meant and made to do. God's ultimate goal in making man and woman was that we would enjoy a relationship with him. John Stott explains, "[Humans'] highest destiny is to know God, to be in personal relationship with God."[10] God created human beings and placed them in the Garden of Eden to dwell as the place where man and woman would live in a relationship of worship and obedience with him.[11] Though God has no needs, he chose to create humanity for intimate fellowship.

---

[9] Kenneth A. Mathews, *Genesis 1–11:26*, The New American Commentary (Nashville: Broadman & Holman, 1996), 1A:160.

[10] John Stott, *Basic Christianity* (Chicago: InterVarsity Press, 1964), 72.

[11] See John Sailhamer, "Genesis," *The Expositor's Bible Commentary*, ed. Frank Gæbelein (Grand Rapids, MI: Zondervan, 1990), 2:45; and Allen Ross, *Creation & Blessing* (Grand Rapids, MI: Baker, 1988), 124. Old Testament scholars John Sailhamer and Allen Ross argue that the better translation of Gen 2:15 should read that God put humanity in the Garden of Eden to "worship and obey." He notes several factors leading to this conclusion. First, the Hebrew word for "placed" used by Moses in v. 15 is not the common word for "placed" as was used in Gen 2:8. The word is used by Moses to refer to an object or person being set apart for service to God. Second, the Hebrew construction of Gen 2:15 makes clear that to "work it and watch over it" does not refer to the garden but to God himself. Third, the terms often translated "work it and watch over it" should be translated "worship and obey." These terms are used throughout the Pentateuch in regard to spiritual service to God. Primarily, the terms refer to worshipping and serving God and obeying his commands. The two terms were often applied to the work of the priests serving in the tabernacle. Thus, humanity was placed in the garden for a relationship of worship and obedience to God. Sailhamer writes, "Man is put in

Fall

Rather than live in worship and obedience to God, humanity believed Satan's lie that they could be worshipped and obeyed as their own gods. Genesis 3 records how Satan entered the garden to tempt Adam and Eve. Satan asserted that God failed to tell them that eating of the tree of the knowledge of good and evil would open up a new world in which they themselves would be like God; they could become deity through disobedience. If they ate of the tree, they would no longer have to worship and obey God.

Scripture records that Satan's lie deceived both the man and woman. First, because they doubted God's goodness, they dethroned him in their hearts.[12] Then, inward rebellion led to an outward disregard for God's command. The woman, and then the man, took and ate of the forbidden fruit. A. W. Tozer writes, "The essence of sin is rebellion against divine authority."[13] The two rebelled against God's command, rejecting God and his rule in an effort to steal his throne away from him.[14] Their sin led to a number of consequences, but as Stott points out, "Perhaps the most dreadful of all sin's consequences is that it estranges us from God."[15] Sin severed our relationship with God and placed us under his wrath.

---

the garden to worship and obey [God]. Man's life in the garden was to be characterized by worship and obedience; he was a priest, not merely a worker and keeper of the garden" (45).

[12] John Piper, "Did Adam and Eve Sin Before the Bite?" *Desiring God*, September 18, 2017, https://www.desiringgod.org/interviews/did-adam-and -eve-sin-before-the-bite.

[13] A. W. Tozer, *Discipleship* (Chicago: Moody, 2018), 63.

[14] A. W. Tozer, *The Knowledge of the Holy* (San Francisco: HarperSanFrancisco, 1961), 30.

[15] Stott, *Basic Christianity*, 72.

Redemption

Even after humanity's sin, God came down to pursue them. They did not seek God but tried to hide from him. They attempted to cover their sin and shame by stitching leaves together to cover their nakedness. God came to the place they committed betrayal. He reminded them that their sin affected every relationship, including their relationship to God, to one another, to creation, and to themselves.[16] Spiritual death and severed relationship with God had already come. Physical death would follow in the days to come. In the midst of declaring such tragic consequences, God uttered the first words of hope and salvation.

God gave a promise of salvation when he declared that a descendant of the woman would come to do battle with Satan. This declaration in Gen 3:15 is referred to as the "protoevangelium," or first gospel. Arthur Patzia and Anthony Petrotta write that it is "the first glimmer of the gospel that God's purpose in creation will be fulfilled in spite of the fall of humanity."[17] God proclaims good news that humanity would one day be restored into right relationship with him as his image bearers. As a result, they would one day once again live in a relationship of worship and obedience with him.

God gave a picture of salvation as well. To show the cost of delivering us from the power of sin and death, God took an animal and put it to death. God said that man would die if he disobeyed. In that moment, however, an animal died in humankind's place. God shed

---

[16] See Francis Schaeffer, *True Spirituality* (Carol Stream, IL: Tyndale House, 1971); and Francis Schaeffer, *Pollution and the Death of Man: A Christian View of Ecology* (Wheaton, IL: Tyndale House, 1970). In these works, Schaeffer notes how sin fractured humanity's multiple relationships, including humanity's relationships with God, each other, oneself, and nature.

[17] Arthur G. Patzia and Anthony J. Petrotta, "Protoevangelium," in *Pocket Dictionary of Biblical Studies* (Downers Grove, IL: InterVarsity Press, 2002), 96.

the innocent blood of an animal as a substitute to cover humanity's sin and shame (Gen 3:21). Sin required that blood be shed to make right what sin made wrong. God clothed man and woman with animal skins to replace the leaves they had sewn together. In this, God revealed his power to cover and heal, as well as declared humanity's inability to provide their own salvation.

The hope pictured in the garden finds its ultimate fulfillment in the person and work of Jesus Christ. Jesus, the eternal Son of God, became man through the incarnation (John 1:14). Descending from Eve as God had declared, he came to seek and to save lost humanity (Luke 19:10, Matt 18:11). Jesus accomplished this mission by living a perfect life of obedience to God. He satisfied the demands of God's Law that qualified him to sacrificially die in our place as our proxy (Rom 5:7–9, 1 Cor 15:3–4). Then Jesus rose again from the dead on the third day to give new life to those held in the grip of sin and its power of death (Ps 34:5; Acts 16:31; Gal 2:20). His death covered our sin with his blood, while covering our shame with his robe of righteousness. The gospel is at the heart of God's story to redeem and restore people into relationship with himself. By faith in Jesus Christ alone, we are rescued from sin and its result of spiritual and physical death. God adopts us as his children who worship and obey him (John 1:12; Rom 10:9–10; Eph 2:8–10).

Restoration

Our disobedience has brought God's creation into disorder, chaos, and brokenness. Every human relationship has been negatively affected. Our lives have been mired in turmoil, sickness, death, and disease. However, the death and resurrection of Jesus Christ is God's means of restoring what sin has broken. Gabe Lyons observes, "While the redemptive Christ event is the apex of the story, it isn't the whole story. The story begins in the context of a perfect garden and continues through God's promise of restoration."[18] God will reverse the curse of sin and restore all things to their proper state through Christ (Col 1:19–23).

Jesus's numerous miracles on the earth, though only a selection are recorded (John 21:25), demonstrate God's restoration promise and power. Every time Jesus acted to alter what sin had corrupted, he pointed humanity to God's promise of a future world without sin and its ill-effects (Rev 21). Tim Keller writes:

> The Bible tells us that God did not originally make the world to have disease, hunger, and death in it. Jesus has come to redeem where it is wrong and heal the world where it is broken. His miracles are not just proofs that he has power but also wonderful foretastes of what he is going to do with that power. Jesus's miracles are not just a challenge to our minds, but a promise to our hearts, that the world we all want is coming.[19]

God will bring into place a new heaven and new earth where no sin exists and no consequences or devastation of sin are experienced. The followers of Jesus will no longer find themselves beleaguered by sinful motives, thoughts, words, or deeds. Once again, Jesus Christ alone will rule and reign. As Lyons notes, "Creation and restoration are the bookends to Christ's earthly work."[20] As it was in the beginning, so will it be in eternity because of the power of the gospel.

---

[18] Gabe Lyons, *The Next Christians* (Colorado Springs: Multnomah Books, 2010), 51.

[19] Timothy Keller, *The Reason for God: Belief in an Age of Skepticism* (New York: Penguin Books, 2008), 95–96.

[20] Lyons, *The Next Christians,* 51.

The Bible is about the mission of God to save sinners and restore the broken world for his glory. But what is our role?

What Is Our Role?

The New Testament makes clear that believers all have an integral part to play in the mission of God's restoring work. All four Gospels and the Book of Acts record a Great Commission mandate from Jesus to all his disciples (Matt 28:19–20; Mark 16:15; Luke 24:46–49; John 20:21–23; Acts 1:8). Jesus instructs his followers to go into the entire world in the power of the Holy Spirit to be witnesses of him and his redemptive work as we call others to follow him by faith. The Great Commission calls all believers to join God in his mission. By proclaiming the gospel to lead nonbelievers to repentance toward Christ for salvation and helping believers follow Jesus, we lead fallen image bearers to return to their created role of reflecting God through worship and obedience.

Equipped to Share the Gospel

Teach Them the Gospel

We must ensure teenagers and adults understand the biblical message of the gospel. A faulty gospel cannot lead others to salvation. Greg Gilbert laments that far too few Christians appear to have an accurate understanding of the gospel.[21] Therefore, if we want to mobilize students for evangelism, we must teach students a biblically faithful gospel.

---

[21] Greg Gilbert, *What Is the Gospel?* (Wheaton, IL: Crossway, 2010), 15.

One helpful way to achieve this is by first helping students know what the gospel is not.

What the Gospel Is Not

First, *the gospel is not a message that we are all God's children who are basically good.* We were created by God, but our rebellion has alienated us from God, making us his enemies. Being the creation of God does not automatically make us the children of God, though a common refrain today states the opposite. Only those who place faith in Jesus are the children of God.

Second, *the gospel is not a message that God is only love.* God is love. He has both declared and demonstrated his love for humanity. Jesus's death on the cross in our place demonstrates this. Proclaiming as the gospel just that God loves us, while neglecting God's wrath and justice against our sin, betrays the biblical message. We need God's forgiveness.

Third, *the gospel is not a message that salvation comes from both God and human effort.* God does not help those who help themselves; God helps those who can never help themselves. Paul writes that Christ died for the helpless (Rom 5:6). He also declares that we are incapable of doing anything to earn our salvation (Eph 2:9). Paul's letter to the Galatians especially deals with the fallacy that salvation comes through both divine work and human effort. The gospel does not urge us to try harder or do better to earn God's favor. The gospel is the message that salvation comes by grace alone, through faith alone, in Christ alone.[22] God showed favor in the giving of his Son, whose death and resurrection alone provides for our salvation.

---

[22] Thabiti Anyabwile, "God Does Not Justify Sinners by Grace Alone through Faith Alone in Christ Alone to Make Salvation Easy for Us," *The*

What the Gospel Is

The best and most concise definition of the gospel message comes from Paul's pen to the Corinthians. He writes:

> For I delivered to you as of first importance what I also received: that Christ died for our sins in accordance with the Scriptures, that he was buried, that he was raised on the third day in accordance with the Scriptures. (1 Cor 15:3–4 ESV)

Paul consistently presented the gospel as "the announcement that Jesus's life, death, and resurrection have brought about salvation for Israel and the world."[23] Jesus lived a sinless life, died a satisfactory death, and rose to new life to save those who trust in him by faith.

Every part of the message—Jesus's life, death, and resurrection— is necessary. Without a sinless life, Jesus could not die a perfect sacrifice to forgive our sin. His perfect life met the standard of God we all failed to meet. Without the death of Christ, there would be no atonement for sin. Without the resurrection, there would be no victory over sin and sin's power of death. In his death, Jesus offered himself as a sacrifice to pay the price for our sin. By his resurrection, Jesus extends new life to us to release us from the power of sin and death. Some commonly share the gospel emphasizing the crucifixion while downplaying the resurrection or never mentioning it. The gospel is the declaration of Christ's sacrifice on the cross, burial, and

---

Gospel Coalition, August 31, 2010, https://www.thegospelcoalition.org/blogs /thabiti-anyabwile/god-does-not-justify-sinners-by-grace-alone-through -faith-alone-in-christ-alone-to-make-salvation-easy-for-us/.

[23] Chris Kugler, "Gospel," ed. Douglas Mangum et al., in *Lexham Theological Wordbook*, Lexham Bible Reference Series (Bellingham, WA: Lexham Press, 2014).

resurrection. Those who will share the gospel well must share the whole message.

Train Them to Share the Gospel

After ensuring students have a correct understanding of the gospel, we must then train them to share the good news with others, and this can only be done using words. G. William Schweer notes, "Evangelism has to do with the proclamation of the message of good news."[24] Living a good life that embodies the gospel of Jesus is not insignificant, but it is insufficient by itself. Paul says we are to live "worthy of the gospel" (Phil 1:27). A life of holiness provides credibility to our message, though we will not live a perfect life. We need to teach Christians that our lives ought to reflect the power and beauty of the gospel. However, the gospel is a message that can only be communicated with words; therefore, students need to be trained how. Michael Green observes how the early church's witness for Jesus Christ regularly included "their public and their private testimony, both in their written and their spoken word."[25]

Sharing through Personal Story

Every believer has a story of coming to faith in Jesus Christ. Our stories are tools to share the gospel. Every person's story bears three common elements: life before Jesus, trusting Jesus by faith, and living as a follower of Jesus. The apostle Paul exemplifies how one's own personal story can communicate the gospel. Paul shared with

---

[24] G. William Schweer, "Evangelism," ed. Chad Brand et al., in *Holman Illustrated Bible Dictionary* (Nashville: Holman Bible Publishers, 2003), 518.

[25] Michael Green, *Evangelism in the Early Church* (Grand Rapids, MI: Eerdmans, 1970), 207.

Agrippa about his life before following Jesus (Acts 26:4–12), the day he came to trust in Jesus (Acts 26:13–18), and how his life had changed since following Jesus (Acts 26:19–23). Like Paul, our story is one we can share in minutes. Our story communicates our personal experience of trusting in the life, death, and resurrection of Jesus. We can walk students, their parents, and our adult leaders through the process of communicating and sharing their story using these same three common elements. As we do, we can seek to give them opportunities to share their story one-on-one with other believers in small groups or during worship services and gatherings. In doing so, they not only gain confidence but also begin to see the power of their story in others' lives.

Sharing through Gospel Presentation[26]

Christians should know how to share the gospel both through their testimony story and via a simple gospel presentation. There are a number of gospel presentations that can be used, but we must take care to select one that accurately presents the gospel message.

One presentation method created by Dare 2 Share Ministries seeks to share the message of salvation by using the word *gospel* as an acrostic. This method presents the message clear and concise, while also briefly capturing the overarching story of the Bible. This method is a tool for both teenagers and adults to share the good news with friends, family, neighbors, and coworkers.

GOD created us to live in relationship with him.

---

[26] Adapted from Dare 2 Share Ministries, accessed July 14, 2021, https://www.dare2share.org/resources/free-teen-resources/.

OUR sin separates us from God and relationship with him.

SIN cannot be removed by doing good things.

PAYING the price for sin, Jesus died on the cross for you and me and rose again.

EVERYONE who trusts in Jesus alone receives forgiveness of sin and eternal life.

LIFE and relationship with Jesus begins at the moment of faith and lasts forever.

The Gospel Travels through Relationships

Most opportunities to share the gospel occur in everyday life with those with whom we already have relationship. We observe this in Scripture with Philip, who went to share with Nathanael (John 1) or the woman of Sychar who went to tell people in her town (John 4). This is not to suggest that we should not seek to share with strangers or those with whom we do not have relationship. Rather, believers should be equipped to seize everyday rhythms and routines and the opportunities they afford to share the gospel. Christians ought to be proactively building relationships with gospel intentionality with unbelievers.

Steps to Starting Gospel Conversations

One common challenge Christians face is how to transition everyday interactions into gospel conversations.[27] We can equip others through both teaching and role-playing and by example how to bridge ordinary

---

[27] "Ask, Admire, Admit," Dare 2 Share Ministries, accessed July 14, 2021, https://www.dare2share.org/outreach-tools/ask-admire-admit/.

conversations to gospel conversations. A technique to impart is the Ask–Admire–Admit method provided by Dare 2 Share Ministries.

The first step in moving to a gospel conversation is to *ask* the other person about his or her life. People like to talk about themselves, generally. We can ask them to share their story. We could ask specifically about their family, work, and interests or hobbies. A significant step is to ask them about spiritual matters and if he or she has any spiritual beliefs. When we ask, we ought to be good listeners as they share. Doing so is important because it demonstrates that we are actively listening rather than merely waiting to be heard.

The second step is to respond with admiration. *Admire* what you can about their beliefs. In some cases, it might be difficult to admire much of anything, except perhaps the person's tenacity or passion in belief. Admire aspects that are true or noble. If through their sharing we learn he or she is a Christian, this should lead us to celebrate our common bond in Jesus. However, when he or she is not a follower of Christ, we move in the conversation to a third step.

The third step is to *admit* that our life was so ruined and messed up that we needed someone to rescue us. This statement positions us to share Christ's salvation through the gospel. Then, we can ask for permission to share what changed our life. If permission is given, we can share our personal story of coming to faith in Jesus and his death and resurrection. This is also a time where the simple gospel presentation may be used. In certain situations, we might notice the other person's restlessness and agitation in the conversation. Instead of forcing a three-minute testimony or a gospel presentation, we can offer a short statement admitting both our need for and faith in Jesus Christ. We admit that our life was so messed up that we needed Jesus Christ to rescue us from our sin and ourselves. When we put our faith in him, he forgave us of our disobedience, restored us into relationship with God, changed our lives, and gave us meaning and purpose.

Leading Others to Trust Jesus

Once a person hears the good news, Christians must be prepared to lead unbelievers to faith in Jesus in order to receive God's gift of salvation. When Paul shared his story, he appealed to others to believe in Jesus (Acts 26:25–29). Students and adults should be prepared to follow sharing the gospel with an invitation to the person to trust in Jesus. A way of extending that invitation is to ask the person, "Has anything like this ever happened to you?" "Have you trusted in Jesus Christ and his death and resurrection to have new life and relationship with God?" If and when an individual states that he or she has never done so, we can then invite them to do so, asking, "Would you like to place your faith in Jesus alone to receive forgiveness of your sin, eternal life, and relationship with God?"

We must prepare students and adults that not every gospel presentation or invitation will be accepted or received kindly. Individuals might respond with anger, mockery, or rude statements. However, when someone desires to trust in Jesus, we must be ready to direct them to exercise saving faith. Scripture does not say salvation comes through praying to ask Jesus into one's heart. Rather, the Bible says we are to confess with our mouths that Jesus is Lord and believe that he died and rose again on the third day for our salvation (Acts 16:31; Rom 10:9). Prayer is the means of confessing one's sin to God, as well as confessing one's trust in Jesus for salvation through his death and resurrection. Thus, knowing how to lead a person to pray to God to acknowledge their need, confess their sin, and declare their trust and hope in Jesus who died and rose again is critical to evangelistic work.

Weathering Objections

Sharing the gospel will lead to the encounter of objections to the gospel message or Christianity. Christians often fear responses and questions unbelievers might raise. Objections might center on a number of things such as the existence of God, the nature of Scripture, the reality of Satan, the history of evils done by the church in Jesus's name, the narrow-mindedness of Christianity, and others. Believers should be ready to address the most common objections in a gentle, patient, and compassionate manner. At the same time, we must bear in mind that God does not need our defense of him or the gospel. We are to be Christ's witnesses and not his defense attorneys. We trust him to work by the power of his Spirit through our witness to convict others of sin and truth and draw them to faith in Jesus. Objections might come for which we do not have an answer. We should never guess at an answer, but rather agree to research and return with one later. Facing objections and pursuing scriptural answers grows us as followers of Jesus and prepares us for future encounters with individuals presenting similar objections.

Engaging the Mission of God through Evangelism

We must teach and equip believers as to the importance of sharing the gospel and in how to share. This, however, can occur regularly without anyone ever actually engaging in sharing the gospel. Therefore, we must exemplify and lead those entrusted to us in sharing the gospel regularly.

The Leader's Example

Those we lead are most likely to emulate our example far more than follow our instructions. "The loudest sermon is the one lived, not the one spoken."[28] Leaders who do not exemplify a life of evangelistic engagement, regardless of their teaching, likely will not produce evangelistic followers. Lee Vukich and Steve Vandegriff write, "We communicate an abundance of information concerning our beliefs and Christian faith, primarily through our lifestyle, in full view of [others]. Our words and actions must be in alignment; otherwise we will fail in our communication efforts."[29] What you want to see in the lives of your people must be conspicuous in your own. They must see and hear about our gospel efforts and conversations. Even more, taking Christians along with us as we seek to have intentional gospel conversations provides both teaching and example. We should tell them of moments in our lives when we were both obedient and disobedient to share the gospel. Especially reporting about gospel conversations where you led another person to faith in Christ can wield significant influence and inspiration.

We must acknowledge that teenagers' faith and practice is most influenced by their parents.[30] Kenda Creasy Dean notes, "Research is nearly unanimous on this point: parents matter most in shaping the religious lives of their children. This is not to say that parents determine their children's spiritual destinies."[31] God established the parent–child relationship as the primary relationship for children to learn by precept and example. If we desire to see evangelistic teenagers, we must aim for the hearts of both parents and teenagers to be

---

[28] Eric Geiger and Jeff Borton, *Simple Student Ministry* (Nashville: B&H, 2009), 54.

[29] Lee Vukich and Steve Vandegriff, *Timeless Youth Ministry* (Chicago: Moody, 2002), 270.

[30] Smith and Denton, *Soul Searching*, 261 (see chap. 8, n. 21).

[31] Kenda Creasy Dean, *Almost Christian* (New York: Oxford University Press, 2010), 112.

enthralled with Jesus and passionate to live obediently in proclaiming the gospel.

Intentional Course

Missions and evangelism will not be prominent in our ministry without intentionality. What we plan is what we really value. What we do not plan often does not get done. Planning for evangelistic activity and engagement helps you communicate what is important to students, parents, and volunteers. Planning for this also invites them to join in God's mission through strategic and intentional efforts you and your team prayerfully set forth. Involvement in God's mission is more than just events and activities the church plans. Yet these events and activities can serve to ignite a passion for gospel involvement in the everyday life of those you lead. The following are a few ways you can intentionally prioritize advancing the gospel.

Praying Intentionally

The role of prayer in evangelism cannot be overstated. First, Christians should pray for those who have not heard or believed the gospel. Paul reminds us in 2 Cor 4:4 that Satan has blinded unbelievers' minds from seeing the glory of the gospel. We must pray that God opens the eyes of unbelievers to see the beauty of the gospel and believe. Second, Christians should pray for those tasked with sharing the gospel. Jesus called us to pray that God would send more laborers into the fields where many needed the gospel (Matt 9:38). Our prayers should focus on asking God for boldness to share the gospel and that he would give us eyes to see opportunities.

Praying for the salvation of others, as well as our involvement in the mission, can be a regular part of corporate gatherings. We can lead others to pray for friends, family, coworkers, and neighbors by name. We can identify and adopt a particular country or people group and pray for God to work to bring his message of salvation to them.[32]

Planning Intentionally

No matter where our church is located, we have people living near us who have no relationship with Christ. They might be far from God but they are near to us, and we have the message of the gospel of hope. Identify ways to mobilize students to engage in local evangelism and missions right where the church meets and its members live.

We can do this by pointing students to see their school campus, sports teams, friend groups, social media platforms, and so on as places where unbelievers are present before whom they can live out and speak the gospel. We can resource families and students to gather friends and unbelievers at their home for block parties that intentionally include a time of sharing the gospel. We can lead students to provide free car washes where you seek to share the gospel with the owner while others wash the car. We can go door to door to do evangelism. We can partner with a new gospel-centered church plant or other churches nearby to be in neighborhoods or malls sharing the gospel. We can take students with us to visit first-time guests that have visited our church or student ministry gathering or event with the hope of sharing the gospel.

---

[32] "Global People Groups List: An Overview," Joshua Project, accessed July 14, 2021, https://joshuaproject.net/resources /articles/global_peoples _list_comparison.

Leading Short-Term Mission Trips

Short-term mission trips provide a life-changing experience for participants. Those who participate often experience the power of God outside their own culture, routines, and abilities. There are opportunities for short-term missions nationally and internationally. Giving students and adults an opportunity to engage in both national and international settings would be powerful. Not all mission trips are explicitly gospel-centered and gospel-advancing, though. Be careful that the short-term mission endeavor seeks to be sharing the gospel to meet the greater spiritual need even if the trip is also meeting real, tangible, physical needs.

Students today are considering the possibility of a gap year before entering college or taking a full-time job after high school. This presents a prime opportunity for parents and the church to encourage young people to serve a semester or year in missions through a church-plant partnership, serving with an international missionary, or being sent by a mission organization to serve in an area. Even more, after a gap year, students can choose a college or job in a place where there is great need for the gospel or where they can partner with a church or church planter to share the gospel and lead people to follow Jesus.

Conclusion

God's mission from the beginning has been to gather a people who walk in a relationship of worship and obedience with him. Humanity's rebellion severed the relationship between humankind and God. Only through the death and resurrection of Jesus Christ and our faith in him can this relationship be restored. Thus the gospel must be proclaimed that others may hear and believe. Every follower of Jesus has been entrusted with the gospel and commissioned to share the gospel in order to lead others to faith in Jesus.

Student Ministry
and Discipleship

• R. SCOTT PACE •

A biblical and balanced approach to discipling teens requires a holistic ministry philosophy that embraces the complex reality and the formative potential of the teenage years in an effort to facilitate authentic spiritual development. But this type of balanced approach to discipleship requires us to expand the concept of student discipleship beyond the typical theistic-behavioral modification we often promote and the group discipleship model we typically practice.

A more holistic philosophy for discipling teens involves a multidimensional strategy that facilitates progress through our ministry design—making disciples, mentoring disciples, and mobilizing disciples. This approach meets students where they are in their spiritual journey, has a variety of on ramps and growth opportunities, and is not a spiritual cul-de-sac that leaves them wandering in circles when they graduate. It is also relationally designed and depends on a collaborative effort between the parents/guardians and youth leaders. This is to collectively facilitate student discipleship in the context of the local church community.

But this holistic approach must be more than philosophical, it must be practical. As we dive into these three dimensions of a discipleship strategy, we can discern the implications for student ministry.

Making Disciples

As elementary as it might sound, an effective strategy for discipleship must begin with a clear understanding of the goal in Jesus's command to "make disciples" (Matt 28:19–20). In simple terms, a "disciple" is in fact a follower, an understudy, a protégé. Jesus clearly understood the process of discipleship to include learning and obedience ("*teaching* them to *observe* all that I have *commanded* you," emphasis added). But, that's not where it began. The regeneration of the heart and a personal relationship with the Lord ("baptizing them in the name of the Father, the Son, and the Holy Spirit") is the essential first step of discipleship that cannot be assumed or avoided. In other words, the Great Confession (Matt 16:13–18) and the Great Commandment (Matt 22:37–40) are the foundational building blocks of "making disciples" in order to fulfill the Great Commission (Matt 28:18–20).

Teach Them to Love Jesus

Sadly, as we work with students, too often we begin with and focus on a lifestyle of moral compliance. Our approach to discipleship essentially becomes teaching teenagers to adopt biblical virtues and values. But this is not the essence of true spiritual growth. Genuine discipleship is summarized by Jesus's invitation: "If anyone wants to *follow after me*, let him . . . *follow me*" (Luke 9:23, emphasis added).

You might be thinking, *Wait! You left out the most important part!* But this is the mistake. What discipleship requires, "deny himself" and "take up his cross daily," is the *means* by which *the goal* is accomplished. Authentic discipleship is not focused on the responsibility of the follower, it centers on the relationship with the One we are following. This common and tragic misstep alters the trajectory of our discipleship plan from the moment we invite people to follow Christ.

Practically speaking, this begins with how we share the gospel with students. We often define salvation in destinational terms (heaven/hell) or situational terms (better life/improved circumstances), but Jesus defined salvation in relational terms (John 17:3). This means that the real decision we are inviting students to make is primarily and ultimately a decision to follow Jesus through personal faith in him as their crucified Savior and risen Lord. Forgiveness, power over sin, hope for their earthly life, and the promise of eternal life are all glorious benefits of salvation. But the foundational core of salvation and discipleship is the personal relationship with Christ made possible by his redemptive work on the cross and his regenerative work in their heart.

Everything we teach students regarding discipleship has to be predicated on this relational truth of salvation. Discipleship is then cultivated through authentic love for Jesus in response to his sacrificial love for us. This means that our behavioral instructions for them must be rooted in a soil of sincere affection for Jesus. Our love for him is a response to his love for us (1 John 4:10, 19), and our love for Christ is expressed through our obedience to him (1 John 5:3).

While we may affirm these doctrinal truths, is it evident in our lives and ministry? Do our students see us model a lifestyle that is compelled by love for Jesus or that is obligated by our moral convictions and cultural opposition? Does our guidance and instruction for them always point them back to evaluating their hearts and making decisions that reflect a love for Christ? And do we consistently exalt Jesus as the One who is worthy of our adoration and affection?

Loving Jesus might sound elementary, but that does not mean it is rudimentary. It is foundational to every step they will make in their journey of following Christ. And it is within this loving context that they find the acceptance, affirmation, and affection that they so desperately seek from a world that cannot ultimately provide it. Loving Jesus is also where they will experience the deepest joy and find the greatest hope. Making disciples begins by teaching students to love Jesus.

Teach Them to Live for Jesus

The love of Jesus not only compels us to love him, it compels us to live for him. While we easily recognize the selfish nature that exists within all teenagers, the truth is that we all gravitate toward a me-centered reality that operates with self as the center of the universe. But the Scripture reminds us, when our hearts are captured by the love of Christ, we are compelled to no longer live for ourselves, but to live for the One who died and rose again on our behalf (2 Cor 5:14–15). Therefore, the natural result of a heart that loves Jesus will be a heart that lives for Jesus.

This is where our focus on the practical part of Jesus's invitation to be his disciple is rightly emphasized, "let him deny himself, take up his cross daily" (Luke 9:23). Following Jesus requires an ongoing discipline that seeks to align the positional reality of our death and new life in Christ with the practical reality of living for him (Gal 2:20). As we disciple teenagers, we should explain the biblical aspects of what this self-denial means. Consider just some of the aspects it involves while also noticing the magnitude of the responsibility.

It requires walking in the Spirit and not carrying out the desires of the flesh (Gal 5:16–25; Rom 13:14). It includes waging war against the desires of the flesh and claiming the victory that is ours in Christ (Rom 6:12–14). Denying ourselves and taking up our cross also involves dying to the world (Gal 6:14), not loving the world (1 John 2:15), not being conformed to the world (Rom 12:2), and not being polluted by the world (Jas 1:27). We are not to be "friends" with the world (Jas 4:4), but we are called to be in the world to engage the world (John 17:16–18). Even reading through this brief summary of "dying to self" can be exhausting and seem overwhelming! And many times, this is what our discipleship strategy can seem like to our students.

While this should not keep us from teaching our students these aspects of discipleship, it does remind us that we need to help them boil it down and maintain the proper perspective. Think about it this way—if the essence of his *invitation* is to "follow him," what is the essence of his *instruction* "to deny ourselves" and "take up our cross"? In its simplest form, it is to live *for* him by living *like* him. Denying himself and taking up his cross is exactly what Jesus did spiritually in his incarnation (Phil 2:6–7). It is also what he did literally in his crucifixion (Phil 2:7–8). And it is what he calls us to do practically by way of imitation (1 John 2:6). This is what it means to be a disciple, to be a Christ-follower. It simply means we are called to be like Jesus.

The Bible clearly teaches us that becoming like Christ is the purpose of our salvation, which requires the process of our sanctification (Rom 8:29). Being conformed "to the likeness of the Son" should encourage our students to claim their positional status in Christ as a child of the King (1 John 3:1; John 1:12), who is a new creation (2 Cor 5:17), and one who is righteous before God (2 Cor 5:21).

It also should challenge students to embrace the practical reality of conforming their lives—their affections, their attitudes, and their actions—to the likeness of Jesus. By God's Spirit they can be transformed into his likeness (2 Cor 3:18), and they grow in the grace and knowledge of our Lord (2 Pet 3:18).

For us, as student leaders, this clarifies the starting point for discipleship. The mission begins with making disciples—followers of Christ who love Jesus and live for Jesus.

Ministry Implications

When we know the desired outcome of discipleship, we can then develop a corresponding strategy to achieve it. It also allows us to evaluate our existing approach and modify it accordingly. Since "making disciples" defines our mission, we can begin by establishing a "target student." This does not identify the type of student you are attempting to reach, but the intended student you are trying to produce.

If our goal is to produce followers of Christ who love Jesus and live for Jesus, we can determine the attributes they should possess and the character they should embody. Take a few moments to list those descriptive characteristics that you desire to see in students who graduate from your student ministry. This may include everything from specific devotional habits, certain levels of biblical literacy, and personal life skills, to their servant's disposition. It can be as specific and comprehensive as you desire. You may work through this together with some of your ministry leaders and parents. Ultimately, this picture should be a prototype of what a teenage Jesus-follower will look like.

Once you have established these intended attributes, begin to evaluate your ministry philosophy and practices. Consider how your current activities, Bible studies, curriculum, trips/retreats, and budget are designed to produce students who reflect this ideal. While you might be able to easily identify some aspects of your ministry that are not effectively contributing to the desired outcome, you might need to look more closely at those that are not being optimized and need modification. This process can require some hard looks in the mirror that challenge us to swallow some difficult medicine for the health of our ministries.

Some of these questions might be program- or event-specific. How do you leverage those social and fellowship-oriented events to stir affections for Christ? Are your Bible studies designed more for formation or information? Does your budget and calendar reflect more of an event-oriented approach that measures success by attendance or a people-oriented focus that emphasizes spiritual growth? What are some ways our ministry platforms can be enhanced or more strategically designed to accomplish the mission of making disciples?

Sometimes it might not be about the things you are currently doing. It might be something that you are not doing. Are there any glaring absences that are expecting discipleship fruit to be produced that do not have corresponding "seeds" being planted or a ministry soil to grow in? In other words, if you desire a student to be able to defend their faith and withstand the cultural attacks they will undoubtedly face, when would they be equipped to do so in your ministry? These types of questions can determine whether we should add a platform to our ministry or repurpose an existing avenue for discipleship.

This also requires us to evaluate our ministries beyond a single year in order to achieve the holistic goal. Do you have a curriculum strategy for your small groups that is designed to address various aspects of the target student throughout their journey in your student ministry? Do you have broader teaching times that foster spiritual community in a corporate setting? At the same time, do you provide small-group opportunities that might be gender-specific? Are there dedicated times that are more specifically designed for seniors or those transitioning into the youth group (sixth or seventh graders)? Are there middle school and high school platforms that tackle age-appropriate issues?

Maximizing the designated days/times we have is essential. While no one has enough time in any given week to accomplish all of these things at once, this highlights our need to be more strategic in our overarching plans for making disciples. The current demographics of our groups, the established pattern for our ministries, or the brevity of our expected tenure at a specific church are not valid reasons to avoid designing a broader discipleship strategy.

Mentoring Disciples

We all know that relationships are *the* platform for any effective ministry. But beyond the relational component that is so essential for growing in community, there must be an intentionality as to how we leverage these relationships. Jesus modeled this throughout his ministry. Certainly, Jesus led his disciples to places they had never been, showed them things they had never seen, taught them how the truth of the Scriptures should inform their view of the world, and involved them in the gospel mission. But he did not primarily teach them all of these things sitting in the temple. He deliberately spent time with his disciples by being involved in their lives, wrestling through theological questions, frequently sharing meals together, discussing current events, and dealing with social and cultural challenges. This sounds exactly like student ministry!

These aspects of Jesus's relational approach were not simply the result of living in first-century Palestine, and they were not intended to be unique features of his ministry. They were all strategic efforts in the mentoring aspect of discipleship that is so critical to our spiritual development. Our ministry requires this same strategy. By necessity, *making* disciples requires us to be *mentoring* disciples.

Mentoring Requires Our Personal Investment

Oftentimes in our ministry the concept of mentoring is either assumed or ignored. We either assume that we are mentoring students by being friends and spending time with them; meanwhile, we never actually disciple them. Or, we are so focused on the group as a whole that we are distracted away from the individuals and never truly invest in them. Both of these common pitfalls are deceptive because we can be convinced that our ministry is healthy when in reality it's not designed to produce the lifelong disciples that we so desperately desire.

Mentoring is a concept that is modeled and endorsed throughout Scripture. In the Old Testament we see examples of personal support and guidance such as Jethro with Moses (Exod 18:1–27). We also see models of influence and tutelage through divine plans for succession with Moses and Joshua (Num 27:18–23) and Elijah and Elisha (1 Kgs 19:16, 19–21). In the New Testament we see Jesus establish the model for mentoring through his investment in the twelve apostles (Luke 6:12–16). He also exhibited an intentional effort to particularly invest in Peter, James, and John (Matt 17:1; 26:37). While Jesus certainly might have taught the multitudes, his discipleship strategy was clearly focused on investing in individuals through a mentoring relationship.

Likewise, the apostle Paul enlisted and invested in traveling companions throughout his ministry. He ministered with less-recognizable names such as Erastus, Gaius, Aristarchus, Sopater, Secundus,

Tychichus, and Trophimus (Acts 19:22, 29; 20:4); more notable partners Barnabas (Acts 13:46–49) and Silas (Acts 15:40); and others like Timothy (Acts 16:3; 1 Tim 1:2) and Titus (Titus 1:4), who became "sons" in his ministry.

Beyond his own ministry, Paul's exhortations throughout his letters direct believers to invest in others through active mentoring (Titus 2:1–8). His instructions also provide various elements of mentoring that give us insight into some of the essential elements for discipling students. For instance, mentoring requires a sacrificial commitment that stems from genuine affection, models a godly lifestyle, provides encouragement and counsel, and instructs others to grow in their walk with God (1 Thess 2:8–12). It involves living as an example that models Christ-likeness and invites others to pursue it for themselves (1 Cor 11:1).

Personal investment of this caliber requires our personal involvement. Our relationships with students must extend beyond the weekly gatherings on the church calendar. The scheduled church times can provide an initial platform for our relationship, but if we are going to invest in our students, we must look for ways to engage beyond these limited occasions. Their family, schoolwork, sports, clubs, jobs, and social activities dominate their time and demand their attention. But rather than trying to compete with these, we should leverage them when possible. They can provide points of common interest, opportunities to support them, and platforms to demonstrate genuine care that warrants their trust. They also serve as practical avenues for our students to live out their faith, and our involvement allows us to provide counsel and spiritual encouragement in these areas.

In addition to being involved in their lives, we can also invite them to be involved in ours. This can include hosting them in our homes, working on personal projects together, sharing our family time, and giving them responsibilities within the ministry.

Ultimately, sharing our lives and being involved in theirs provides natural pathways to offer spiritual guidance as we mentor them through our personal investment.

Mentoring Requires Our Practical Instruction

Based on the biblical precedents and principles, mentoring students also requires us to leverage our relationships by teaching them to walk with Christ. While personal investment provides the platform for these formative relationships, we must also make intentional efforts to provide the practical guidance necessary for them to spiritually mature and live out their faith. At its core, mentoring is implied within the concept of a disciple as a "learner." It also corresponds to Jesus's command to "make disciples" by "*teaching* them" (Matt 28:19, emphasis added). This process is meant to be replicated and perpetuated by passing along the truths of the faith to others who are "faithful" and will "teach others also" (2 Tim 2:2).

We must start by imparting biblical truths that will shape their thinking and renew their minds (Rom 12:2). Practically speaking, this may include walking through passages of Scripture together, working through a particular Bible study, or providing verses related to relevant issues or particular struggles. When we help them see the rich beauty of God's Word, our students will develop a hunger that can only be satisfied by the timeless truth of the Scriptures!

We should also encourage them to read God's Word on their own, not simply to maintain a personal devotion, but to thirst for God's Word and be satisfied with its soul-nourishing truth. This requires us to do more than simply *tell* them to study the Bible, we must *teach* them to study God's Word! Providing them with the basic tools necessary will equip them to feed themselves and sustain their spiritual growth far beyond their time as part of our student ministries.

In addition to studying Scripture, we should also personally mentor them in other essential spiritual disciplines including praying, giving, witnessing, serving, and worshipping. These are all concepts we regularly mention to our students, but we rarely mentor our students in them. Our guidance must provide both the "why" and the "how." In other words, as we leverage our personal relationships with students, we must take the time to provide them with a biblical understanding of the disciplines as well as the useful instruction of how to practice them.

Mentoring our students in the faith requires us to model the disciplines in our own lives, to invite them to participate in them with us, and to help them maintain a proper perspective of their function. We must consistently teach and continually remind them that the spiritual exercises have no transforming power in and of themselves. Otherwise, the disciplines will become obligatory duties that unnecessarily burden them with guilt when they fail to practice the disciplines or self-righteously puff them up with pride when they habitually perform them.

Instead, a healthy understanding of the disciplines recognizes that they are simply God's designated means to position us beneath the transforming power of his grace. Transformation occurs through the finished work of Christ in our lives as his Spirit conforms us to his image (2 Cor 3:18). Some of our well-meaning but flawed approach stems from our own distorted view of spiritual maturity that equates performance with progress. We can be guilty of unintentionally causing them to be satisfied with a moral lifestyle that affirms biblical values and performs religious rituals. We have to be careful that we do not blur their understanding of their relationship with Christ by emphasizing the disciplines at the expense of the intended intimacy they are meant to help facilitate.

The level of involvement and practical instruction that mentoring requires also highlights the need to enlist others in the mentorship process. Not every student will relate to us, but we should do our best to involve a variety of leaders who can provide a listening ear, an influential voice, and a formative influence. While some of our volunteers might serve in a specific capacity, we should do our best to recruit those who have the availability and spiritual maturity to invest in students.

Ministry Implications

Sometimes we can be guilty of overcomplicating clear and simple principles. Mentoring students can easily become a complex program that is an overstructured, rigid attempt to manufacture moral and religious robots. To be clear, this isn't our intention, but it can easily become our approach as we meet with students in an attempt to mentor them. Our time with students may focus on certain tasks to be completed or expectations to be met. And while we should set strategic goals to maximize our time together and utilize helpful resources, we can never mistake busyness for effectiveness.

Adopting a mentoring philosophy and developing a corresponding strategy might require us to begin by recalibrating our hearts. Oftentimes we pursue the students that we believe have the greatest potential, possess social influence, and have exceptional personalities or abilities. While these students can certainly be used to make a difference for Christ, the beauty and power of the gospel is magnified through the lives of those who aren't wise or significant by worldly standards (1 Cor 1:26–31).

As a student minister, I remember exactly where I was when my ministry philosophy changed and mentoring became a more concerted effort. I was lamenting the news with one of our ministry leaders that a couple of our "premiere" students were living in sin and had been successfully covering up their sinful lifestyle. I was devastated. I even posed the rhetorical question, "If these are some of our best students, and this is how they're living, what are we doing?" All of my standard measures of success were unraveling before me. The influential and popular high schoolers, their endorsement of our ministry by their involvement, and my approval rating based on my "friendship" with them were all supposed to translate into a strong ministry and making a difference for Christ.

At that moment, my phone rang. It was a student who was socially awkward but very kind and extremely committed. He was the type of young man everyone liked having around, but no one necessarily wanted to hang around. I did my best to minister to him and his family because his mom had passed away when he was young, his dad was physically disabled, his stepmom was doing her best, and he didn't have a lot of friends. But I never knew what all the rides home, the prayers after worship time, and the simple jokes we exchanged meant until he called that day. He simply reached out to say thank you for all I was doing, to let me know that it was making a difference, and to encourage me.

Of course, he had no idea what was going on with these other students, but I hung up the phone, and from that point forward my approach to making disciples changed forever. Instead of putting most of my efforts into trying to reach the most *influential* students, I began to focus on the *incidental* students who were eager to become *instrumental* students. Sometimes we do not get to choose who we mentor. Either the selection of students is limited, or certain students gravitate toward us. But when we are praying for students to mentor, we should pursue those students who are teachable and hungry to grow. They don't have to have the greatest ability, just availability.

Another important implication for mentoring students involves leveraging the parental influence as the primary avenue for mentoring.

While our culture and our churches have a growing number of broken and blended families, God's design for the home includes discipleship through personal investment and instruction. Although we must be careful not to overstep with parental advice, we can provide resources, training, and encouragement for parents and guardians as they navigate the difficult waters of raising teenagers. Some of the greatest influence we have in the lives of our students might be through the relationships we forge with their parents that unite our efforts to mentor their teens.

Mobilizing Disciples

Oftentimes our assessment of a student's growth as a disciple focuses on the consistency of their devotional habits, a lifestyle marked by moral behavior, and their level of ministry involvement through their regular attendance. While these can be important indicators of spiritual health, Christian maturity according to the Scriptures should also be measured by a heart that beats for the mission of God and takes personal responsibility to participate in the cause of Christ.

Our failure to properly emphasize the missional component of spiritual growth often derives from our own false dichotomy between evangelism and discipleship. But these two aspects of following Christ are inseparable and must operate in reciprocating harmony. Although we would never knowingly advocate for this unbiblical separation, we can subtly segregate them from one another by rarely emphasizing the missional aspect of practical application in our Bible studies or by relegating evangelism to designated events or trips. Tragically, when we do, we unintentionally implement and reinforce this unbiblical distinction through our ministry philosophy and practice. As a result, we must adopt a process that not only makes and mentors student disciples but mobilizes them as well.

Living with Gospel Purpose

Sometimes it is difficult for students to see beyond their immediate stage of life and circumstances. But as we teach them to love and live for Jesus, we must also help them see that Jesus desires to redeem their passions and pursuits. This expands the discipleship conversation beyond their current struggles and social challenges. God's work during this season of their lives is formative preparation for his extended will for them.

As we help them look beyond their teenage years to the future, it does not minimize the significance of their present potential. Actually, it helps provide a broader context and perspective for their current service that is not limited to the opportunities we are able to provide for them. Ministering to others as members of the local church translates beyond the demographic category of student and should begin to influence how they view their college choice, future vocation, and purpose in life.

In other words, when we reference God's plan for students' lives, we should be pointing to the kingdom impact he desires to make with them. We must help them understand that the significance they crave isn't measured by number of friends, social media followers, or material possessions. We have to help our students define the measure of success as "faithfulness"—being good stewards of God's saving grace (1 Cor 15:10), their spiritual gifts (1 Pet 4:10–11), and the truth of the gospel (Rom 1:16).

In discipleship terms, this means helping students realize that following Christ is more than just a private journey. It's a personal mission that enlists them as soldiers who serve valiantly in an effort to honor the King (2 Tim 2:3–4). As we help prepare them for a lifetime devoted to serving Jesus, there are several timeless truths that can capture their hearts and provide ongoing motivation to live with a gospel purpose.

The primary impetus for leveraging their lives for the cause of Christ certainly must be the glory of God. In addition to the selfish depravity of the human heart, our world entices and conditions students to seek and pursue their own notoriety for selfish gain. We must give them a vision for God that marvels at the glorious majesty of his transcendence and cherishes the personal intimacy of his immanence. We must exalt his worthiness to be worshipped and adored by all of his creation. More specifically, we should accentuate the glory he receives through the salvation of souls that was secured by the sacrifice of the Son (Phil 2:10–11). When we elevate the glory of God, we help our students reorient their perspective so that they're not at the center of their own universe and can fulfill their created purpose of glorifying him. It also motivates them to devote their lives to sharing the gospel so that others can ascribe to him the glory he is worthy to receive!

The glory of God in salvation also highlights the tragedy of lostness, the brevity of this life, and the gravity of eternity. While our world convinces people to live for the moment, the temporary nature of our earthly existence and the momentary satisfaction of fleshly indulgence should compel our students to give their lives for the eternal cause of Christ. While we are rightfully disgusted by the immorality of our culture, we must make sure that our students recognize that our disdain for the sins of society does not translate into taking pleasure in the eternal punishment of the lost. We must teach them to grieve over their desperate condition and to devote our lives to the gospel that can remedy their hopeless condition. The finality of death and brutality of God's judgment should foster an urgency in them that is desperate to see people find forgiveness and freedom in Christ.

All of these factors should culminate in a personal understanding of "calling" for our students. This generation, along with previous generations of young people, crave a sense of purpose for their lives. To help them live with gospel purpose, we should continually encourage them to fulfill their personal calling as followers of Christ. This does not always translate to vocational ministry. In fact, it will not for most of our students. And while we cannot dismiss or ignore the possibility of a vocational calling to ministry or missions for some, we must help all of our students to understand their vocation as a calling.

In other words, whatever career capacity corresponds to their interests, abilities, and opportunities can be leveraged for the cause of Christ when pursued according to his will and performed according to his Word. This mindset will help set the trajectory of their lives, including significant college, career, and companion decisions. It will also affirm their value in God's kingdom and not limit their significance based on perceived importance or positional prominence. We must teach our students that as Christ's disciples, God has created, converted, and called each of them to achieve a particular part of his divine plan. Therefore, we should mobilize them to live with gospel purpose.

Living with a Global Perspective

Just as this generation desires significance and purpose, they also have a heightened sense of global awareness. The growing international and ethnic diversity of our country has broadened their understanding of various cultures and given them an appreciation for all people. Combined with the global technology that is not bound by geographical distance and the accessibility of worldwide travel, our students are more naturally inclined to operate from a global perspective.

But as with anything else, familiarity can breed apathy. Instead, we must leverage it for opportunity. The beauty of our country's growing diversity is the removal of personal discomfort that stems from the unknown and unfamiliar. The possibility for demolishing ethnic barriers, which Christ came to spiritually remove (Eph 2:11–22), is more naturally plausible because of our cultural integration. But we cannot allow a naïve sense of comfort to grow from a broadened sense of community diversity that would ultimately diminish our students' awareness of the desperate need for Christ that still exists around the world.

To combat the gravitational pull toward indifference, we must expose them to the needs of countries with little to no gospel exposure. We must highlight the physical needs of underprivileged countries that can be served as a means to meet their spiritual need for Christ. We can celebrate the value of an international career that can be leveraged as a platform for the gospel and encourage our students to consider the possibilities. And we can prayerfully and financially support international and domestic missionaries through our ministries that can introduce our students to the beauty and significance of a life that is called to the mission field.

Ultimately, our desire for our students should reflect God's desire for all people. He does not discriminate (Acts 10:34–35), and he desires all people to come to a saving knowledge of Jesus Christ (1 Tim 2:3–6). Therefore, in order to mobilize our students effectively, we should begin by welcoming students from diverse backgrounds into our ministry. We must be willing to cross social barriers in our communities and encourage our students to do the same in their schools. We also should express and embody the desire for the church on earth (including our student ministries!) to reflect the church in heaven (Rev 7:9).

As we promote growth by reaching various areas of our own communities, we should also look for ways to expose our students to international experiences around the world. We can invite families and students to participate in churchwide mission trips. We can also provide short-term international opportunities for older students that include less travel and are somewhat less expensive. And we can encourage parents to take their students on international trips for family vacations or personal milestones that can serve as bridges for missional awareness. Collectively, these efforts are meant to mobilize students by encouraging them to live with a global perspective.

Ministry Implications

If we truly desire to mobilize our students on a mission for Christ, we must honestly evaluate the missional thrust of ministries. In addition to teaching the biblical and theological truths as the foundation, and providing opportunities with practical experiences, a missional heartbeat and mindset must permeate our ministries. Our students' passion for the nations will be sparked and stoked through the missional culture we cultivate.

As we affirm their current value and God's future plans for their lives, we must also equip them to share the gospel. This does not require a scripted presentation. We should help them see the value of conversational evangelism that builds genuine relationships and provides a natural opportunity to tell others about Jesus. We can teach them simple ways to tell their own story of salvation, express the truths of the gospel, and invite others to follow Christ. We should also emphasize the importance of a godly lifestyle as a testimony for Christ that is accompanied with a clear and unashamed explanation of the hope within them (1 Pet 3:15).

In our current culture and climate, our students also need to be prepared to endure the hostility that a sincere and faithful testimony can invite. We must encourage them to exercise wisdom toward outsiders, make the most of every opportunity, and season their conversations with grace as they respond to each person (Col 4:5–6). As they engage the world around them, we must help them model the balance that Christ embodied, being "full of grace and truth" (John 1:14). This certainly is not an easy task, especially considering that the world of teenagers is oftentimes an amplified version of the culture at large. Preparing them accordingly is essential and demonstrates our appreciation for the difficulty of the task.

In order to further equip them for mobilization, we must also prepare them with foundational training in key doctrines of the faith. Entry-level apologetics might not be necessary for every student, but it can be beneficial, particularly as we help them anticipate questions and objections to their faith or prepare for college. Additionally, we cannot avoid difficult cultural issues that people raise that often hijack their evangelistic efforts. While we won't be able to equip them to fully respond to every doubt or difficult question, we can give them permission to pursue additional answers and promote ongoing conversations.

In our student ministries, missions and evangelism must become a demonstrated priority that is reflected in every aspect of our budget, calendar, activities, and events. When we prioritize missional living, we honor the Lord Jesus, not simply through obedience to the Great Commission, but by reflecting his heart that he demonstrated by leaving his home in heaven to deliver salvation to those who desperately needed it and otherwise could have never secured it on their own. Therefore, we must constantly remind ourselves, our efforts to make and mentor student disciples should always seek to culminate in mobilizing student disciples.

Conclusion

Student discipleship is an ongoing process that requires a concerted and collective effort. We must approach the discipleship task strategically and holistically as we devote ourselves to the process of making, mentoring, and mobilizing student disciples. As we evaluate our ministries, we must be intentional to leverage every opportunity and every relationship for the goal of producing genuine followers of Christ who love and live for Jesus. As we personally invest in our students and provide practical instruction to promote their spiritual growth, we must help them realize their potential to be used by God as they live with gospel purpose and a global perspective.

The breadth and depth of the discipleship task, combined with the gravity of our personal responsibility, should humble us to renew our own walk with the Lord. It should also challenge us to invite mentoring influences into our own lives and to live on mission for the sake of the gospel. We also have to recognize the importance of the local church community and the collaboration with parents that is essential for students' spiritual growth. And as we cooperate together, may we be humbled by the privilege of ministering to families, discipling students, and serving our King!

Student Ministry
and Technology

• SAM TOTMAN •

In the Beginning

Imagine for a moment the challenges early mariners faced as they set out to travel uncharted waters in search of new lands and the vast treasures waiting to be unearthed. As long as ships remained close to land, they could use landmarks to guide their journey. While still dangerous, failure did not necessarily mean death. Traversing the deep waters of the world's oceans called for a new set of skills and tools. In the high-stakes world of ocean navigation, success meant new lands, opportunity, and wealth. Failure almost certainly guaranteed death for everyone on board.

Initially, sea captains used natural elements such as celestial bodies, wind, and currents to determine their position and heading. In short, these were educated guesses often foiled by turbulent seas and bad weather.[1] Sea travel only became safer and faster as inventors developed new technologies to improve navigation amid the storms. Navigating student ministry can feel like making educated guesses, particularly when it comes to integrating technology. To make matters worse, the ministry is a perilous journey with cloudy skies and turbulent seas ahead. Fortunately, unlike those first navigators, this is a time of technological advancement, and with a proper understanding of the resources and tools available, one has the highest chance of success. This chapter introduces various ways technology can be used in student ministry. It will explore different technological innovations and how they can serve student ministers and their youth groups.

Five Questions One Must Ask First

In 1998, Neil Postman laid out five concepts everyone should know to confront technological change. Postman was a prolific author, writing eighteen books, including *Amusing Ourselves to Death* and *Technopoly: The Surrender of Culture to Technology*, and numerous journal articles in the area of media ecology. He was a professor at New York University for forty years and served as chairman of the department of culture and communication before his death in 2003. His teaching continues to influence technological discussions today. In any dispute about the inclusion or exclusion of technology in ministry, it is beneficial to hear Postman's concerns to make appropriate precautions before blindly accepting a practice that could potentially have negative consequences. Each concept helps to reinforce and

---

[1] "Challenges of Sea Navigation," *Time and Navigation*, Smithsonian, April 15, 2020, https://timeandnavigation.si.edu/navigating-at-sea/challenges.

strengthen one's development of digital discernment, which is so vital to determining one's chances of success.

What Foreseeable Changes Will this Technology Introduce?

Postman often raised two related questions: "What will a new technology do?" and "What will a new technology undo?"[2] The fact that youth ministries might be able to make use of their smartphones during a service is no guarantee that this ability is without cost. The benefit might outweigh that cost, but when the beneficiaries of such a change include teenagers, students will ultimately pay the price.

A student minister may consider encouraging students to take advantage of a Bible app instead of a physical copy of God's Word. Students already carry their smartphones with them, and student ministers might determine this to be a great way to connect with teenagers. Using digital apps offers a different experience for teenagers rather than turning actual pages of a Bible or searching for verses through skimming their contents as opposed to using a search box. Making further application, how would encouraging people to share their faith online encourage or discourage witnessing offline? Social media and virtual communities provide points of connection for some and yet lead to disconnection for others.[3] What foreseeable changes will this technology introduce, and how can student ministers limit or eliminate the harmful effects of introducing technology?

---

[2] Neil Postman, "Five Things We Need to Know about Technological Change" (lecture, Denver, CO, March 28, 1998), 2, http://web.cs.ucdavis.edu /~rogaway/classes/188/materials/postman.pdf.

[3] Sherry Turkle, *Alone Together: Why We Expect More from Technology and Less from Each Other* (New York: Basic Books, 2011), 154.

Will Students Benefit or Suffer?

Social media companies offer a service, seemingly for free, but in reality, these companies profit from the content users provide. Participating in virtual communities often comes at the price of one's privacy. As technology seemingly becomes a natural part of adolescent life, teenagers are inadvertently dropping their defenses and releasing higher amounts of personal information, more than any other generation before them.[4] Even if students, by some measure, limit the amount of information they provide about themselves, every choice they make online is tracked across multiple devices and platforms. Media companies sell this data to advertisers who tailor their marketing approaches to persuade teenagers to buy their products and services.[5]

One might consider avoiding these privacy issues altogether and end social media use, but disconnecting from social media becomes a social challenge for teenagers. People in general feel like social networks and connectivity are inevitable and that disconnecting from them is too complicated and will be next to impossible within the next ten years.[6] Palfrey and Gasser wrote, "For youth, it would mean opting out of much of social life and being deprived of the wonderful opportunities for self-expression, learning, and entrepreneurship that come with digital technologies."[7] Many are willing to give up

---

[4] John Palfrey and Urs Gasser, *Born Digital: How Children Grow Up in a Digital Age* (New York: Basic Books, 2016), 53–54.

[5] Palfrey and Gasser, 57.

[6] See Theme 1 and Theme 2. Lee Rainie and Janna Anderson, "The Internet of Things Connectivity Binge: What Are the Implications?" Pew Research Center, 2017, http://www.pewinternet.org/2017/06/06/the-internet-of-things-connectivity-binge-what-are-the-implications/pi_2017-06-06_future-of-connectivity_0-01/.

[7] Palfrey and Gasser, *Born Digital*, 55.

personal information to gain entrance into public spaces and social gatherings that are increasingly taking place online.

What Is the Technology Teaching Teenagers?

Postman noted that every technology is embedded with powerful ideas that are often hidden from the participants. Every digital application includes a value system that is usually accepted by those who allow it to do so. The internet places emphasis on endless amounts of information. What often gets lost—devalued—is knowledge and wisdom.[8] While young people quickly adapt and learn new technology, it stands to reason that one crucial building block for life, in general, is the development of knowledge and wisdom. Here student ministers can contribute to the use of technology both within the student ministry as well as student use. Technologies often are merely new methods of dealing with old challenges. People who have navigated real-world problems are better equipped to educate those who are now facing those challenges anew in the virtual space of the internet.

In today's culture, speed is valued over depth of learning. Search engines have, in many ways, replaced the necessity to drive to the library, and spend countless hours scouring musty bookshelves hoping to find that one book that could have the content you seek. Search engines such as Google make it easier to access a world of information that was previously only held by experts. It's a fantastic tool, but the consequence of efficiency and devaluing the classroom or library might ultimately stunt learning. To what extent does the capability of instantly searching the Bible for a particular verse on any given topic limit one's ability to understand the context or how

---

[8] Postman, "Five Things We Need to Know," 3.

to apply a verse to their lives properly? One might also ask even if a student can instantly locate a verse, and by chance or divine intervention can understand the authorial intent of the said verse, how much is lost in skipping over the journey to find it? Some of the greatest lessons might go unlearned because teenagers read the end of the book without experiencing the story along the way.

When Marshall McLuhan wrote "The Medium Is the Message," what he was attempting to communicate is that inherent in every medium is an influence that changes everything, including the message at least on some level.[9] If it is true that the medium has a transformative effect on the message, then ministers must consider how introducing new technology will alter their teaching and, ultimately, the gospel.[10]

McLuhan and his son Eric McLuhan taught that every new medium enhances, amplifies, or extends some human capacity.[11] Since the fall of mankind in Genesis 3, humanity has been trying to survive in a broken world. The development of technology is, in many ways, an effort to fix and correct course. With each innovation, society convinces itself that this new tool will bring about a better world.[12] The great danger here is that humanity puts its hope in its creation—technology—dismissing what broke the world in the first place. This misplaced hope might lead to incredible inventions, technologies that will benefit humanity greatly, but technology is just as broken and

---

[9] Marshall McLuhan, *Understanding Media: The Extensions of Man*, 1964, http://web.mit.edu/allanmc/www/mcluhan.mediummessage.pdf.

[10] Justin Wise, *The Social Church: A Theology of Digital Communication* (Chicago: Moody, 2014), 103.

[11] See Shane Hipps, *The Hidden Power of Electronic Culture: How Media Shapes Faith, the Gospel, and Church* (Grand Rapids, MI: Zondervan, 2005), 41.

[12] John Dyer, *From the Garden to the City: The Redeeming and Corrupting Power of Technology* (Grand Rapids, MI: Kregel, 2011), 35.

limited as its creators. Psalm 115:4–7 speaks of humanity's idols and their inherent weakness in comparison to God. The psalmist wrote, "Their idols are silver and gold, made by human hands. They have mouths but cannot speak; eyes, but cannot see. They have ears but cannot hear; noses, but cannot smell. They have hands but cannot feel; feet, but cannot walk. They cannot make a sound with their throats." Technology is not the devil, but neither is it a savior. This role is one only Jesus Christ can fulfill. John Dyer wrote, "Technology plays a role in [God's] story, but it is a subservient role, not an ultimate one. The only true salvation offered to humanity comes from God himself, through his Son Jesus Christ."[13] The psalmist continued with a striking warning, "Those who make them are just like them, as are all who trust in them" (115:8). When humanity fails to see technology as an extension of itself, what results is a culture that becomes enslaved to its tools, powerless and unfulfilled.[14]

What Ecological Changes Will Technology Bring?

Next, Postman instructed his audience that technological change is not additive but ecological.[15] Ecology refers to how environments change in response to makeup.[16] Introducing technology into ministry does not equate to ministry as usual plus technology; instead, what results is an entirely different ministry. More significantly, not only will the new technology change the student ministry, but it will also have transformative effects on the students and not necessarily for the better.[17] For example, projecting Scripture on a screen or

---

[13] Dyer, 41.

[14] Hipps, *The Hidden Power*, 35.

[15] Postman, "Five Things We Need to Know," 4.

[16] Hipps, *The Hidden Power*, 40.

[17] Dyer, *From the Garden to the City*, 35.

allowing students to access their Bible from their smartphone might result in fewer students bringing their physical Bibles to the youth group. Without understanding the ecological changes that will occur, student ministers run the risk of adapting their ministries to meet the demands of the tool instead of choosing the tools that will fulfill the needs of the ministry.[18]

Has Technology Become a Myth?

Finally, Postman warned that media would often become mythic to the people who have no recollection of life without it.[19] Dyer defines a myth as a "story that develops over time about how the world works and what makes sense to a group of people."[20] When technology becomes mythic, people begin to trust it without question and exalt it to a position of perfection. They forget that the programmers who engineer technological applications themselves experience the effects of their sinful nature, which limits their ability to understand their creation's influence on its users.[21]

Enthusiasm for technology can turn into a form of idolatry, and our belief in its beneficence can be a false absolute. The best way to view technology is as a strange intruder, to remember that technology is not part of God's plan but a product of human creativity and hubris, and that its capacity for good or evil rests entirely on social awareness of what it does for us and to us.[22] Technology can benefit

---

[18] Dyer, 25.

[19] Postman, "Five Things We Need to Know," 4.

[20] Dyer, *From the Garden to the City*, 25.

[21] Tim Challies, *The Next Life: Life and Faith after the Digital Explosion* (Grand Rapids, MI: Zondervan, 2011), 26–27.

[22] Postman, "Five Things We Need to Know," 5.

its users, but there always exists the potential for harm, and it is wise to approach it with skepticism and forethought.

The Connected World

In 1991, Tim Berners-Lee created hypertext transfer protocol, or HTTP, for accessing files within a computer network, laying the foundation for the World Wide Web. As monumental as this development was, his decision to not limit it through a patent opened the door to allow any computer to become an integral part of the Web; anyone could become a contributor and user of the internet.[23] Unlike the broadcast age, which was primarily dominated by media corporations, the Web channels open communication.[24]

Since its birth, the internet has become an integral part of nearly all aspects of life, from the mobile smartphones people carry in their pockets to the appliances that have become servants to voice-operated digital assistants such as Apple's Siri or Amazon's Alexa. Computers continued to increase in power and shrink in size, allowing for the development of cellular networks and mobile technology.[25] Smartphones enable individuals to not only connect with others via the phone but also take full advantage of the internet. Users could maintain their connection to technology twenty-four hours a day, seven days a week. Amanda Lenhart of the Pew Research Center found that in terms of the American teenager, accessing the Web through their mobile phones had become a way of life and an integral part of personality and identity development, with 92 percent reporting that

---

[23] Rudi Volti, *Society and Technological Change*, 7th ed. (New York: Worth Publishers, 2014), 264.

[24] Wise, *The Social Church*, 45.

[25] Challies, *The Next Life*, 57.

they go online daily and 24 percent saying they do so almost always.[26] Connecting to technology is no longer an event, but a lifestyle.

The Age of Distraction

According to Sherry Turkle, professor of the social studies of science and technology at the Massachusetts Institute of Technology, teenagers today are increasingly growing up in homes in which they rarely experience intentional, uninterrupted conversations.[27] Youth ministers also experience these interruptions as teenagers disengage during youth meetings and other inappropriate times to use their smartphones. Youth workers often attempt to deal with the challenges of discipling always-on, always-connected students by taking up mobile devices during their youth service. Turkle noted these strategies might not be enough to address the problem. She wrote that the mere presence of a mobile phone invites distraction even if it is turned off.[28]

Without continued discussion in properly addressing these challenges, student ministers might find themselves in a war for the focus and attention of their teenagers. Michael Hausauer, a psychotherapist in Oakland, California, told a reporter for the *New York Times* that teenagers are deeply interested in their friends' lives, but overexposure to the newsreel of their lives leaves teenagers feeling anxious about missing out on opportunities.[29] Youth pastors must find new ways to engage students, or else they might find themselves competing

---

[26] Amanda Lenhart, "Teens, Social Media and Technology Overview 2015," Pew Research Center, 2015, 2, http://www.pewinternet.org/files/2015/04/PI_TeensandTech_Update2015_0409151.pdf.

[27] Sherry Turkle, *Reclaiming Conversation: The Power of Talk in a Digital World* (New York: Penguin Press, 2015), 16.

[28] Turkle, 4.

[29] Katie Hafner, "Texting May Be Taking a Toll," *New York Times*, May 26, 2009, http://www.nytimes.com/2009/05/26/health/26teen.html.

against a virtual space of endless amusement and distraction. Merely taking phones away or turning them off might not be enough to engage adolescent minds. New strategies need to be developed in order to address these challenges.

Historians have identified and defined past generations by the major military, political, and cultural events of that time, but Gardner and Davis predict the identification of future generations will be dependent on the shelf-life of their gadgets.[30] Social media, in particular, has come to have a dominant presence in adolescent life. Social media refers to social networking sites that emphasize relationships and encourage participants to post images, videos, and links as well as create and display their own content through blogging, micro-blogging, developing art portfolios, and maintaining video albums. This is so others can share in their interests and make comments.[31] Social media networks have come to dominate the world of many teenagers today. A recent census taken by the Common Sense Media group noted 54 percent of teen social media users agree that it often distracts them when they should be paying attention to the people they are with compared to 44 percent in their previous 2012 census.[32]

The Five Categories of Mobile Apps

Mobile applications, commonly referred to as "apps," have made these social media services easily accessible to students. They have

---

[30] Howard Gardner and Katie Davis, *The App Generation: How Today's Youth Navigate Identity, Intimacy, and Imagination in a Digital World* (New Haven, CT: Yale University Press, 2014).

[31] Boyd, *It's Complicated*, 6–7 (see chap. 7, n. 17).

[32] "Social Media, Social Life: Teens Reveal Their Experiences," Common Sense Media, 2018, https://www.commonsensemedia.org/sites/default/files /uploads/research/2018-social-media-social-life-executive-summary-web.pdf.

provided these teens with a plethora of tools through which to broadcast their lives and creatively express themselves. Understanding the various types of apps students have on their smartphone provides a valuable window into their life, identifying their interests, habits, and social connections.[33] Mobile apps typically fall in one of five categories: texting, photo and video sharing, microblogging, live streaming, or self-destructing. One should note, however, there is much overlap between these categories as social media developers broaden the functionality of their applications.

According to Christine Elgersma of Common Sense Media, teenagers prefer a variety of social media networks rather than limiting themselves to a particular favorite. She compiled a list of currently trending web and mobile apps among teens.[34] They include GroupMe, Kik Messenger, WhatsApp, and Discord. These allow users to primarily send text messages in addition to photos, videos, and calendar links without limits of direct or group messaging. Photo and video-sharing apps include Instagram and the increasingly popular TikTok–Real Short Videos, which allows users to pair their short videos with a sound clip. Microblogging apps such as Tumblr and Twitter are typically a collection of text content, photos, and audio clips that users find funny and share with their friends. Live-streaming video apps such as Houseparty, YouTube Live, Live.me, and YouNow allow teens to stream and watch live video. Snapchat continues to be a favorite among teens, allowing users to post pictures and videos that will disappear after a limited time. Concerning this last category of apps that produce self-destructing or secretive content, Elgersma writes, "With all

---

[33] Gardner and Davis, *The App Generation*, 60.

[34] Christine Elgersma, "18 Social Media Apps and Sites Kids Are Using Right Now," Common Sense Media, 2019, https://www.commonsensemedia .org/blog/16-apps-and-websites-kids-are-heading-to-after-facebook.

the emotions running through teens, anonymous outlets give them the freedom to share their feelings without fear of judgment."[35] This list will change over time, but one should note the various forms of interaction and expression each of these social applications provide teenagers.

Identity, Community, and Intimacy

Regardless of the type of app, each of these platforms allows teenagers to develop their identity and community even if those two concepts are, at best, virtual. Teenagers, like all of humanity, are hardwired to desire relationships with others, and these apps allow teens to feel connected even when they are apart from their friends. There might be a biblical precedent or connection here as suggested by Daniella Zsupan-Jerome, author of *Connected toward Communion*. She references the triune nature of God, the commune between the Father, Son, and Holy Spirit, as the origin of humanity's innate desire (as personified through Adam and Eve) for intimacy and the theological foundation upon which society seeks community and communication.[36] As God looked upon what he had made, Adam and the rest of creation, as good as it was, he assessed that it was not good for man to be alone; he needed another to complete God's grand design (Gen 2:18). So, he crowned his work with the creation of a suitable helpmate, a woman, and it was not only good but very good.

Since that moment in time, humanity continues to gravitate toward and congregate with like-minded people, with whom they

---

[35] Elgersma, "18 Social Media Apps."

[36] Daniella Zsupan-Jerome, *Connected toward Communion: The Church and Social Communication in the Digital Age* (Collegeville, MN: Liturgical Press, 2014), 49.

can share their ideas, passions, and even the most intimate details of life.[37] Psychologist Janet L. Surrey wrote that authentic connection is essential for growth and healing. That's because it allows people to escape the bonds of isolation and develop a type of communal resilience that is formed from groups of all sizes, from intimate relationships to large networks.[38] In this sense, social media feels almost intuitive, natural even. The reason social media has resonated with modern culture is that it has provided the means through which humanity can pursue constant connection.

Social media platforms find impetus and profit from their ability to provide people with effective means for establishing these connections. Jesse Rice, contemporary worship arts director at Menlo Park Presbyterian Church, writes, "The kind of connection we're longing for—whether consciously or unconsciously—is the kind that creates a sense of belonging within us, a sense that we are 'safe, cared for, protected, and loved.' In other words, we feel most at home—most *ourselves*—around people with whom we experience that deep and authentic connection."[39]

In 2014, the Information School at the University of Washington brought together thought leaders in the area of technology and adolescence to discuss current policy and ongoing research as well as exchange ideas and address challenges facing study and learning from digital youth. These were certainly high-level discussions, but what drew the most attention was a small panel of teenagers

---

[37] Terrace Crawford, *#Goingsocial: A Practical Guide on Social Media for Church Leaders* (Kansas City, MO: Beacon Hill Press, 2012), 32.

[38] Janet Surrey, "Relational Psychotherapy, Relational Mindfulness," *Mindfulness and Psychotherapy*, ed. C .K. Germer, R. D. Siegel, and P. R. Fulton (New York: Guilford Press, 2005), 92.

[39] Jesse Rice, *The Church of Facebook: How the Hyperconnected are Redefining Community* (Colorado Springs: David C. Cook, 2009), 47.

who were willing to share their experiences with using social media and mobile technology. One of the young female panelists stated, "Technology opens doors, you can communicate. Like on Snapchat, you can share what's going on with friends really quickly, and it lets them see what's going on. You could just tell them. But it's different when they can see it by sending them a photo. You can share more of your life. Like, I can take a picture of being on this panel and send it to them."[40] The highly relational and personal nature of this young woman's comment brings clarity to how teenagers perceive their use of technology. There is an adolescent desire for continuous connection in the world that is increasingly disconnected.[41] Author Andrew Zirschky noted, "The irony is that youth ministers who try to stay 'relevant' by adopting the latest social media apps secure their own irrelevance if they fail to understand the true attraction of youth to social media and fail to offer the deep community that God intended and that youth long for."[42]

Teenagers want continuous communication with their network of communities. The combination of social media and increased access to mobile technology has provided a mechanism through which teens can maintain this constant connection. As teenagers develop relationships with others, they naturally want to establish places where they can hang out with those friends and be themselves. These places used to be physical locations such as the local mall or movie theater, but since the advent of social media, social networking sites more

---

[40] Karen Fisher, Katie Davis, Jason Yip, Negin Dahya, Elizabeth Mills, and Michael Eisenberg, "Digital Youth Seattle Think Tank" (White Paper, Information School, University of Washington, May 2016), 7, http://dystt .ischool.uw.edu/wp-content/uploads/2015/10/DigitalYouthSeattleThink Tank2016.pdf.

[41] Zirschky, *Beyond the Screen*, 5 (see chap. 7, n. 18).

[42] Zirschky, 6.

often today have surpassed the mall in popularity.[43] Teenagers who have grown accustomed to the always-on, always-connected lifestyle often experience intense anxiety when separated from the networks and mobile devices that allow this way of life to be possible. This has led to a phenomenon among teenagers abbreviated as FOMO, which stands for "fear of missing out," in which teenagers feel perpetually locked in a state in which they must maintain their digital connections in order to prevent exclusion from their social circles.[44]

Much of adolescent identity development is connected to their roles within their network of relationships, which is only amplified by the public nature of social media networks. Justin Wise wrote that technology takes the natural "adolescent assumption that the world is watching, and offers us a spotlight, a microphone, and a stage as vast as cyberspace from which to act out our assumption—with our legion of friends serving as an invisible entourage."[45]

As much as social media connects communities, it also creates additional challenges both for teenagers and the adults responsible for their welfare. When an individual communicates, he or she often assesses the environment and context in order to determine his or her subject matter and vocabulary. For example, a teenager might speak and act differently around their peers than they would in front of their parents, teachers, or employers. Social media collapses or collides these various contexts for all to see.[46] Offline, students can easily compartmentalize their various contexts, but online, teenagers, to some extent, lose this choice.

---

[43] Zirschky, 6.

[44] Palfrey and Gasser, *Born Digital*, 153.

[45] Justin Wise, *The Social Church: A Theology of Digital Communication* (Chicago: Moody, 2014), 111.

[46] Boyd, *It's Complicated*, 31.

As vast as the internet is, social media and networked life have created a small room in which all of one's social circles get to judge, engage with, and comment on every expression. Online, unintended audience members, such as one's parents or potential employers, see shared content originally intended only for the student's peer audience. Teenagers have to learn how to communicate in multiple contexts simultaneously. Boyd wrote that in order to stabilize their contexts online, teenagers would often create an imaginary audience, much like journalists and politicians imagine the audience they are trying to reach.[47] This imaginary audience becomes the dominant force and filter for all content shared online.

Teenagers have developed ways of protecting their social media activity, such as obfuscation, deliberately providing false information about themselves, which is easily recognized and decoded by their close network of friends.[48] What makes perfect sense to one social circle might be confusing and even disconcerting to another. In their attempt to gain back control in their networked world, teenagers might find that their actions can have significant consequences, especially in their professional endeavors. Posts can be misinterpreted or taken out of context by unintended viewers.[49]

Ministry in the Digital Age

The church of the twenty-first century needs highly efficacious student ministers, capable of meeting student needs, whether offline or within their digital hangouts. Youth ministers have to make the best use of the short amount of time they spend with teenagers to engage

---

[47] Boyd, *It's Complicated*, 31.

[48] Palfrey and Gasser, *Born Digital*, 73.

[49] Boyd, *It's Complicated*, 33.

them in the process of discipleship, not just the practice of Christian education but in the endeavor to develop self-directed students, capable of furthering their own spiritual development. Neither cultural acceptance nor the pursuit of relevance should determine one's acceptance of technology into ministry. Instead, that decision should be grounded in one's biblical calling to change lives through intentional and purposeful discipleship. Youth ministers need to be able to assess whether a tool is beneficial to their vision as well as approach popular applications with an open but discerning mind. Rejection of technology should not be determined by fear of the unknown but rather by its inability to fulfill purpose or add value. Challenges can be overcome, but these efforts will lack direction if the student minister or the church does not have a clearly defined purpose.

Formal educators might be well-trained and knowledgeable in the Word of God but inadequately prepared to engage youth culture in a beneficial way. Without question, biblical literacy must always have primacy over digital literacy. The message, especially as it concerns the Word of God, must always take precedence over the medium. Still, digital literacy can support one's efforts to develop biblical literacy more effectively in others. Youth ministers need to understand how to wisely model technology use given their unique position to speak into the lives of teenagers who have grown up in a world in which internet technology has always existed. Gardner and Davis note that teenagers long for mentors to help them deal with the personal ethical dilemmas they face online—dilemmas that formerly were comparatively simple analog problems now manifesting themselves in a new digital environment. They need wise individuals to come alongside them to help them address the challenges of an always-on, always-connected life.[50] The internet can be a dark place,

---

[50] Gardner and Davis, *The App Generation*, 171.

but ministers of the gospel have the tools and systems necessary to be beacons of light.

Zirschky, who has written extensively in the area of student ministry and technology, warns that much of the discussion about technology integration centers around determining whether technology is good or bad, or whether it should be accepted or rejected, and is not given proper perspective as to the church's responsibility and influence in a technological society.[51] While this chapter seeks to highlight and address some of the challenges of practicing ministry in a digital world, it is ultimately not a chapter about technology. Instead, it is about the various people involved in the process of passing on the truths of God's Word from one generation to the next. Technology is not a savior but a tool, a means to an end, and the goal should always be a more robust student ministry, a ministry that uses every resource it can to point as many people as it can to Jesus Christ. This is a nearly impossible task without knowledge and discernment, without the ability to properly evaluate their choices, actions, and tools. Marc Prensky writes concerning one's pedagogy: "Our task is to best configure students' brains so they can constantly learn, create, program, adopt, adapt, and relate positively to whatever and whomever they meet, (and in whatever way they meet them, which increasingly means through technology)."[52] While Prensky certainly had the classroom in mind in writing this, it has far more significant implications for those in ministry and the students under their leadership. In addition to becoming scholars of the gospel, the most important message on earth, student ministers should examine the tools through which they will communicate it. Youth ministers

---

[51] Zirschky, *Beyond the Screen*, 6.

[52] Marc Prensky, *From Digital Natives to Digital Wisdom: Hopeful Essays for 21st Century Learning* (Thousand Oaks, CA: Corwin, 2012), 12.

and the teenagers under their care live their lives, both offline and through social media. To focus only on one half of the equation will leave these ministers ill-prepared to address the challenges of modern society with its online/offline lifestyle. Youth ministers need to have a basic understanding of how to use technology so that they can make the best use of their time and resources.

Youth ministers must not forget the purpose of social media; at least for teenagers it is to be social. When ministries follow the practices of the business world, a field dominated by the desire for profit and brand recognition, they primarily use social media as a promotional tool to send out informational content. While social media networks can be a powerful tool to promote the ministry, it makes the ministry the commodity, not the means through which one comes to know the love of Christ. To effectively use these kinds of technologies, youth leaders should seek to encourage personal and meaningful involvement between students and adults and thereby extend community and service beyond the walls of the church.[53] In this way, the focus is less about attractive branding of a ministry, and more about the relationships through which modern technology can support and enhance.

Youth ministers can utilize social media to promote interactivity and encourage users to comment on, create, and share content themselves.[54] Wise suggested that it might be time to consider how social media has created an atmosphere in which the members of one's congregation want to have a more interactive experience.[55] This interactivity does not mean control over the content. Ultimately, this is determined by Scripture and the ministers who are called to

---

[53] Zirschky, *Beyond the Screen*, 38.
[54] Gardner and Davis, *The App Generation*, 23.
[55] Wise, *The Social Church*, 30.

proclaim it. Interactivity has more to do with a conversation than it does with any particular content.

For example, interactivity can take place before the sermon, after the sermon, and even during the sermon. A student minister can use social media before his or her sermon to engage the online community with a discussion question to assess their understanding of a particular passage or topic. The minister could then use that information to address any challenges and correct misunderstandings in his or her sermon. The minister could also use social media to extend the points after the sermon by training his or her congregation to post examples of how the sermon impacted their life that week. He or she could also create social cards for each of the sermon points. Social cards are graphic representations that members can easily share and spread throughout their social networks.

Adventurous ministers could even utilize social media during their sermon, allowing their members to post questions on social media and addressing those questions live. In each of these examples, the preacher remains in control of the content while allowing his audience members to interact with each other, the minister, and the content. Ministry 2.0 looks beyond the primary worship experience in that it provides a platform for members to dwell on what has been presented, to ask questions they would never have an opportunity to ask within the time constraints and structure of a youth group or sanctuary. This is not to say that every church, every youth group, should integrate all technology or all of these approaches in the same sermon; it is merely to say that a discussion needs to be ongoing in how technology is influencing the church and how to utilize it correctly for the advancement of God's kingdom. Social media has advanced resources of the church and additional means through which ministry leaders can offer community, pastoral care, and discipleship on an ongoing basis.

Considering the works of Marshall and Eric McLuhan, Neil Postman, and countless others who raise questions about technology use, it becomes clear that technology is not a neutral invention of humanity. It has the power to advance humanity but also the potential to cause great harm. Social media has had unprecedented success in connecting people, but as the literature has highlighted, studies have demonstrated that users increasingly feel disconnected. Before student ministers attempt to incorporate technology into their mix of ministry tools, they should weigh its cost and assess its benefit. One cannot be so overcome by optimism that he or she neglects to consider the inadequacy of technology to do what only the Holy Spirit can do in a biblical community of believers.

Conclusion

Technology has been shaped in the image of man and man in the image of God. Therefore, technology has the power to bring glory to God, but like all of creation, it has the potential to become an idol and misperceived to possess the ability to save. Technology is such a dominant force in the lives of teens that it has come to define their identity, intimacy, and community. Just as it has shaped the lives of teenagers both positively and negatively, it will influence one's ministry as well. Technology will continue to evolve, and it will always have its advocates and its detractors. Ministry leaders must push past irrational concerns and ignorant optimism and instead use biblical and purposeful discernment in deciding whether technology should be integrated into their ministry contexts.

Welcome to the Future:
Student Ministry *Next*

• TROY TEMPLE •

The hardest thing about understanding the future is that it is entirely unknown to us. To know the future requires great responsibility. It comes with an incredible amount of pressure as one could imagine. Just think about it. When you see what is in front of you, you have the responsibility of making preparations and acting on it. Your knowledge of the future makes you responsible for all those affected by it. Don't get me wrong. I grew up just like every one of you, always wishing I knew what was going to happen next. Isn't that what's really behind the question when kids ask, "Are we there yet?" We think about problems like these because we're worried about what might or might not happen. But sometimes we ask this question because we genuinely want to know what's coming next and we don't want to miss it. Many times, we don't want to miss the experience. At other times, we don't want to miss the opportunity.

Remember When? Remember When You Wished Things Could Be Different?

I dream about the future all of the time. One of my favorite songs from Brad Paisley is a song about the future. The name of the song is "Welcome to the Future."[1] The song captures the dreams of a child who thinks of extended family trips in the car and wishes that he could watch TV or have his own Pac-Man video game. His dreams come true, and they are wrapped up in a cell phone in the palm of his hand. Those aren't his only dreams. He also wishes for days when racial reconciliation can be celebrated, after all of the harsh days of discrimination suffered by so many. When we wish about the future, our dreams are shaped by what's missing or by the things that we love. Sometimes, it's a combination of both. One thing is for sure; human beings love to dream.

As children, we dreamed about being adults or at least about being free enough to do the things we wanted to do without someone else telling us what we can and cannot do. When I was a kid, I always wished for a time when I could play outside as long as I wanted and never have to take a bath, never have to eat my vegetables, never have to make my bed . . . well, you get the picture. I'm sure you can identify with me. As children, we dream. We dream about being rich. We dream about being in control. We even dream about being Michael Jordan stealing the ball and hitting the game-winning dunk! (OK,

---

[1] Brad Paisley, "Welcome to the Future," track 3 on *American Saturday Night*, Arista Nashville, 2009, compact disc.

maybe that was just me? But I did this every Sunday after church playing basketball at the neighborhood court.) The reality is we all dream about the future, and we rarely envision a future that isn't one that we want. However, many people do dream about the future, and what they see doesn't encourage them. Instead, it lays a foundation for great discouragement. In the end, the future can give us hope, or it can completely scare us to death. The future of student ministry is no different. As we look toward the coming decades, there are many things in which we can find great encouragement, and there are many things that will require caution.

Every generation dreams about the future. Take a second right now and think back on when you were younger. What did you dream about? Did you ever dream about what it would be like if you won the lottery? I bet you did. And I bet you and your friends told each other how you would spend your money. But once we get past the childhood dreams that sometimes are just unrealistic, we can start to dream about things that really might change the world. When we look around us and take a hard look at the things that we wish were different, our dreams start to take shape.

Dreams Are Shaped by What We Lack or What We Love

During college, I would think back on my days in high school. There were many times when I would think about the experiences that I had in my youth group and my church. And while I had so many memories that I will keep with me forever, there were many memories that I wanted to make sure I never repeated when I stepped into my first opportunity as a student minister. Even though I had a rich experience in my youth group back in high school, I saw a lot of things that were missing. It wasn't hard to see how my church put a lot of pressure on young people to look a certain way and always be in attendance at every church event. My friends and I had such a great time in our youth group that we often felt like we were missing the mark if we didn't look the right way or if we happened to miss a church event.

I knew what was missing from the moment I sat in my first student ministry class, like many of you are doing right now. The church had plenty of rules and expectations of perfection, but the depths of relationships were so lacking that it often left all of us feeling insignificant. This experience explains why I dreamed about doing student ministry in a way that would emphasize the relationship before the rules. I remember a quote from Dick Day in his book *How to Be a Hero to Your Kids*: "Rules without relationships lead to rebellion."[2] As a freshman sitting in that first student ministry class, I determined then I would always lead with an emphasis on relationships. Young people need to know that they are valued because God has created them. I knew then, and I still believe it now, the gospel is unconditional. It's not by works of righteousness that we do but according to his mercy that he saves us. There was something severely lacking in my experience from my student ministry days in high school—genuine relationships. These factors have shaped the way I do ministry and the way I lead every single day right up until this very moment. What started as a dream has become a defining value for every aspect of my life. This value was developed by reflecting on what was missing.

When I look back, there are also things that I dreamed about that were born out of what I genuinely love. It's a kind of a combination of both what was missing and what I love. You see, much

---

[2] Josh McDowell and Dick Day, *How to Be a Hero to Your Kids* (Nashville: Thomas Nelson, 2008), Kindle loc. 563 of [*].

of my lived experience as a teenager was shaped by that rigid structure and incredible predictability. Those things were held in high regard as profoundly spiritual and set apart for God's service. That just sounded so weird to me. God had created this world for us to subdue and have dominion over and, well, enjoy! And the "mature" Christians that I saw were pretty sad, tired, and just flat-out dull. Those experiences created a desire in me to always look for the opportunity to give somebody a unique experience and connect it with the bountiful treasure that we find in our relationship with Jesus Christ. This desire wasn't merely a desire to have fun. It was a driving motivation to help young people see that living for Christ was exciting because of the life that he gives, abundantly (John 10:10)! I have always been eager to step outside the box and do things in a way that many said couldn't or shouldn't be done.

Now, don't miss this. Please, don't miss this! Our dreams are shaped by what we lack or what we love, and many times by a combination of both. A quick way to get a snapshot of the future of student ministry is to make a list of what's lacking in student ministry today or to identify what our young generation loves and places a high value on in their culture. You will quickly understand what the future holds, and that gives us the foundation for preparation. Make no mistake. The future of student ministry will not be the same as it is right now. But it is being shaped by what is lacking and by the things we love in our culture today.

Past Behavior Can Help Predict Future Realities, or Does It?

How can we put our finger on what student ministry will look like in the years ahead of us? I think we could start by looking to the past. We have heard it said that the past is the best predictor of the future.

While that statement might hold some truth, it doesn't always seem to be the case, or is it? This statement may not ring true when you look at your own life, or maybe it does. Even at this point in your life, you can reflect on your life and see things that had to change. This fact is real whether you're new to your studies in preparation for a vocation in student ministry, or whether you've picked up this book after you've been in student ministry for several years and are now looking for some inspiration. The past might not always predict the future accurately. What can we learn from our past? We can reflect and see how things changed over the years. When it comes to student ministry, there are at least four historical changes that can today give us insight into the future of student ministry.

From Bible Knowledge to Relational Relevance

In the late 1700s, we saw the beginning of what came to be known as Sunday school. Sunday school originally began in 1780 in England as a program to educate, and it persisted throughout the 1800s. The focus of Sunday school programs was to teach religious education. In Great Britain and America, Sunday schools gave opportunities for children affected by poverty to learn to read, write, develop math skills, and receive religious education. Over time and as cultures progressed, the religious education content was eventually abandoned and no longer compulsory. Churches picked up the banner and developed robust Sunday school programs that would fill in the gap left by public education. Throughout the middle of the twentieth century, churches invested much energy and resources in Sunday school curriculum programs and continued efforts. The emphasis of the Sunday school program was to teach Bible knowledge. For a season, this propelled the growth of the church and provided the foundational knowledge needed for every follower of Christ. But as we look back, there was a considerable gap. The church had filled the gap by strengthening Sunday school programs. However, eventually, another gap developed. Churches had taught Bible knowledge but had lacked relevance and relationship in much of the teaching. The focus was on content and had abandoned or simply neglected the value of relationship and the application of that knowledge to living life in contemporary society.

Youth ministry filled the gap that it was uniquely shaped to meet. Various parachurch organizations were established to meet the needs of religious education for children from poverty and broken homes who were seldom connected to a local church. These organizations even collaborated with public schools. A new world of student ministry began. Eventually, these organizations sought to balance the need for religious education and authentic relationships. The local church student ministry movement that burgeoned in the 1970s brought an added dimension and filled the gap left by Sunday schools and religious education in the church. Local church student ministry learned from the parachurch student ministry organizations such as Youth for Christ and Young Life. Youth ministry had to change in the church. The local church began to establish programming that was both culturally relevant and biblically sound. The final twenty-five years of the twentieth century saw an explosive increase in full-time, multiple-staff, local church student ministry across all denominations in the United States. Churches had seen what was lacking and connected the loves of a generation to the discipleship strategy it was commissioned to accomplish.

Two Decades: Mission and Community

As we crossed into the twenty-first century, student ministry responded to a new lack and love of a generation. A brief history of student ministry would demonstrate that young people had always responded to opportunities to serve and meet a need to help impact the lives of people. Throughout the 1980s and '90s, local church youth ministries developed a healthy blend of biblical teaching and cultural relevance wrapped up in engaging programming. But they had also sprinkled in mission trips and local service projects in addition to various outreach opportunities for teenagers in their churches. As we moved into the new century, the desire to serve and make an impact had grown and become a defining value of a generation.

The dawn of the twenty-first century saw the growth of many humanitarian organizations with evangelical moorings. Local church youth ministries became increasingly involved in organizations such as Samaritan's Purse, Compassion, World Vision, and Operation Blessing. These organizations have been around since as early as 1950, but their respective missions collided with the growing desire of a generation to make an impact and change the world. Church ministry responded and often partnered with organizations such as these or at least strengthened their work with their own denominational agencies to provide more missional opportunities. This would be demonstrated as much in the student ministry of the church as anywhere else.

Youth ministry had stepped up to fill a missing component that a generation was longing to see in the church. The emphasis on mission and changing the world was part of that missing component. What was lacking in a generation was a purpose. However, a new generation was also reaching to fill another void that was deeply connected to a passionate soul cry. Authors and researchers were identifying the predominant descriptors of a new generation. Alongside mission and purpose, the generation of a new century was craving authentic community.

Filling the Gaps

As life moves forward, we look back and see things more clearly. When we reflect on where we have been, we undoubtedly see gaps or ways that we could have done things more effectively or simply better. This shouldn't be an exercise in regret, though. This should be an opportunity to learn. In that sense, the past *might* not be the best predictor of the future, but it can teach us. When we learn from the past, we can build on success, amend mistakes, and walk away from failures. Let's take a quick look back and identify some student ministry gaps that have been filled in by the next generation.

The Relational Gap Left by the Church

In the latter part of the nineteenth century, with an emphasis on Sunday school and Christian education, conservative churches saw unprecedented growth across the country. There is no question that these churches provided a strong biblical foundation for young people and for those who were new in the faith. Each one of these churches placed an incredible emphasis on biblical knowledge. But as these churches grew in Bible knowledge, where understanding biblical content was about being able to memorize facts, it created a new need in the body of Christ. What happens when we focus too much on content and too much on facts, and not enough time on relationship, is that we end up with a disconnect between what we know and the relationships we have with each other and ultimately the relationship that we have with Christ. Looking back on the past, we can learn to not let relationships fall to the wayside and trade them off for biblical knowledge. Make no mistake; biblical knowledge is essential. The absolute truth of God's Word is irreplaceable in guiding us to understand that God, our Creator, has given us specific revelation and absolute truth found in his Word. Many times we can become so emphatic on the *what* that we don't spend time on the *who*. Not only do we lack in our relationship with each other as we seek to lead, disciple, and evangelize those in the community around us, but we also end up lacking in our relationship with God himself.

Think of it this way: you can spend so much time knowing the facts that you don't spend enough time enjoying the fellowship. That's one of the things that we saw come out of this emphasis of the church, especially as it relates to student ministry. There was undoubtedly a lack of understanding of biblical knowledge, of not being able to connect the dots while just reading words on a page. But when that emphasis grew, it created a relational gap between those who were discipling and those being discipled.

The Relevant Biblical Teaching Gap

Life is lived in cycles. We can see cycles all around us in the way our families grow and in the ways that we live and learn, generation to generation. We also can see cycles in our own personal lives in how we relate to others, in the kinds of relationships we establish, as well as in some of the habits we create or the habits that we *should* create or maybe the ones that we should forget.

Likewise, the church goes through cycles, often in terms of what is emphasized. We can look back in history and see a relational gap that was created by an overemphasis on biblical knowledge without relationships. We can also see that when you start to emphasize the relational aspect of our faith and life in the church, the foundational biblical wisdom can be hijacked by a relativism that develops in response to prioritizing relationships, even to the neglect of God's truth.

Youth ministry hinges on building relationships. When the main focus is on building relationships with young people, the church can fall into patterns of ease regarding Bible teaching. This develops out of a desire to minimize personal offenses that can arise when we are confronted with biblical truth—we don't want to hurt anyone's feelings when discussing those truths. Consequently, teaching that becomes relative more than truthful will result in irrelevance, producing a new gap—the relevant biblical truth gap. Somewhere in there, in trying to make sure that we taught the right things about God's Word and ultimately about God and his kingdom, we missed an opportunity to balance the gaining of Bible knowledge with a deepening of true fellowship among the body of believers. Then, as we began to address and fill in that relational gap, we created a new gap by emphasizing *relative* biblical teaching rather than *relevant* biblical teaching. Youth ministry struggled to retain the relationships, sometimes at all costs.

But let's not blame all of this on student ministry. The emphasis on biblical knowledge and teaching biblical facts that yielded a relational gap also left us with the beginnings of the relevant teaching gap. Youth ministry had seen and lived through the season where we emphasized Bible knowledge to the degree that we never made a connection to life and how we live our faith in the community. As student ministry responded to the relation gap, it didn't initially press forward to connect the relevance of biblical truth to real life— authenticity was lacking. When we understand biblical truth, value relationships, and live it out in real life, we can begin to experience authentic biblical community.

Missional Mobilization Gap

There was a long season of student ministry in the church that emphasized activity. We witnessed youth culture spinning out of control throughout the 1980s. Youth ministry was tasked with creating attractive programming to pull young people into the church, or at least get them on the property twice a week. But such programs without purpose will eventually run their course and leave people looking for better programming or starving for a significant purpose; most often, it's both. After the residual effects of a church student ministry philosophy that emphasized Bible knowledge while leaving the significant gap of intentional relationships, student ministry responded by creating space for genuine relationships that sought to bring about transformation instead of simply a transaction. Following that with a drive to provide relevant biblical teaching that offered answers to young people's lives, local church student ministry was on the verge of something more powerful than we could have imagined. Youth ministry needed purpose behind the programming and, more importantly, an intentional connection to mission.

As the gaps appeared in recent student ministry, they all led us to redirect it back to mission. Mission is the most recent gap that we have seen in student ministry through the first two decades of the twenty-first century. Student ministry has stepped up to bridge the gap between programming activity and mission. Relevant biblical teaching gave student ministry the tool to solidify purpose. It provided a *why* behind the *what* of biblical knowledge and placed a *how* front and center. The most recent generation of young people is poised to discover their purpose found in God's Word and engage in the mission. Mission is the action that follows the foundation laid by faithful, biblical, relevant teaching. It takes biblical knowledge and wraps it in a cultural awareness of our world's brokenness. Jesus, the Word made flesh, has the answer, and we have a mission to carry that answer to a hurting culture.

Looking Back to Move Forward

While there are certainly other gaps that we could identify in recent student ministry history, these profoundly shaped the future of student ministry. The impact of the three gaps just discussed can still be observed in student ministry today. As we think about the future of student ministry now, we must look intently at the current realities in youth culture and the global culture in all aspects before we can chart a path toward a fruitful time to come.

To make this process more accessible, it will require a purposeful investigation of where student ministry has been. Is the past the best predictor of the future? There are times when it might be. So, as we look to student ministry past, how can we identify the building blocks that can help forecast student ministry next? We can look at the past and list the behaviors, habits, and values that were present and begin to place them into three categories: reinforcement, correction, and elimination. Too many times, we remember the past with regret. At other times, we remember the past with warming nostalgia. In either case, we can often recall events that seemed worse than they were or better than they were. Reflection must include these memory walks, both fond and fearful. In the end, we can find anchor points in reflection that offer stability for laying a trajectory for the future.

Past Behavior Reinforcement

It is a dangerous decision to categorically walk away from our history and dismiss it as a story from the past. To consider the recent history of student ministry and reject aspects that were positive is a crucial mistake. Rather than taking a dismissive stance when looking back at the past, we are wise to reflect with prayer and discernment that comes from God.

Recall the three student ministry gaps that were described earlier in this chapter. Would you consider each one of those an opportunity to only learn from the mistakes of previous church ministry leaders? Or, could you look under the surface and focus on the underlying concern that was initially good but developed into something less helpful and more hurtful? The gap that was left by the sole emphasis on teaching biblical knowledge in previous seasons of student ministry opened a door of opportunity for relational student ministry. But the desire that young people would know God's Word was nothing less than admirable and necessary.

As we look to student ministry next, Bible knowledge would be a great example of a past behavior or value that we could shape or reinforce based on what we know about young people now. *Youth ministry must reinforce biblical teaching with a faithful biblical theology that connects the dots.* The goal isn't to make every teenager a biblical scholar. The goal becomes helping every Christian young person understand the facts that support Christian faith and places a better story to tell in our hands.

The second gap that we discussed was the relevant teaching gap left by an overemphasis on relational ministry to the softening of gospel truth. Situations and relationships arise, and we can have such a strong desire to see friends, family, and others understand the love that Jesus has poured out for anyone who will call upon him that we make it as *easy* as possible without an accurate picture of the mercy and grace that he makes available. Make no mistake, the gospel message is simple, but it is also hard. A true friend cares enough to speak the truth in love, even if it means that people might reject it, at least temporarily. If we only share the saving part of the gospel and leave out the living part, we miss the opportunity to connect biblical truth to real life. Young people may find Jesus's salvation but reject his way. That's where student ministry stepped in and raised the call to teaching biblical truth and connecting it to the better story that Jesus has written for his people.

We know that relationships are important. God created us for relationship. In Genesis 1 and 2, he gave Adam and Eve each other because it was never his plan for man to be alone. That's why *we must reinforce the need for relational student ministry by building environments that help authentic communities flourish.* These would be places to carefully and lovingly walk with each other in the fellowship of the Word. Encouragement and accountability would be the values that strengthen the student ministry.

The missional mobilization gap presents student ministry with a third opportunity for reinforcement to propel the kingdom mission. The development of the programming model that created numerous opportunities for young people to get involved in a local church student ministry imposed an underlying value in two specific ways— genuine engagement and participation in spiritual maturity. (The second will be addressed under in the next section, "Past Behavior Extinction.") At its heart, what the programming model set out to accomplish was genuine engagement. It had the best intention of connecting young people to the body of Christ. And, in some instances, it did just that. *Youth ministry next must reinforce genuine engagement that connects with the biblical mission.* We capture the underlying positive and accentuate it for future kingdom advancement and building up the body of Christ.

This is how we take what we can observe from our past and reinforce it with a faithful, biblical understanding of what Jesus commanded us to do. Youth ministry next will require an accurate understanding of the world, now! Then, it can effectively carry the timeless values that student ministry past once affirmed into the coming decades.

Past Behavior Correction

Sometimes we need a course correction. Similar to reinforcement, there might be behaviors and values from the recent student ministry past that were good. However, at some point, they went off track. Again, let's look at the three gaps. The relational gap that resulted from the emphasis on Bible knowledge shouldn't cause us to cast off the need for Bible knowledge. *The goal for student ministry next is to correct the emphasis and place in perspective a balanced picture of student ministry.* The programmatic elements that involve gaining biblical knowledge are a building block for relevant teaching, authentic community, and the church's mission.

The relevant teaching gap birthed from the stress placed on relational student ministry is intricately connected to relationship building. Discipleship is best communicated through environments of relational groups. *Youth ministry next will see great fruit when it corrects wayward agendas in relational ministry and weaves it into a discipleship strategy connected by relevant biblical truth.* Highlighting relationships for effective student ministry is not the error. Doing it apart from a biblical community is.

Programming has taken a beating in student ministry over the last three decades or more. Are student ministry programs really the problem? Or are student ministry programmers the problem? This correction is simple. Youth ministry programs must be intentional. They must have a purpose. I can list dozens of student ministry leaders who have been experts at purposeful programming. And while many of these student ministry leaders have been given a voice in the student ministry universe, there are still youth leaders who slide off the rails on one of two sides. Some will decry programs and activities under a banner of an anti-entertainment platform, while others will forge ahead and flood the student ministry calendar with events that leave little to no room for family or life in general. *Youth ministry next will correct purposeless programs or, even better, replace them with mission.* This will generate numerous stories of spiritual victory in the lives of young people and impact the world!

Past Behavior Elimination

The lessons that we can learn from the past, in addition to reinforcement and correction, can lead us to another conclusion—elimination. There are simply things in the past that just need to stay there, never to return. This extinction is a healthy reality that allows culture and organizations to mature and release behaviors and values that were only around for a season. When we refuse to move on, we bind the church to chains instead of anchoring it to the immovable truth of God's Word. For example, although much of the activity that flooded the typical student ministry calendar in the past offered opportunities for students to be part of something positive, it often resulted in an overcrowded schedule that was competing with other healthy ventures. It was good and right to let the intense orchestration fade away to provide room for more intentional student ministry movements that demonstrated a sensitivity to the needs of families and their young people. Remembering can be the best option for some of these behaviors that held meaning in the past but could not continue as the world changed.

Youth Ministry Next Framework: Timeless Tasks for Anticipating Future Ministry Opportunities

This chapter has the task of equipping you to see the future of student ministry. Some might have used a forecasting approach, and they might have been able to hit that nail on the head. Many leaders throughout history have made assertions regarding the future and how the world will look one day. In the early twentieth century, authors and influencers alike predicted that current realities such as wireless communication, cashless financial transactions, and even digital currency would come to a societal realization. You must know that no one has ever been able to predict the future. Reading the tea leaves most often yields statements that describe future realities as guesses.

Even though we cannot predict the future, we can learn from the past and anticipate new realities that will present new opportunities for student ministry. Instead of laying out a list of predictions, I have laid a foundation for a framework that you can use at any point in time. A framework gives you the guidelines and structure to take in the current behaviors and values and find a valuable new map for student ministry next. We will walk through a five-step framework and show how you can keep student ministry next within reach. (Note: This chapter has not addressed the underlying leadership skills and competencies necessary for executing this framework process.)

Start by Restating the Mission

The first time you lead your student ministry team through the process of articulating the mission, it can take a considerable number of meetings, phone calls, emails, texts, direct messages, and whatever tool is being used at that time. Mission identification and articulation must not be taken casually! They will determine the target, and everything you do from there must aim for the target. The mission should focus on what we have already been given in the Great Commission (Matt 28:19–20; Luke 24:44–49; John 20:19–23; Acts 1:8). The mission for any student ministry will rely heavily on the biblical direction given in these passages while describing it in the context of a more specific expression of the church in its local community. You will always be able to return to this mission as you face difficult questions and decisions. For example, *The mission of student ministry is to develop culturally appropriate programs where young people will hear the gospel, have the opportunity to respond, and spiritually mature.*

Identify Variables That Weren't Realities in Recent History

Once the target has been defined, now you are ready to take aim. Start by creating a list of current observable variables that were not realities in recent student ministry history. You will want to consider this question from a total church perspective as well as the surrounding community, national, and global culture. Take ample time for this exercise.

I have found it helpful to begin by selecting a point in history that you and your leaders remember well. Reflect back at least three to five years, maybe more. (Some cultural experts state that culture, especially youth culture, experiences significant changes every three to six months.) Begin the list with the most obvious items. These may involve foundational cultural components such as family, education, religion, climate, technology, government, and economy. You will also want to think about more leisure cultural components such as recreation, entertainment, social media, fashion, hobbies, and trends or fads. Think through these cultural components and identify three to five items that have changed and weren't realities until recently. Categorize each of these by their behavior and value. Then create a statement that summarizes those cultural components' benefits or influence in current culture.

Connect Felt Needs to Cultural and Individual Values

One of the most difficult tasks for church student ministry leaders is putting your thumb on the pulse of the values beneath the felt needs of young people and families in your church or community. A felt need is one that we experience at a physical or emotional level. It is connected to real needs that we have and is driven by our spoken and unspoken values. When we have hunger, we feel it. The real need is for physical nourishment and health. Loneliness is a common felt need that results from the real need for relationships. This second step in the Youth Ministry Framework demands that you have a relational connection with the community of young people around you and in your community.

Once you have identified the most pronounced or prevalent felt needs, you can then list key statements that describe the opportunities that exist to meet real needs by beginning with felt needs. Youth ministry has a glaring opportunity to recognize and respond to the epidemic of relational brokenness. It exists in families, on every middle and high school campus, and in your church. These felt needs also paint a vivid picture of the values that lie under the surface but are the cause of what stands above the surface.

There is always a handful of felt needs within reach of your student ministry. This connects the heart with mission and provides a powerful opportunity to bring the transformative power of the gospel to so many hurting young people. Youth ministry next will be fruitful when it seizes that opportunity. The goal is to connect felt needs to real values.

Rethink Current Program in Light of New Realities and Values

Once you have solidified your mission, listed the new variables, and collected the felt needs, you can now begin to align your current program with this new understanding. This step will involve a comprehensive inventory of all student ministry programs throughout the calendar year. You will take each program and ask if that program needs to change in light of new variables, or if it helps meet felt needs and speaks to the underlying values of current culture. Each program should be filtered through the Youth Ministry Next Framework to determine its past effectiveness in order to project its future success. The outcome for each program will be determined by whether it can adjust to the new variables and speak to the real needs and values of contemporary youth culture.

Map Out a New Journey

The final step is to create a student ministry next map that pulls all of this new insight together and leads to a future that responds quickly to the cultural gaps with precision. This is one of the most exciting parts of this process. You have the opportunity to draw a clear path for the coming year and beyond that shows how the student ministry next will reinforce timeless, biblical behaviors and values, correct the past behaviors that have gone off course, and eliminate past behaviors that simply need to end. The map that you design will look like a calendar, only it will connect to the mission intentionally. It will capitalize on new realities that were absent from the recent past and meet the felt needs of the young people in your community. This will bring greater clarity to where your student ministry is and sharpen the focus for where your student ministry needs to go.

Scroll Down: What Will It Look Like?

It's one of the most common activities in life today. We do it on our computers. We do it on our phones. We do it on our tablets. On all of those devices, we open up a website or app and view content. As we read or view the page, we will eventually scroll down to see more content. If you are like me, you open up a blog post or digital article or social media post, and the title immediately grabs your focus, and then you scroll to the bottom of the page to see what else it says. I eventually jump back to the beginning and read all the way through the post. I wish we could do that with the future of student ministry! Wouldn't it be cool if we could scroll down to see where the story goes, then come back to the beginning and absorb all of the rich experiences that student ministry gives us? Well, maybe we can.

While we might not be able to see into the future, we can look in the mirror. In some ways, student ministry next will resemble student ministry now. This chapter has guided us to look back to look forward. We can reflect and grab the most timeless aspects of what we see that will persist into the future.

First, young people will still need the gospel! That will never fade away. They need relationships beginning with their relationship with Jesus Christ. The message is constant and desperately necessary in the lives of every young person. That will continue for the future. Second, student ministry will still instruct in righteousness. The apostle Paul tucked that initiative into 2 Tim 3:16. That's what God's Word is designed to do. It will continue to be the mission of student ministry. Stability is found in the absolute truth of God's Word. Third, student ministry next will be dialed in on the mission. Everything that is done throughout the student ministry year will have to connect young people with the mission. Building a student ministry with an overarching purpose will yield eternal fruit for the kingdom.

This is where student ministry is going!

Conclusion: Student Ministry Philosophy and Strategy Development

• TIM McKNIGHT •

We all looked at the map and referred to the quarter-scale model of the battlefield. One hill stood out as the highest point on the map. That hill was our objective.

It was time to formulate a strategy to move from our current location to seize that objective. That was the mission. Take the hill represented by a six-digit grid coordinate on the map.

Our soldiers would execute the mission guided by the army core values: leadership, duty, respect, selfless service, honor, integrity, and personal courage. These values formed the bedrock for every soldier in the battalion.

To plan our strategy, we needed to bring battlefield experts from every area into the planning process. The personnel section briefed us regarding our combat strength, how many soldiers were able-bodied and could take part in the operation. Our intelligence officer taught us about the battlefield's terrain, the size of the enemy force, and what weapons they possessed. The operations section described the mission, including what units would be involved and how they would maneuver to the objective, and the air and artillery support available for the mission. Supply officers explained how fuel, food, equipment, and ammunition would reach each unit. Signals personnel briefed our leaders regarding how we would communicate on the battlefield. Our medics explained our evacuation plan for wounded soldiers and where they would locate the battalion aid station. Before we began, we listened carefully to all the important voices.

As we wrapped up our mission planning briefing and prepared to write up the operations order that would outline our strategy, I was struck by how many parts of the battalion would comprise the operation. It was always awe-inspiring to see how each part of our team worked together to accomplish our strategy. Each of us had a role in making up the very different aspects that formed a cohesive strategy to achieve our mission to take that objective.

You are likely in the same position regarding your ministry. You are getting ready to navigate an incredible journey or accomplish the mission of your student ministry. In each chapter of this book, like the section heads of my battalion, academicians and practitioners in student ministry communicated helpful principles and information regarding subjects ranging from a biblical foundation for student ministry to using technology as a tool to help you teach and minister to your students. Now, it is time for you to draw from what you have read in this book to formulate your mission, core values, vision, and strategy for your student ministry. These four components comprise your student ministry philosophy of ministry. This concluding chapter will help guide you through that process so that you can venture out on your journey to navigate to your objective.

Student Ministry Philosophy Development

There are many approaches student ministers can take to develop their philosophy and strategy for student ministry.[1] Each model focuses on different aspects of philosophy and strategy. The process I find most helpful for student ministry teams who are new at developing a student ministry philosophy is one proposed by Duffy Robbins in his book *This Way to Youth Ministry: An Introduction to Adventure.* The questions and comments regarding the development process are beneficial. For our purposes, we will use his approach.

Robbins contends that a student ministry philosophy must contain the following elements:

- **Phase One:** Mission—the "Why?" question. Why does the ministry exist?
- **Phase Two:** Core Values—the "How?" question. How will the ministry conduct its mission?
- **Phase Three:** Vision—the "What if?" question. This provides a mental picture of what this organization or ministry should look like.

---

[1] For some approaches to creating philosophies and strategies of ministry, see Will Mancini, *Church Unique: How Missional Leaders Cast Vision, Capture Culture, and Create Movement* (San Francisco: Jossey-Bass, 2008); and Mark H. Senter III, Wesley Black, Chap Clark, and Malan Nel, *Four Views of Youth Ministry and the Church: Inclusive Congregational, Preparatory, Missional, Strategic* (Grand Rapids, MI: Zondervan, 2001).

- **Phase Four:** Strategy—the "What now?" question. How can we accomplish this mission?[2]

The remainder of this chapter will focus on unpacking each of these elements, including explanations and questions that will help you and your student ministry team during the student ministry philosophy and strategy development process. These steps will help you develop a philosophy and strategy that will guide you well as you navigate student ministry.

Mission Statement

If your church already has a mission statement, use it. Creating a new statement when one already exists for the congregation will likely cause disunity and separation of the student ministry from the congregation. The student ministry team might change the language of the church's mission statement to communicate aspects that relate specifically to student ministry; however, the substance of the church's mission statement should remain intact.

In the absence of a church mission statement, the student ministry leadership team must carefully deliberate the mission of the student ministry. They should ask questions such as, Why does the student ministry exist? What purpose does it seek to accomplish? What are the objectives of the student ministry? What does Scripture say about the mission of the student ministry? How does our mission align with the Bible?

---

[2] Duffy Robbins, *This Way to Youth Ministry: An Introduction to the Adventure* (Grand Rapids, MI: Zondervan, 2004). Robbins attributes his approach to Aubrey Malphurs, *Ministry Nuts and Bolts* (Grand Rapids, MI: Kregel, 1997), 9–10.

The first chapter of this book is a helpful resource for your student ministry team in writing your mission statement. It describes the biblical foundation for student ministry and how it relates to the church and family. The discussion of how contextualization of the gospel and the overall redemptive metanarrative of Scripture relate to student ministry can assist your team in thinking about the big picture and grant them a kingdom perspective in approaching mission development.

Although the mission statement includes the big picture and foundational concepts, it is essential to keep it short. You want your mission statement to be simple but not simplistic. Your student ministry team and church members should find the mission statement easy to memorize. Some examples of mission statements are:

Mosaic Church of Anderson: Mosaic Church of Anderson exists to reflect God's mosaic in the community by making disciples of people in the community and on the campus.

United States Army Infantry: Our mission is to find, fix, and destroy the enemy.

Both of these statements are easy to remember yet contain thought and depth concerning the mission.

Communicate your student ministry mission to people at every level of the church's ministry. It should be accessible to the church member on the fringes of your student ministry as well as your core leaders. One reason for mission success in the military is that the mission is known by the generals and the privates. This widespread knowledge of the mission helps lend to its success in the church.

Do not be surprised when your mission statement's development takes more time and effort than you anticipated. The student ministry mission statement is crucial to the student ministry philosophy and strategy. It is well worth the time and effort your student ministry team invests in formulating it.

Core Values

Core values are the building blocks on which the student ministry philosophy is grounded. If your church already has a list of core values, use them in developing your student ministry philosophy and strategy. Otherwise, discuss what biblical doctrines, practices, and characteristics are vital to your student ministry. Some critical questions to ask in developing core values are:

- What are the priorities of the student ministry?
- How would you want people to describe the student ministry?
- What are the essential biblical beliefs upon which you base your student ministry?
- When students graduate from the student ministry, what values do you want them to possess?

Answering these questions will help you discover or develop the values that are most important to your ministry.

Though this list is important, it doesn't have to be long. Make it a goal of limiting your list of core values to about six or eight items. This number makes the core values easier to manage and memorize. For example, the list of core values for the church I pastor, Mosaic Church of Anderson, are:

1. **Servant Leadership**: Like Jesus, we lead by serving.
2. **Gospel Community**: Like the early church, we show hospitality, love, and unity in the gospel.
3. **Scriptural Authority**: The Bible is our authority in all matters of faith and life.

4. **Gospel Witness**: We must share the gospel in what we say.

5. **Gospel Action**: We must share the gospel in how we live.

6. **Kingdom Diversity**: We must seek to reconcile everyone to God and everyone to each other.[3]

After you finalize your core values, intentionally communicate them to the adult leaders, parents, students, and congregation. Describe the biblical and theological support for each of your values. Do a series on your values, teaching on one value per week. Such communication and teaching will help your values become part of the student ministry's DNA and strategy.

Vision Statement

The vision statement refers to what the student ministry looks like when you achieve your mission with a successful strategy based on solid core values. Adopt your church's vision statement if one already exists and adapt it to your student ministry. If not, create your vision statement by answering the following questions: What is your God-sized dream for the student ministry? What kingdom goal do you want your student ministry to accomplish by the grace of God and through the power of the Holy Spirit?

Duffy Robbins offers some other helpful questions to help student ministry teams form the vision statement. He queries:

1. Is it clear enough to be grasped and owned by people within the ministry?

2. Does it offer a clear challenge?

---

[3] Mosaic Church of Anderson, *Church Planting Prospectus* (Anderson, SC: Mosaic Church of Anderson, 2019).

3. Does it offer a picture?
4. Is it future-oriented?
5. Is this vision feasible?
6. Is there firm commitment to this vision?[4]

One of the challenges with formulating a vision statement is making it large enough that you must depend on God to attain it while keeping it small enough that it is within reach of your student ministry team. The vision of the student ministry should motivate people who serve in every area of your ministry. It should prompt them to visualize themselves working to help achieve the vision.

Like the mission statement and core values, the student minister must consistently communicate the vision statement throughout every facet of the student ministry. Explain how the student ministry's mission serves to accomplish the vision. Tying the two together shows the intentionality of the student ministry's philosophy of ministry to the church members, parents, adult leaders, and students.

Strategy

The strategy component of the student ministry philosophy is its largest component. It comprises the steps that the student ministry will take to achieve its mission and vision. The student ministry strategy involves every element of student ministry represented in each chapter of this book. The more detail the team includes in the strategy, the more helpful it will be in serving the church and everyone involved in the student ministry.

In this final section, I will review elements necessary to help you use your strategy to navigate student ministry. We will review how

---

[4] Robbins, *This Way to Youth Ministry*, 464–65.

to obtain direction for the strategy and discuss the context or map within which we operate. The last part of this section offers necessary categories and helpful questions for creating each part of the strategic component of the student ministry's philosophy of ministry.

The Compass. As you review the chapter on biblical foundations for student ministry, remember that Scripture is your compass. Every element of your student ministry strategy should be founded in Scripture. The Bible presents the charge for parents and the faith community to lead the next generation to faith in Christ. The Great Commission calls every Christ-follower to make disciples of people from every culture and subculture. The example of the apostle Paul shows us the importance of contextualization, bridging the gospel to student culture. The metanarrative of redemption in Scripture indicates that every human being, including students, needs redemption and restoration. Return to these biblical principles frequently as you formulate and implement your student ministry strategy.

The Map. Our map involves the environment in which we operate. In this book, you read chapters on youth culture and adolescent development. We must become very familiar with both of these elements of student ministry if we want to create and implement an effective strategy. The culture, the student subculture, in your area is unique. Are you familiar with the specific expressions of youth culture exhibited in your area? Do you know the demographic information about the area surrounding your church? What are the family dynamics in the area? How are the students in your culture utilizing technology? How are the students in your community exploring and expressing their identities? All of these questions relate to how you can contextualize the gospel to engage students in your community. They also help you minister more effectively to the students in your ministry. Knowledge of your cultural context enhances your strategy.

Awareness of your students' developmental stages and their dynamics is also necessary to formulate an effective student ministry strategy. Knowing the differences between middle school and high school students' cognitive development is critical to successfully ministering to them. Are you considering cognitive development stages when you plan your strategy? Do you know what your students' views are regarding sexual identity and sexual norms? How are you helping them develop a biblical understanding of identity and gender identity? What tools are you giving your students to help them interact in a Christlike way with their family members and friends? These adolescent developmental trends also make up the map on which you travel in student ministry. You need to have a good grasp of this map to implement a strategy that will effectually engage people with the truth, grace, and mercy of the gospel.

The Software. Remember our discussion about self-care in student ministry? Student ministers and adult leaders will not navigate this journey or execute your strategy well if they do not take care of themselves physically, spiritually, mentally, and emotionally. Are you exercising the spiritual disciplines consistently? Do you manage your time well on a personal and ministerial level? Are you caring for your relationships, whether you are single or married? Do you see your doctor as recommended? Is exercise a part of your daily regimen? Do you meditate and pray daily? As we read previously, all of these skills will enable us to travel the student ministry journey for the long haul. They will also ensure that we have the health and energy to lead our team in strategy implementation.

Leadership. As you develop your team's strategy, refer back to the chapters on leadership development and leadership between the student minister and the student ministry team. Student ministers must ensure they lead well with the staff, parents, adult leaders, and student leaders throughout every student ministry strategy element. They must strive to collaborate and coordinate with other staff members and church leaders to accomplish the church's mission and to ingraft the student ministry into that mission. Student ministers must lead up, across, and down.

Your leadership discussion should prompt several questions to field with your team: Is leadership development a vital part of your strategy? Do you have a leadership development plan that focuses on demonstrating, delegating, and multiplying leaders? What role does your staff play in coordination and collaboration relating to the student ministry? Are you intentionally involving parents in your student ministry leadership? Do you have plans and processes for recruiting, interviewing, equipping, and deploying adult leaders in the student ministry? How will you train and develop student leaders as an element of your strategy? Answering these questions is a critical step in the planning and development of your student ministry. Your student ministry rises or falls on its leaders.

The Family. Failing to include the family in your student ministry strategy will be a recipe for failure. Understanding that every family dynamic is different, the family still spends the most time with and exerts the most influence on students. Review the chapters on the family and how it is a vital part of the student ministry team. Your student leadership team must keep the family in view throughout the strategy development and implementation process. Remember that we need both the church-as-family and the family-as-church approach. The parents must disciple their students while at the same time adult leaders and church members offer intergenerational discipleship as well.

This discussion of the family and its relationship to the student ministry should prompt several questions: How does our strategy encourage families to engage their students in discipleship? How are we equipping and what resources are we offering parents and legal guardians to disciple their students? How are we promoting intergenerational discipleship and ministry to our students in every aspect of our student ministry strategy? How are we engaging unbelieving parents with the gospel? What are we doing to coordinate between the children, student, and adult ministries of the church to encourage, equip, and engage parents in discipling their students? The family is key to helping students build strong faith foundations before they graduate. The student ministry team must not neglect the family in its planning.

Evangelism and Discipleship. Evangelism and discipleship are the flip sides of the same coin. You cannot have one without the other. An effective student ministry strategy will model evangelism and discipleship as adult leaders live out the gospel in front of students. Also, the student ministry strategy encourages and equips parents to be the primary evangelists and disciplers of their students. The student ministry team must be intentional in planning opportunities for students to study God's Word and see how disciples apply Scripture to their daily lives. They need to hear the content of the gospel and see how the gospel is lived out. Finally, an effectual student ministry strategy will include equipping students to lead their peers to Christ and disciple them.

Some questions to ask when preparing the evangelism and discipleship piece of your strategy include: How will we help students have a biblical understanding of the gospel and conversion? What will we do to teach students the mission of God and how it impacts a local, national, and global focus for missions and evangelism? Are we offering our students opportunities to participate in local, national, and foreign missions? How are we encouraging adult leaders and parents to model evangelism in front of their students? What doctrines do we believe are essential for students to learn, and how do we include them in our planning for teaching middle school and high school small groups? How are we promoting relationships in which students can be discipled? Answering these questions will help the student ministry team incorporate evangelism and discipleship in their student ministry plan.

Technology and the Future. Technology is a way of life in our day and age. Student culture is saturated with technology. Students of Generation Z are more engaged with online activity than any other previous generation. They use technology for relationships yet experience loneliness because social media platforms cannot replace personal interaction. The student ministry team should discuss how to use technology to serve the student ministry and enable it to evangelize and disciple students. Student ministers must practice both biblical and digital literacy in student ministry. The student ministry strategy should include ways to communicate and teach through technology as aspects of the student ministry strategy. If there are ways that technology can make the student ministry more efficient, then student leaders should also include them in the process.

The subject of technology generates several questions that student leadership should ask during strategy development: Where is the line between the student ministry serving technology and technology serving the student ministry? How can we encourage the use of technology without supporting its overuse? What are some ways that the student ministry strategy can incorporate technology to make the ministry more efficient? How can small group leaders use technology to enhance their teaching? How does technology relate to preaching in the student ministry? What are some ways the preacher can utilize technology to reinforce the message? Discussing and finding answers to these questions will help the student leadership team integrate technology into their plan.

Conclusion

Are you ready to start your journey? You have your compass. You know how to read your map. We have discussed how you can care for yourself as you travel on the journey of student ministry. You have heard from numerous guides regarding formulating a strategy for navigating to your objective.

Your journey is a wild one. It will take you over the highest mountaintops and through the deepest valleys. You will experience some of the greatest joys in your life when you see students give their lives to Christ or lead their friends to him. At the same time, there will be grief and sorrow as you witness the reality of sin in the lives of students and their families. All the while, you will see the Lord working his will through you, the adult leaders, parents, fellow staff members, and student leaders to bring himself glory and to advance his kingdom.

His mission is to save people from every tribe, tongue, and nation. That includes students. The Lord has given you the great privilege of being a part of that mission. It is a journey that has the most excellent ending. Describing his vision of what he saw at our destination, John wrote,

> After this I looked, and there was a vast multitude from
> every nation, tribe, people, and language, which no one could

number, standing before the throne and before the Lamb. They were clothed in white robes with palm branches in their hands. And they cried out in a loud voice: Salvation belongs to our God, who is seated on the throne, and to the Lamb! (Rev 7:9–10)

Until we reach that glorious scene, the Lord will walk with us on our journey. He will guide us along the way. As we navigate student ministry, we will not do so alone. We have brothers and sisters in Christ who make up our student ministry team. More importantly, we have the presence of the Holy Spirit and the promise of Jesus Christ. He said, "And remember, I am with you always, to the end of the age" (Matt 28:20). As you navigate student ministry, understand that the good shepherd is leading you.

Blessings on your journey!

Appendix 1

Catechism Classes and Other Surprising Precedents for Age-Organized Ministries

• TIMOTHY PAUL JONES •

I n recent years, a small but vocal cluster of church leaders has contended that age-organized programs and ministries in the church ought to be eliminated. These proponents of "family-integrated churches" have called for congregations to dismantle any programs that practice "age-segregated discipleship," including student ministry.[1] "We do not divide families into component parts," writes one

---

[1] National Center for Family-Integrated Churches, "A Declaration on the Complementary Roles of Church and Family," Articles 13, 14, 16, http://www.ncfic.org/confession. Although family-integrated church leaders frequently use the term "age segregation" to refer to the practice of teaching children or youth in classes that are separated from the intergenerational congregation, the association of "segregation" with the marginalization of African Americans and the systematic deprivation of African American legal rights in the nineteenth and twentieth centuries limits the suitability of this terminology. I have thus utilized phrases such as "age-organized ministry" instead to describe the phenomenon of classes for children or youth that are conducted separately from the rest of the church.

proponent of family-integrated churches. "We don't even do it in
Bible study."[2] One support that has been claimed for this model of
ministry is that age-organized classes for youth and children are a
recent innovation. According to this line of thinking, age-organized
ministry represents the modern imposition of individualistic philosophies in the church.[3]

The purpose of this research is to examine the historical claims
made by advocates of family-integrated ministry. According to
one such proponent, classes where children or youth are discipled
apart from the congregation as a whole originated in the nineteenth and twentieth centuries, when churches began to imitate the

---

[2] Voddie Baucham, *Family Driven Faith* (Wheaton, IL: Crossway, 2007),
191.

[3] NCFIC, "A Declaration on the Complementary Roles of Church and
Family," Articles 13, 14, 16. In the article "My Top Four Favorite Family-
Integrated Church Pastors," Brown asserts that intergenerational worship
services have been the dominant pattern throughout church history but then
follows this assertion with the more dubious declaration that the practices
of family-integrated churches thus stand in continuity with longstanding
historical practices ("what we advocate was practiced by some of our most
treasured pastors and theologians of the past"). See Scott Brown, "My Top
Four Favorite Family-Integrated Church Pastors," December 15, 2012,
https://churchandfamilylife.com/resources/my-top-four-favorite-family
-integrated-church-pastors. The changes demanded by many proponents of
family-integrated ministry have been, however, far more comprehensive than
a call for intergenerational worship and father-led family discipleship. What
family-integrated church leaders have promoted has been the complete or
near-complete elimination of age-organized programs and ministries. What
is disputed here is not the general ubiquity and venerability of intergenerational worship services and family discipleship; it is rather the claim that age-
organized church ministries should be eliminated and that they emerged due
to emulation of patterns in pagan and secular cultures. The primacy of family
discipleship and age-integrated worship does not require the elimination of
age-organized programs or activities.

age-organized structures of the surrounding culture.[4] Age-organized ministries developed, this author claims, over the past two centuries from "the lofty deposits of platonic philosophy, the loamy organic of rationalism, the ethereal waters of evolutionism, and the breathable but allergenic air of pragmatism."[5] The promotional materials for *Divided*—a documentary that calls for the dissolution of student ministry—similarly claim that the film unmasks the "shockingly sinister roots of modern, age-segregated church programs."[6] If these perspectives are correct, classes and programs for particular age groups in the church represent an innovation that has emerged over the past two centuries as a result of imitating pragmatic and progressivist practices in the surrounding culture.[7] The emergence of these age-organized ministries has correlated, according to this

---

[4] Scott Brown, *A Weed in the Church*, rev. ed. (Wake Forest, NC: NCFIC, 2013), 34–35.

[5] Brown, 34, 37.

[6] *Divided*, directed by Peter Bradrick (Wake Forest, NC: Leclerc Brothers, 2010), http://www.dividedthemovie.com.

[7] Although worship practices of the ancient church are not the subject of this research, it should be noted that the notion of nuclear families seated together in an intergenerational worship service does not seem to have been the predominant pattern even in the early centuries of Christianity. According to the third-century *Didascalia Apostolorum*, elders were arranged on the east side of the space designated for worship, followed by the men of the church and then the women. Among both men and women, younger people were to sit separated from the older people if that was practical in the church's meeting space; if space was limited, younger people were to stand in their places instead of being seated separately. Children stood to the side or stood with their parents. Deacons were charged with the responsibility of arranging everyone according to the church's custom. See *Didascalia Apostolorum* 12 in R. H. Connolly, ed., *Didascalia Apostolorum: The Syriac Version Translated and Accompanied by the Verona Latin Fragments* (Eugene, OR: Wipf & Stock, 2010), 119–20. The notion of a nuclear family worshiping together is shaped more by a modern view of the family than by any premodern practice of the church.

interpretation, with an increasing absorption of non-Christian values in churches.

This appendix presents a quite different account of the emergence of age-organized ministries. Three centuries prior to the supposed culprits of "rationalism, . . . evolutionism, and . . . pragmatism," faithful churches systematically offered age-organized classes led by vocational ministers. Far from being an innovation instituted in an attempt to imitate the practices of the surrounding culture, these gatherings were initiated with the explicit goal of reinstituting what was believed to have been the practice of the ancient church.[8] These practices began no later than the sixteenth century as part of an attempt to restore what John Calvin and others perceived as earlier patterns. Furthermore, this attempt at restoring catechetical instruction in the church provided the template for some of the earliest expressions of Sunday school, particularly the forms of Sunday school promoted by Robert Raikes. In addition to critiquing

---

[8] Whether the leaders of the Reformation rightly reconstructed the practices of the ancient church stands beyond the scope of this research. In some instances, the Reformers seem to have erred in their understanding of ancient precedents for the practices they proposed. John Calvin, for example, thought that the Apostles' Creed dated to the first century and that this creed had been part of the catechumenal practices described in the book of Hebrews. The epistle to the Hebrews was, according to Calvin, "written . . . when some pattern of polity had been established in the churches, such as that before the catechumen was admitted to baptism he should make confession of faith. . . . This examination was concerned particularly with what is known as the Apostles' Creed." John Calvin, *Epistle of Paul the Apostle to the Hebrews and the First and Second Epistles of Peter*, trans. William Johnston, ed. David and Thomas Torrance (Grand Rapids, MI: Eerdmans, 1963), 71 (6:1). At the same time, the practices of the second and third centuries do provide some precedent for the catechetical processes that Calvin described. See, e.g., Tertullian of Carthage, *Prescription Against Heretics*, 41, wherein Tertullian criticizes heretics for moving persons from initial profession of faith to full participation in the church without adequate catechetical instruction.

the claim that age-organized ministries such as student ministry emerged due to the church's embrace of non-Christian philosophies, this research will also highlight the willingness of early Reformed churches to modify ecclesial methodologies to disciple young people more effectively.

"The Devil . . . Overthrew This Policy": Calvin's Perception of Children's Catechesis as a Restoration of the Practices of the Early Church

On January 16, 1537, a pastor named Guilliame Farel presented the Little Council of Geneva with a series of proposals for the government of their city. One of Farel's coarchitects in these proposals was a twenty-seven-year-old French theologian who had only recently been appointed to the colloquium of pastors in Geneva. The next year, this same young man would be dismissed from Geneva and make his way to the city of Strasbourg. His name was John Calvin.

The purpose of the articles Farel presented was "to maintain the Church in its integrity."[9] One of the primary means proposed in the articles to maintain ecclesial integrity was the catechesis of children. The articles of 1537 directed parents to "exercise pains and diligence" so their children would "be individually taught" to confess the true faith. At the same time, these articles also called for pastoral instruction of children.[10] Parents in Geneva were instructed to bring their

---

[9] "Articles Concerning the Organization of the Church and of Worship at Geneva by the Ministers at the Council, January 16, 1537," in *Theological Treatises,* ed. and trans. J. K. S. Reid (Philadelphia: Westminster, 1954), 48.

[10] "Articles Concerning the Organization of the Church and of Worship at Geneva by the Ministers at the Council, January 16, 1537," 54. In this research, I am using "catechism" to refer to the text that was taught, "catechesis" to refer to the process of learning the catechism regardless of the context

children before the pastors "at certain seasons." At these designated times, the children would be expected not only to confess their faith but also examined before the church and, if necessary, receive from the ministers "more ample explanation" of the catechism "according to [their] capacity."[11] Even in 1537, the leaders of the Reformation in Geneva saw the need for adapting content and instructional methods to the developmental capacities of the hearers.

Several months earlier, John Calvin had already envisioned how these processes of examining and instructing children might take place in the context of a local church. In the 1536 edition of the *Institutio Christianae religionis*, Calvin described how

> children or those near adolescence would give an account of their faith before the church. But the best method of catechizing would be to have a manual drafted for this exercise, containing and summarizing in a simple manner nearly all the articles of our religion, on which the whole believers' church ought to agree without controversy. A child of ten would present himself to the church to declare his confession of faith, would be examined in each article, and answer to each; if he were ignorant of anything or insufficiently understood it, he would be taught. Thus, while the church looks on as witness, he would profess the one true and sincere faith, in which the believing folk with one mind worship the one God. If this discipline were in effect today, it would certainly arouse some slothful parents, who carelessly neglect the instruction of their children as a matter of no

---

or instructor, and "catechetical classes" to refer to the gatherings wherein the catechism was taught and discussed.

[11] "Articles Concerning the Organization of the Church and of Worship at Geneva by the Ministers at the Council, January 16, 1537," 54.

concern to them; for then they could not overlook it without public disgrace.[12]

Calvin—like many others in the sixteenth century, including Martin Luther—seems to have viewed the development of children and youth as a process that unfolded in three seven-year stages.[13] Calvin's description of catechesis in the *Institutio* focused on the second of these developmental stages ("children or those near adolescence . . . a child of ten")—the cycle that began with the dawning of reason and ended at puberty.

The pastoral practices described in the *Institutio* of 1536 and the articles of 1537 were occasional and seem to have taken place in the

---

[12] John Calvin, *Institutes of the Christian Religion, 1536 Edition,* trans. Ford Lewis Battles (Grand Rapids, MI, Eerdmans, 1975), 130 (5:10). A few months before Calvin's dismissal from Geneva, he produced the short and simple guide to the faith that he had envisioned in 1536, *Instruction et confession de foi.* This instructional guide in French was primarily intended as an instructional tool for the youth of Geneva. A Latin version was published the next year, titled *Catechismus sive Christianae religionis institutio.* See Wullert Greef, *The Writings of John Calvin,* expanded ed., trans. Lyle Bierma (Louisville, KY: Westminster John Knox, 2008), 108–9; and I. John Hesselink, *Calvin's First Catechism: A Commentary* (Louisville, KY: Westminster John Knox, 1997), 40.

[13] For Luther's perspective on children's development, see Gerald Strauss, *Luther's House of Learning* (Baltimore: Johns Hopkins University Press, 1978), 34–36, 54–56, 99–100. In this and in many other areas, Calvin was willing to draw wisdom from sources with which he disagreed. According to Calvin, "persons are superstitious who do not venture to borrow anything from heathen authors. All truth is from God, and consequently if wicked men have said anything that is true and just, we ought not to reject it; for it has come from God. . . . The invention of arts and of some other things which serve the common use and convenience of life [are gifts] by no means to be despised, a faculty worthy of commendation." John Calvin, *Commentaries on the Epistle to Titus,* trans. William Pringle (repr., Grand Rapids, MI: Baker, 2009), 300; John Calvin, *Commentaries on the First Book of Moses Called Genesis,* trans. John King (repr., Grand Rapids, MI: Baker, 2009), 217.

context of the entire congregation. Nevertheless, it is clear Calvin expected those who led Reformed churches to commit themselves to the training of children. The purpose of this increased engagement was not to replace parents as trainers of their children but to arouse parents to become more committed to their children's spiritual training.[14]

From the perspective of Calvin and his compatriots, the institution of catechesis for children and new converts represented the recovery of a long-lost practice that had characterized Christians in the apostolic era.[15] According to the ecclesiastical articles to which Calvin contributed in 1537, ancient Christians had employed "a definite catechism" to instruct children in the fundamental truths of the Christian faith.[16] After being instructed, "children of the faithful" presented themselves before the church for examination. If they were capable of rightly confessing their faith, they were received into the church's full fellowship.[17]

The practice of catechism and public profession had been, Calvin claimed, "abolished some centuries ago under the papacy." This abolition was a disastrous act by which "the devil . . . overthrew" catechetical instruction and set about "miserably rending the church of God

---

[14] Robert Kingdon, "Catechesis in Calvin's Geneva," in *Educating People of Faith*, ed. John Van Engen (Grand Rapids, MI: Eerdmans, 2004), 295. Luther had similar expectations for parents: "God has appointed you [as] a master and a wife in order that you should hold your family to [teaching the catechism]. . . . Every father of a family is a bishop in his house and the wife a bishopess." Martin Luther, "Sermons on the Catechism," in *Luther's Works*, vol. 51, ed. John Doberstein (Philadelphia: Fortress, 1959), 136–37.

[15] See, e.g., Calvin, *Institutes of the Christian Religion, 1536 Edition*, 130 (5:10).

[16] "Articles Concerning the Organization of the Church and of Worship at Geneva by the Ministers at the Council, January 16, 1537," 54.

[17] Calvin, *Epistle of Paul the Apostle to the Hebrews and the First and Second Epistles of Peter*, 71 (6:1).

and bringing upon it his fearful destruction."[18] What had replaced catechesis in the Roman Catholic Church was, according to Calvin, confirmation. Confirmation was a "sign, which, invented by the rashness of men, has been set out as a sacrament of God."[19] By the sixteenth century, the confirmation of children had degenerated into a ritual that was—in Calvin's words—"decked out like a prostitute" and filled with "gesticulations which are more than ridiculous and suited rather to monkeys."[20] The Roman Catholic rite of confirmation included a slap on the cheek of the child being confirmed;[21] this may have been one of the ritual gesticulations that Calvin deemed "suited rather to apes."[22]

Calvin's vision was to see in his own lifetime a divine "restitution of the church" through a renewed understanding of divine truth.[23]

---

[18] John Calvin, "The Catechism of the Church in Geneva, That is a Plan for Instructing Children in the Doctrine of Christ," in *Theological Treatises*, ed. and trans. J. K. S. Reid (Philadelphia: Westminster, 1954), 88. Of course, the practices of the ancient church were more variegated and the demise of catechetical instruction more complex than Calvin's rhetoric would suggest.

[19] Calvin, *Institutes of the Christian Religion, 1536 Edition*, 125 (5:2).

[20] Calvin, "The Catechism of the Church in Geneva, That is a Plan for Instructing Children in the Doctrine of Christ," 88.

[21] For descriptions of this rite, which persisted into the twentieth century as a gentle tap on the child's cheek, see Anscar Chupungco, *Liturgical Inculturation* (Collegeville, MN: Liturgical, 1992), 33–34; A. C. A. Hall, *Confirmation* (London: Longmans, 1904), 33; and Frank Senn, *Embodied Liturgy* (Minneapolis: Augsburg Fortress, 2016), 198.

[22] Martin Luther likewise rejected confirmation as practiced in the Roman Catholic Church, though Luther's reasons were grounded in a rejection of the Roman Catholic teaching that the Holy Spirit was not fully given in baptism but in the chrism and laying on of hands that accompanied confirmation. For further discussion, see Arthur Repp, *Confirmation in the Lutheran Church* (St. Louis: Concordia, 1994), chap. 1.

[23] Calvin, "The Catechism of the Church in Geneva, That is a Plan for Instructing Children in the Doctrine of Christ," 90. For the recognition that this work would only be accomplished by means of divine power, see John Calvin, "Letter 229, To The Protector Somerset," in *Letters of John Calvin*, vol.

The recovery of catechesis was so central to Calvin's vision that, when he agreed to return to Geneva in 1541, retention of the catechism was one of the two conditions that he required. "I would never have accepted this ministry," Calvin later declared, "if they had not pledged me these two things; namely, to keep the catechism and the discipline."[24]

Soon after his return to Geneva, John Calvin drafted a series of ecclesiastical ordinances for the city of Geneva. In these ordinances, he reshaped the catechetical ideals that he had outlined in 1536 and 1537 into a detailed plan for the discipleship of children and younger youth. Calvin never retreated from the priority he placed on parental catechesis of children.[25] At the same time, his plan for catechizing grew more precise and moved closer to a partnership between the church and the home. Most important for the purposes of this

---

1, ed. Jules Bonnet (repr, Eugene, OR: Wipf & Stock, 2007), 195: "Above all, we must cling to this maxim, that the reformation of [God's] church is the work of [God's] hand."

[24] William Monter, *Calvin's Geneva* (Eugene, OR: Wipf & Stock, 1967), 97. Catechism and discipline were intertwined in Calvin's perspective to a greater degree than one might think at first. Catechism classes could be (and often were) applied by the consistory as discipline to provide an antidote for ungodly behaviors. Changes in Geneva suggest that this might have been effective. Until the mid-1560s, about one out of every ten Genevans were subjects of church discipline; by the end of the sixteenth century, this number had dropped to less than 1 percent. See Scott Manetsch, *Calvin's Company of Pastors* (New York: Oxford University Press, 2013), 273; and Karen Spierling, "Putting 'God's Honor First,'" *Church History and Religious Culture* 92 (2012): 101–3.

[25] The section of the *Institutio* in which Calvin urges parental engagement in catechesis is one of the least-changed sections of the *Institutio* from the first edition in 1536 through the final edition in 1559. Compare Calvin, *Institutes of the Christian Religion, 1536 Edition*, 130 (5:10) with John Calvin, *Institutio Christianae religionis*, 4:19:13.

research, these ordinances included a clear and comprehensive role for pastors.[26]

"At Midday, There Is to Be Catechism": Pastoral Responsibility for Catechesis in Sixteenth-Century Geneva

In his ecclesiastical ordinances, John Calvin placed his catechetical instructions in the same section of the ecclesiastical ordinances in which he described the frequency and locales for pastoral proclamations of Scripture. He directed that each Sunday "at midday, there is to be catechism, that is, instruction of little children, in all the three churches."[27] The individual responsible for this instruction was the pastor—and this was not a peripheral function for the pastor. Rather, "the catechizing task of the pastors in Geneva occupied much of their ministerial activity."[28]

------

[26] The ordinances of 1541 did not essentially alter the ideas found in the articles of 1537; however, greater elaboration and precision marked these later ordinances. See Williston Walker, *John Calvin* (New York: Schocken, 1969), 266.

[27] "Draft Ecclesiastical Ordinances, September and October 1541," in *Theological Treatises,* ed. and trans. J. K. S. Reid (Philadelphia: Westminster, 1954), 62. In Geneva, there were three services every Sunday. The first service of Sunday began at 6:00 or 7:00 a.m., followed by the main service at 8:00 a.m. and an afternoon service at 3:00 p.m. Between these two later services, at noon, catechism classes met. See Jean F. A. L. Gomes, "Reforming the Church, Home, and School," *Fides Reformata* 24 (2019): 90; and Barbara Pitkin, "Children and the Church in Calvin's Geneva," in *Calvin and the Church* (Grand Rapids, MI: CRC, 2002), 156.

[28] Gomes, "Reforming the Church, Home, and School," 96. Pastoral responsibility for children's catechesis seems to have been an innovation when compared with medieval practices, at least in England. See Nicolas Orme, "Children and the Church in Medieval England," *Journal of Ecclesiastical History* 45 (1994): 565–66. In 1281, the Council of Lambeth did envision

These weekly catechetical classes were designed as a distinct and separate gathering for children, and attendance was not optional. "All citizens and inhabitants," the ordinances declared, "are to bring or convey their children on Sundays at midday to catechism" to be instructed by the pastor. If children were absent from the classes, parents were to be "called before the company of the elders, and, if they will not yield to good advice, they must be reported to their lordships."[29] Calvin's ordinances spelled out not only the participants but also the content and the goal of these classes:

> A definite formulary is to be composed by which they will be instructed, and on this, with the teaching given them, they are to be interrogated about what has been said, to see if they have listened and remembered well. When a child has been well enough instructed to pass the catechism, he is to recite solemnly the sum of what it contains, and also [or, "and so"] to make profession of his Christianity in the presence of the church.[30]

The catechism that Calvin would compose the following year was to provide the content for the curriculum, and the method of instruction would be pastoral teaching followed by the posing of

---

parish priests teaching in the vernacular at least four times each year the Apostles' Creed, the Ten Commandments, seven works of mercy, seven virtues, and seven sacraments; however, these teachings seem to have been directed primarily toward adults. See Kevin Lawson, "Light from the 'Dark Ages,'" *Christian Education Journal* 14 (2017): 340–41.

[29] "Draft Ecclesiastical Ordinances, September and October 1541," 69.

[30] "Draft Ecclesiastical Ordinances, September and October 1541," 69. Four times each year on the Sunday before communion, children of about ten years of age were questioned and required to answer catechetical questions. See A. I. C. Heron, "Calvin and the Confessions of the Reformation," *HTS Teologiese Studies* 70 (2014): 3.

questions to test children's knowledge. Calvin's first instructional booklet for the youth of Geneva had been a confession of faith. This work had proved too difficult for many children to memorize.[31] The new catechism that was published in 1542 was constructed in a question-and-answer format, following a trend that would in time characterize Protestant catechesis.[32] Three years later, seeking to multiply the impact of the Genevan Reformation, Calvin translated the text of this catechism into Latin.[33]

In 1547, Calvin adapted his original ecclesiastical ordinances to take into account the challenges faced by churches in the rural regions surrounding Geneva. Each pastor in these contexts served two congregations. As a result, a pastor was only available every other week, and the adjustments that Calvin made in the catechetical classes revealed the importance, in his mind, of a trained minister overseeing catechesis. The significance of the pastor as a teacher of children was such that catechetical classes occurred only on the weeks when the pastor could be present. Fathers were apparently required to be

---

[31] James Edward McGoldrick, "John Calvin—Erudite Educator," *Mid-America Journal of Theology* 21 (2020): 129. See also Dustin Bruce, "John Calvin: Teacher in the School of Christ," in *A Legacy of Religious Educators*, ed. Elmer Towns and Benjamin Forrest (Lynchburg, VA: Liberty University Press, 2016).

[32] Ian Green, *The Christian's ABC* (Oxford: Oxford University Press, 1996), 16. The question-and-answer format was not a Protestant innovation; it was a recovery of an older form. "Luther in his Shorter (though not in his Larger) Catechism had resuscitated this form from the dissuetude into which it had lapsed." J. K. S. Reid, *Theological Treatises* (Philadelphia: Westminster, 1954), 83. The questions and answers in earlier catechisms had, in some cases, been coordinated with confession to the priest. For the function of Roman Catholic catechetical literature prior to the Reformation, see Mary Haemig, "Recovery Not Rejection," *Concordia Journal* 43 (2017): 43–49; Gottfried Krodel, "Luther's Work on Three Catechisms in the Context of Late Medieval Catechetical Literature," *Concordia Journal* 25 (1999): 364–72; and John Nordling, "The Catechism," *Logia* 16 (2007): 5.

[33] Gomes, "Reforming the Church, Home, and School," 90.

in attendance only if one of their offspring was being baptized; even then, fathers might be absent if a "legitimate excuse" was submitted to the consistory.[34] By 1560, in certain regions ruled by Geneva, families were fined if they failed to send not only their children but also any servants or chambermaids who were "old enough [to] have the knowledge to learn" to catechism classes.[35]

The training of youth and children in Christian doctrine had been—according to the preface of the new catechism that Calvin had produced in 1542—part of the "practice . . . of the church" from ancient times.[36] In the past, parents had been encouraged to prioritize the training of their children, and schools had been founded to train children and youth "more conveniently."[37] In Calvin's mind, however,

---

[34] "The ministers are always to exhort the people to link [baptism] with the catechism. Children are to be brought at the beginning of catechism or sermon. Fathers are to be present, unless they have legitimate excuse of which cognizance will be taken by the consistory." John Calvin, "Ordinances for the Supervision of Churches in the Country, February 3, 1547," in *Theological Treatises*, ed. and trans. J. K. S. Reid (Philadelphia: Westminster, 1954), 78.

[35] Emile Rivoire, ed., *Les sources du droit du canton de Genève*, vol. 2 (Aarau, Switzerland: Sauerlander, 1927), 117.

[36] Calvin, "The Catechism of the Church in Geneva, That Is a Plan for Instructing Children in the Doctrine of Christ," 88. For further discussion of Calvin's perception of the function of the catechism in the church, see Richard Osmer, *A Teachable Spirit* (Louisville, KY: Westminster John Knox, 1990), 129–34.

[37] Calvin, "The Catechism of the Church in Geneva, That Is a Plan for Instructing Children in the Doctrine of Christ," 88. In the preface to his Small Catechism, Martin Luther mentioned the same three entities—schools, families, and churches—as having a role in the training of children in the faith. After visiting churches in Saxony, Luther seems to have placed less confidence in parents and pastors than did John Calvin: "The deplorable, wretched deprivation that I recently encountered while I was a visitor has constrained and compelled me to prepare this catechism, or Christian instruction, in such a brief, plain, simple version. Dear God have mercy, what misery I beheld! The ordinary person, especially in the villages, knows absolutely nothing about Christian teaching, and unfortunately many

neither the presence of schools nor the priority of parents precluded the establishment of regular classes that separated children and younger youth from the rest of the congregation for instruction at their developmental level. Catechesis had a strategic role in Calvin's thought precisely because of its implementation not merely in the home but also—separate from the parents—in church classes and in school.[38]

Between the first edition of the *Institutio* in 1536 and Calvin's return to Geneva in 1541, the Reformer's recommendations regarding the catechesis of children became both more comprehensive and more precise. Over the space of five years, Calvin's expectation for pastors grew from occasional instruction in the context of a worship service into a systematic age-organized program for children. In the minds of Christians in Geneva, "catechesis led by professional clergymen should supplement home instruction."[39] In time, Calvin's

---

pastors are completely unskilled and incompetent teachers." Martin Luther, "Handbook, the Small Catechism for Ordinary Pastors and Preachers," in *The Small Catechism, 1529: The Annotated Luther Study Edition,* ed. Timothy Wengert and Mary Jane Haemig (Minneapolis: Fortress, 2017), 212. What Luther observed in the villages of Saxony might have contributed to his emphasis on the establishment of schools in which children would be instructed in Christian doctrine, though the growth of Lutheranism in contexts where monarchs and princes generally supported the movement might also have contributed to this pattern. Reformed churches grew with less external political support and relied more on a strong and well-disciplined church and less on state-sponsored schools. For further discussion, see Strauss, *Luther's House of Learning,* 123–31; and Alister McGrath, *A Life of John Calvin* (Oxford: Blackwell, 1990), 111. Luther's emphasis on schools did not, however, result in any deprecation of the role of parents or pastors. Parents were to engage in catechetical instruction as part of their daily lives with their children, and pastors were to preach the catechism as part of Christian worship.

[38] Gomes, "Reforming the Church, Home, and School," 88.

[39] "A degree of religious education at home was already established prior to the conversion to Protestantism. It was related to memorization of a few prayers and the Apostles' Creed. Mothers trained their children with the

catechetical patterns would shape not only the Reformed congregations on the European continent but also the Reformation that was quickly gaining ground in England.

"The Church of God Will Never Preserve Itself Without a Catechism": Confirmation and Catechetical Instruction in the English Reformation

Following the death of King Henry VIII in 1547, Archbishop Thomas Cranmer grew a beard that declared his theological solidarity with the continental Reformers.[40] It was not, however, merely in his pogonotrophic proclivities that the Archbishop of Canterbury imitated what was happening on the other side of the English Channel. Cranmer—not unlike Calvin—required catechesis of children and younger youth in the context of the church.

---

basic expectation that they would be capable to say these prayers and attend the Mass. The most important prayers at that time were the *Pater Noster* and the *Ave Maria,* memorized in Latin." Gomes, 99–100. Godparents might also have participated in the teaching of these prayers and the Apostles' Creed. See Lawson, "Light from the 'Dark Ages,'" 330; and Orme, "Children and the Church in Medieval England," 564. The Reformation marked a movement away from this pattern that characterized medieval Roman Catholicism, toward catechesis, which was understandable for children and young people (and thus prepared children and youth to participate with understanding in the church's worship) and which involved pastors and parents, particularly fathers.

[40] "At the time, everyone realized the significance of this: throughout northern Europe, clergymen wearing beards equated with Protestantism (Renaissance popes and Cardinal Pole being the exceptions to prove the rule). When Cranmer grew his beard in 1547, he was making an emphatic rejection of the old Church." Diarmaid MacCulloch, *All Things Made New: The Reformation and Its Legacy* (Oxford: Oxford University Press, 2016), 268.

It seems that John Calvin might have influenced catechetical instruction in England through his correspondence with Edward
Seymour, the self-proclaimed Duke of Somerset and the Lord Protector
of England during the early years of the minority of Edward VI.[41] In
Calvin's correspondence with the Duke of Somerset in the autumn of
1548, catechesis was clearly a topic of concern. According to Calvin:

> There ought to be . . . a common formula of instruction
> for little children and for ignorant persons, serving to make
> them familiar with sound doctrine so that they may be able
> to discern the difference between it and the falsehood and
> corruptions which may be brought forward in opposition to
> it. Believe me, Monseigneur, the church of God will never
> preserve itself without a catechism, for it is like the seed to
> keep the good grain from dying out, and causing it to mul-
> tiply from age to age. And therefore, if you desire to build
> an edifice which shall be of long duration, and which shall
> not soon fall into decay, make provision for the children
> being instructed in a good catechism, which may show them
> briefly, and in language level to their tender age, wherein
> true Christianity consists. This catechism will serve two pur-
> poses: an introduction to the whole people, so that everyone
> may profit from what shall be preached, and also to enable
> them to discern when any presumptuous person puts forth
> strange doctrine. Indeed, I do not say that it may not be well,

---

[41] One other precedent for the requirement of catechesis prior to confirmation might have been John Hilsey's recommendation in the 1530s that
confirmation should be delayed until an age of discretion (which had already
been recommended in the fourteenth century by canon lawyer William of
Pagula) and preceded by an examination of the child's understanding of the
Christian faith. For further discussion, see Orme, "Children and the Church
in Medieval England," 577.

and even necessary, to bind down the pastors and curates to a certain written form.[42]

As in Calvin's ecclesiastical ordinances, catechetical instruction is—according to this admonition—not only a parental but also a pastoral duty, linked with proclamation of the Scriptures. Immediately before his recommendations regarding catechism, Calvin urged the cultivation of "lively preaching" in English churches and the provision of an "explicit summary of the doctrine which all ought to preach." After addressing catechesis, Calvin also urged the elimination of chrism, the application of oil by which the power of the Holy Spirit was—according to Roman Catholic tradition—conveyed to the individual.[43]

When the *Book of Common Prayer* was published the next year, Thomas Cranmer retained the rite of confirmation but eliminated chrism. At the same time, the *Book of Common Prayer* included a catechism.[44] Before a young person could be confirmed and receive

---

[42] Calvin, "Letter 229, to the Protector Somerset," 191. In this letter, Calvin urged the elimination of chrism, unction, and prayers for the deceased in English churches. Nevertheless, he did not mention confirmation itself, only the claim that chrism in confirmation conveys the empowerment of the Holy Spirit.

[43] For chrism as the material means by which the fullness of the Holy Spirit is conveyed to the individual, see Thomas Aquinas, *Summa theologiae*, 3:72:2, 4: "Chrism is the fitting matter of this sacrament. . . . In this sacrament the fullness of the Holy Ghost is given for the spiritual strength which belongs to the perfect age. . . . In this sacrament the Holy Ghost is given for strength in the spiritual combat."

[44] On the matter of Christ's presence in holy communion, the 1549 *Book of Common Prayer* expressed Thomas Cranmer's conviction that Christ was not corporally present in the elements; however, the verbiage simultaneously provided enough latitude for traditionalists to treat communion much like the Mass. The title at the beginning of the eucharistic service refers to communion as "the supper of the Lord and the holy communion, commonly called the mass." See Diarmaid MacCulloch, *The Boy King* (Berkeley: University of California, 1999), 89. The presentation of confirmation in the *Book of Common Prayer* similarly retains much of the traditional rite of confirmation

holy communion, he or she was called to commit to memory "all that is here appointed for them to learne" in the *Book of Common Prayer*. Thus, confirmation and communion became contingent on catechesis. In reality, however, the practice of catechesis grew far more significant in Anglican congregations than the rite of confirmation.

> In the reign of Edward VI, visitation articles, which formed the means by which bishops set norms and queried compliance within their dioceses, largely ignored confirmation. By contrast, the articles did reflect an effort to impose a basic test of doctrinal knowledge before admission to communion. . . . Catechizing, rather than confirmation, was the real gate to the sacrament of the eucharist.[45]

Most important for the purposes of this research, the *Book of Common Prayer*—much like the ecclesiastical ordinances that John Calvin wrote for the Genevan churches—required pastors to conduct catechetical classes. The context for this instruction was a Sunday evening gathering that occurred, at minimum, once every six weeks:

> The curate of every parish once in sixe wekes at the least upon warnyng by him geven, shal upon some Soonday or

---

but simultaneously requires a catechism similar to those formulated by the continental Reformers.

[45] James Turrell, "'Until Such Time as He Be Confirmed,'" in *The Seventeenth Century* 20 (October 2005): 205, 217. In *The Christian's ABC*, Ian Green argues that, with the abolition of confirmation in the mid-seventeenth century, catechesis was substituted for confirmation as the requisite requirement for admission to communion. Turrell, however, provides extensive evidence to suggest that that "the substitution had taken place far earlier—and that is highly significant, showing two approaches to Church life within the formularies of the Church of England, one rite-centered and one word-centered, with the latter generally prevailing in practice long before the religious upheaval of the civil war and interregnum" (217).

holy day, half an houre before evensong openly in the churche instructe and examine so many children of his parish sent unto him, as the time wil serve, and as he shal thynke conventiente in some parte of this Catechisme. And all fathers, mothers, maisters, and dames, shall cause theyr children, servountes, and prentises (whiche are not yet confirmed), to come to the churche at the daie appoynted, and obediently heare and be ordered by the curate, until suche time as they have learned all that is here appointed for them to learne. And whansoever the Bushop shal geve knowlege for children to be brought afore him to any convenient place, for their confirmacion: Then shal the curate of every parish either bring or send in writing, the names of al those children of his parish which can say the articles of theyr faith, the lordes praier, and the ten commaundementes. And also how many of them can answere to the other questions conteined in this Cathechisme. And there shal none be admitted to the holye communion: until suche time as he be confirmed.[46]

It is clear these classes were for children ("so many children of his parish") and that they entailed not only review but also teaching ("instruct and examine . . . as time wil serve . . . in some parte of this Catechisme").

Three years after the first *Book of Common Prayer*, Thomas Cranmer—in consultation with German reformer Martin Bucer—produced a revised edition of the prayer book.[47] The rubric in the

---

[46] *The Book of Common Prayer*, ed. Brian Cummings (Oxford: Oxford University Press, 2011), 63.

[47] "Bucer submitted approximately 60 criticisms, of which certainly 23, perhaps 25, were embodied in the book and an equal number were ignored," according to G. J. Cuming, *A History of Anglican Liturgy* (New York: MacMillan, 1969), 100. For further discussion of Bucer's influence on the

revision increased the expected frequency of catechetical classes from every sixth week to weekly ("upon Sundaies, and holy doies halfe an hour before Evensong") but also allowed curates to delegate the responsibility of teaching ("The Curate of every Parishe, or some other at his appoynctmente"), making it possible for other ministers or teachers to undertake this task.[48] The 1552 revision also made explicit what had been implicit in the 1549 edition, that none were to partake in communion until they were able to recite the catechism ("there shal none be admitted to the holy Communion, until suche time as he can saye the Catechisme, and bee confirmed").[49]

Ian Green summarizes the perspective of the English church on catechesis in this way:

> The attitude of the English church to basic catechizing was not very different from that of the mature Luther or Calvin in the stress that was put on the role of the minister. . . . In England from an early stage the brunt of the burden of ensuring the basic catechism was mastered and understood, especially by those who never attended a school, fell on parish clergy. . . . That the clergy were aware of their duty to catechize can be demonstrated by the number who in their publications insisted that catechizing was enjoined by public authority, or cited the appropriate rubric or injunction for

---

1552 *Book of Common Prayer*, see Diarmaid MacCulloch, *Thomas Cranmer* (New Haven, CT: Yale University Press, 1996), 505; Basil Hall, "Martin Bucer in England," in *Martin Bucer*, ed. David Wright (Cambridge: Cambridge University Press, 1994), 158–59; and David Wright, "Martin Bucer (1491–551) in England," *Anvil* 9 (1992): 253–54.

[48] "Confirmacion," in *The Book of Common Prayer, Printed by Whitchurch 1552, Commonly Called the Second of Book of Edward VI* (repr., London: Pickering, 1844).

[49] Turrell, "'Until Such Time as He Be Confirmed,'" 204–5.

their action, or praised the authorities for their care in insisting on the regular performance of catechizing in church.[50]

What becomes clear from the ecclesiastical ordinances of Calvin and the prayer books of Cranmer is that, in the sixteenth century, children and younger youth were expected to attend catechetical classes in their churches; this practice was neither sporadic nor informal but quite regular. Both in Calvin's Geneva and among the English reformers, pastors were called to assemble young people on a weekly basis for catechetical instruction.

"This Day We Restored Our Primitive Practice": Recontextualization of Catechesis in Colonial American Churches

The expectation of pastor-led catechetical classes for children was so engrained in the churches of England in the sixteenth and seventeenth centuries that the practice persisted in both Conformist and non-Conformist churches. Furthermore, by 1570, the Church of England had authorized the printing of an even more extensive catechism than the one found in the *Book of Common Prayer*; this new catechism had been prepared by Alexander Nowell for grammar schools. The ongoing expectation that children and youth

---

[50] Green, *The Christian's ABC*, 98–99. This is not to suggest that Luther and Calvin dismissed the responsibility of parents to catechize with their children. The recurrent clause in Luther's Small Catechism "as the head of the family should teach it in a simple way to his household" reminds the reader of his expectation for fathers. However, Luther in time came to emphasize the role of schools taught by trained professionals, while Calvin not only founded schools but also required weekly pastoral catechetical instruction. For Luther's reliance on schools for the discipleship of children, see Strauss, *Luther's House of Learning*, 4–12, 24–39.

should participate in catechetical instruction is clear from the pro-liferation of catechisms in English throughout the seventeenth and eighteenth centuries.[51]

This expectation was so strong that the ideal of weekly cat-echetical classes followed English settlers across the Atlantic Ocean. On December 6, 1674, a certain apostle Eliot recorded these words regarding the First Church of Roxbury, Massachusetts:

> This day we restored [our] primitive practice for the train-ing up [our] youth, first [our] male youth (in fitting sea-son, stay every sab[bath] after the evening exercize, in the Pub[lic] meeting house, where the Elders will examine theire remembrance [that] day, [and] any fit poynt of cat-echise [*sic*]. Secondly [that] [our] female youth should meet in one place, where the Elders may examine [them] of theire remembrance yesterday. [And] about catechisme or what else may be convenient.[52]

Here, the practice of catechetical classes in the church was perceived as the restoration of a "primitive practice." These classes entailed not only gatherings of particular age groups but also the separation of students according to gender. Once again, pastors led these gatherings through processes that included both examination and instruction.

In seventeenth-century Plymouth, Massachusetts, one pastor likewise conducted catechetical classes for children "once a fort-night, the males at one time and the females at the other" with

---

[51] Stephen Orchard, "From Catechism Class to Sunday School," in *The Sunday School Movement,* ed. Stephen Orchard and John H. Y. Briggs (Eugene, OR: Wipf & Stock, 2007), 4–7.

[52] *A Report of the Record Commissioners Containing the Roxbury Land and Church Records,* 2nd ed. (Boston: Rockwell and Churchill, 1884), 191.

one of his fellow elders "accompanying him therein constantly."[53] Such practices were not perceived in any way as innovations. By the closing decade of the seventeenth century, these classes had been revived as a weekly practice in the church that took place "between the morning & evening worship, the males one sabbath & the females another."[54]

During the Great Awakening, Jonathan Edwards seems to have reintroduced this pattern of gathering the young people after morning worship:

---

[53] *Plymouth Church Records 1620–1859, Publications of the Colonial Society of Massachusetts,* vol. 22 (Boston: Colonial Society of Massachusetts, 1920), 145. In 1669, the church used William Perkins's catechism, published in 1592 under the title "The Foundation of Christian Religion." In 1678, catechism classes were renewed, using one of the Westminster Assembly's catechisms (154). By 1684, the church had returned to William Perkins's catechism (256), and then later returned to the Westminster Shorter Catechism (175). In Plymouth, classes were offered both for males and females. In other locations, catechetical classes were limited to males in a particular age range. According to a church covenant renewal ceremony in 1675 "in Norwich in Connecticut Colony," "all the Males who are eight or nine years of age, shall be presented before the Lord in his Congregation every Lords [*sic*] Day to be Catechised, until they be about thirteen years in age." The reason for this covenant renewal had to do with conflicts between settlers and natives "in this Calamitous Year 1675, the Year of *Jacobs* [sic] trouble in the Wilderness, in which the Lord doth scourge *New England* by the Outrage of the Heathen; a Year never to be forgotten." James Fitch, *An Explanation of the Solemn Advice, Recommended by the Council in Connecticut Colony, to the Inhabitants of That Jurisdiction, Respecting the Reformation of Those Evils, Which Have Been the Procuring Cause of the Late Judgments upon New-England,* 67–69, http://name.umdl.umich.edu/N00267.0001.001.

[54] *Plymouth Church Records 1620–1859, Publications of the Colonial Society of Massachusetts,* 175. In 1696, "July, 26: at the conclusion of the sacrament, the Pastor called upon the chh . . . to command their children etc to attend more upon & not neglect the ordinance of publick catechizing, wherein of late there had bin some remisnesse, upon which followed a Reformation in that respect" (178).

At the conclusion of the public exercise on the Sabbath, I appointed the children that were under sixteen years of age to go from the meetinghouse to a neighbor house, that I there might further enforce what they had heard in public, and might give in some counsels proper for their age. . . . About the middle of the summer, I called together the young people that were communicants, from sixteen to twenty-six years of age, to my house; which proved to be a most happy meeting. . . . We had several meetings that summer of young people.[55]

Although catechetical instruction is not mentioned in this description from the pen of Jonathan Edwards, it seems likely that the existing template of Sunday afternoon gatherings to be taught by a pastor influenced the pattern that he chose. "That summer of young people" also explicitly included not only children ("under sixteen years of age") but also older teenagers and young adults ("from sixteen to twenty-six years of age").

"To Hear the Children their Catechism": Robert Raikes's Sunday School as an Extension of Catechetical Instruction to Marginalized Children and Youth

It seems that these existing templates were the ones that shaped the earliest expressions of Sunday school. Before examining this particular connection, however, it will be helpful to examine a common narrative related to the origins of Sunday school. According to this

---

[55] Jonathan Edwards, "Letter to the Reverend Thomas Prince of Boston," December 12, 1743, in *The Works of Jonathan Edwards: Volume 4: The Great Awakening*, ed. C.C. Goen (New Haven: Yale University Press, 1972), 546–47.

reconstruction of the origins of Sunday school, the initial purpose of Sunday school was to battle juvenile delinquency and moral degeneration by teaching children to read. The following descriptions from widely used texts reveal the widespread acceptance of this narrative:

> Sunday was the day when bands of wandering, unsupervised and often lawless children inflicted damage on the outlying areas. . . . Soon after Raikes succeeded his father as publisher of the *Journal* in 1757, he committed himself to jail reform and the moral education of criminals. His attention moved from *crime* to *ignorance* as a cause of crimes and then to *children* and their ignorance. . . . In modern terms, he wanted to shape preventive measures against juvenile delinquency.[56]

> Raikes felt that education was an effective tool in battling vice and moral degeneration. He determined to develop an experimental school to test his theory. However, he was legally barred from doing so. Until the passage of the Enabling Act in 1779, persons outside the Church of England were prevented from having schools. In 1780 he and [Thomas] Stork enlisted children from the lowest rung of the socioeconomic ladder in Gloucester in their first Sunday school. . . . The primary aim of Raikes's school was literacy training.[57]

> What was needed was an impassioned reformer who could integrate the educational possibilities that Froebel and other Enlightenment educational reformers brought to light with the biblical teachings of Protestant theology. This individual

---

[56] Robert Lynn and Elliott Wright, *The Big Little School* (Nashville: Abingdon, 1980), 24–25.

[57] Ronnie Prevost and James Reed, *A History of Christian Education* (Nashville: B&H, 1993), 256–57.

came in the unlikely figure of an English newspaper owner named Robert Raikes, Jr. . . . Raikes used his influence in the community to draw his readers' attention to the plight of individuals who were imprisoned and in desperate need of assistance. . . . Raikes set about to address the needs of the many juvenile delinquents who were running wild in the streets after work and on Sunday.[58]

These narratives are not wholly inaccurate. Most of them rightly recognize that the role of Robert Raikes in the genesis of Sunday school was not as a founding father but as a popularizer and prophet. There is, however, at least one point at which these reconstructions should be modified: *the initial aim of Raikes's school was not merely— or perhaps even primarily—literacy training.* Catechetical instruction was also a primary aim, and the template for this instruction seems to have been the venerable pattern that can be traced back through the Church of England to the ecclesiastical ordinances of sixteenth-century Geneva.

In eighteenth-century England, the capacity to provide priests with an income in many locations depended on gaining the favor of wealthy landowners. As a result, thousands of parishes in the Church of England had no pastors at all, and many of the church's leaders were sons of aristocrats with little interest in religion and even less interest in the urban poor. Catechetical instruction, when it existed at all, seems to have taken place only in higher social classes.

In this context, Sunday school emerged, in part, to make the ideal of weekly catechetical instruction accessible to urban children who lacked any meaningful connection to the churches. The

---

[58] Michael J. Anthony and Warren Benson, *Exploring the History and Philosophy of Christian Education* (Grand Rapids, MI: Kregel, 2003), 260–61.

instructions provided by Raikes to the first four women who taught in his Sunday schools were specifically catechetical. The women were, in the words of Raikes, "to receive as many children as I should send upon this Sunday" and to instruct them "in reading and in the Church catechism." Later, Raikes described the early emphases in his Sunday schools:

> One or two clergymen gave their assistance by going around to the schools on the Sunday afternoon to hear the children their catechism. This was of great consequence. Another clergyman hears them their catechism once a quarter publicly in church, and rewards their good behaviour with some little gratuity.[59]

When abolitionist William Wilberforce visited Raikes's Sunday school, what he witnessed was a group of children who could "repeat simple prayers and the catechism, and answer Bible questions, and then sing Dr. Watts's hymns."[60]

Raikes's template for a Sunday afternoon class "to hear the children their catechism" seems to have been the classes that had long been mandated for the Church of England in the *Book of Common Prayer*. If so, what happened in the early days of Sunday school was not an innovation. It was the extension of a practice with a venerable history to include children who had become disconnected from the church. Both the Sunday afternoon form of the classes and the

---

[59] Alfred Gregory, *Robert Raikes* (London: Hodder and Stoughton, 1877), 58–61.

[60] J. Henry Harris, *The Story of Robert Raikes* (Philadelphia: American Sunday School Union, 1900), 60. This account fits with the recollection of a student in an early Sunday school, who remembered "standing up in a row with many other children, to say our catechism, and sing one of Watts's children's hymns." Anne Boylan, *Sunday School* (New Haven, CT: Yale University Press, 1988), 45.

catechism as the central content can be traced back to a long-standing ecclesiastical system with roots in sixteenth-century Geneva.

This emphasis on catechetical instruction in Sunday schools did not end with Robert Raikes. It persisted throughout the eighteenth century, even as literacy did become an increasing focus. According to the 1787 book of discipline of the Methodist Episcopal Church, the purpose of Sunday school was to "procure our instructions" and to assist the children in the memorization of these instructions; for Methodists in the eighteenth century, "our instructions" referred to a catechism that John Wesley had published in 1745.[61] The emphasis on catechism was made more explicit a few years later in the Methodist *Book of Discipline*, when "or catechisms" was added after the word "instructions," probably to allow for usage of the new catechism that John Dickins had produced.[62]

By the end of the eighteenth century, the focus of Sunday school does seem to have turned toward expanding literacy.[63] "What can be done," Methodists lamented in 1790, "for the instruction of poor children (whites and blacks) to read? Let us labour, as the heart and

---

[61] Regarding John Wesley's "instructions," see James Kirby et al., *The Methodists* (Westport, CT: Greenwood, 1996), 168.

[62] Addie Wardle, "History of the Sunday School Movement in the Methodist Episcopal Church" (Ph.D. diss., University of Chicago, 1918), 45; Kirby et al., 169.

[63] E. P. Thompson argued in *The Making of the English Working Class* (New York: Pantheon, 1964) that Sunday schools in England had served as an agency by which the middle class attempted to impose its values on a nascent working class. In Thompson's thinking, Sunday schools forced children into a new universe of disciplined time that took away their pre-industrial freedom. For the most part, however, Sunday schools empowered marginalized people, first by extending the privilege of catechetical instruction to lower classes (if my interpretation is correct) and then by providing opportunities for literacy. Furthermore, the values of Sunday school curricula generally reflected the aspirations not of the middle class but of the working class. See Thomas Laqueur, *Religion and Respectability* (New Haven, CT: Yale University Press, 1976).

soul of one man, to establish Sunday schools, in, or near the place of public worship."[64] Even so, a focus on "our scripture-catechism" as the primary curriculum persisted.[65] The Sunday school overseen by William Fox worked to make the lower classes literate, but the learning of catechism was considered to be a crucial component in the curriculum.[66] In the opening decades of the nineteenth century, Sunday schools seem to have shifted from their catechetical foundations, particularly in the United States. Some American Sunday schools became ecumenical in nature, deemphasizing catechisms and focusing on literacy and citizenship; others retained a stronger Christian identity and centered on evangelism even as they also worked to develop literacy.[67]

Many of these Sunday schools were open not only to children but also to adults. Since African Americans had been largely excluded from public education, these Sunday schools provided an opportunity for free African Americans to learn to read. In many northern Sunday schools, adult African Americans working to expand their opportunities by becoming literate outnumbered juvenile pupils of all races.[68]

---

[64] Wardle, "History of the Sunday School Movement in the Methodist Episcopal Church," 52.

[65] Wardle, 53.

[66] Joseph Ivimey, *Memoir of W. Fox, Esq.* (London: Wightman, 1831), 20, 24, 30, 32, 59–61, 77.

[67] K. E. Leal, "'All Our Children May Be Taught of God,'" *Church History* 87 (2018): 1061. Episcopal bishop William White exercised a significant influence on the rise of literacy-focused Sunday schools in the United States. An emissary from the London Missionary Society named Robert May was instrumental in the rise of the evangelistic model of Sunday school, which grew to dominate the American Sunday school movement by the mid-nineteenth century. See Edwin Rice, *The Sunday-School Movement and the American Sunday-School Union* (Philadelphia: ASSU, 1917), 45–52.

[68] Boylan, *Sunday School*, 22–33; Leal, "All Our Children May Be Taught of God," 1077–78.

Occasional efforts were even made to provide Sunday schools for enslaved African Americans in the South. In a home-based Sunday school in Virginia, William Elliott taught not only his own children and white indentured servants but also enslaved persons, albeit not at the same time. In these classes, "all were taught the rudiments of reading, in order that they might be able to read God's Word."[69] The education of enslaved African Americans could not, however, survive the entrenchment of systemic racism in the American South. In the opening years of the nineteenth century, a certain George Daughaday was "severely beaten on the head with a club, and subsequently had water pumped on him from a public cistern" in South Carolina because he taught African American children in a Sunday school.[70] By the midpoint of the nineteenth century, any provision of literacy for African Americans had been severely restricted or rendered illegal throughout the American South.

Complements, Not Competitors

The documented practices of the sixteenth-century Reformers discredit any suggestion that church-based classes for children or youth did not exist prior to the eighteenth and nineteenth centuries. Furthermore, it is clear such classes did not arise due to the assimilation of practices in the culture. The institution of catechesis in the churches was perceived and presented by John Calvin as a restoration of the practices of the ancient church, with a flexible manner of implementation. This pattern became part of the pastoral expectations in sixteenth-century Anglican congregations and eventually wove its way into churches in the American colonies.

---

[69] Wardle, "History of the Sunday School Movement in the Methodist Episcopal Church," 46.

[70] Wardle, 47–48.

Scripture never explicitly commands catechetical classes for children and youth. This did not, however, prevent the Reformers in Geneva and England from implementing such classes on a regular basis for the purpose of fulfilling mandates that they did find in Scripture. Their ideal seems to have been a weekly gathering. This ideal schedule could, however, be freely adapted and modified based on the needs and context of each church.

Age-organized gatherings for youth and children did not diminish the expectation that parents were called to train their progeny in biblical truth. Although the Reformers were at times skeptical about the capacity of parents to fulfill this task, specialized instruction in the context of the church was seen as a complement to parental instruction, never as a competitor. Sunday schools emerged in part as an attempt to extend the ideal of weekly catechetical instruction to children and youth whose parents were disconnected from the churches in England. In time, the Sunday school movement would influence the emergence of early societies for the discipleship of young people, such as the Young People's Society of Christian Endeavor, which provided a template for many early youth ministries.

Regardless of what one thinks of student ministry, the claim that age-organized groups for youth or children emerged from a cesspool of modern pragmatism is unsustainable. The roots of age-organized groups in the church are not "shockingly sinister," as some proponents of family-integrated ministry claim.[71] These roots can be traced back at least as far as John Calvin's Geneva, and the initial goal of these classes was to restore an ancient church practice so that children and youth could be trained in the gospel-rich truths of the Protestant Reformation.

---

[71] *Divided*, directed by Peter Bradrick.

Appendix 2

Student Ministry and Parachurch Organizations

• JAY STRACK •

Perhaps one of the greatest and most powerful resources a young minister has are highly effective parachurch organizations, ready and waiting to assist you in your work. These organizations are filled with trained, compassionate men and women who are ready to come alongside to help in your ministry efforts. The word *parachurch* comes from the Greek *parakletos*, which is used in John of the Holy Spirit, sent to us as The Counselor or Helper, the One who *comes alongside* (see John 14:16–17 NKJV).

Not only is the parachurch wisdom available to you, but also ideas, resources, relationships, and successful projects with which to partner. Ancillary student ministries create extended arms to encircle our treasured youth. Please allow me to introduce you to a handful of battle-tested organizations that I personally partner with in order to grow the effectiveness of the ministry I am called to facilitate.

I want to begin with a ministry that all of us have a heart for but are often unequipped to conduct; that is, underresourced communities.

Idlewild Baptist Church is a megachurch, but when they wanted to go big on an inner-city project, they knew they needed a strong partnership. They united with One More Child to grow and sustain a joint "Hope Street" project to transform lives in the inner city of Tampa though Christ-centered services and community development. Their "Adopt a Block" strategy is simple and effective: the first and third Saturdays of each month, volunteers visit the neighbors on their block to encourage them, pray with them, and assist with needs they might have. Sometimes "old school" is the most effective way.[1]

Dr. Jerry Haag is president of One More Child, a parachurch organization feeding, resourcing, and protecting families regardless of background or culture. I watched this gentle, brilliant man develop relationships over a span of years that came back to him in donations, important introductions, and faithful staff. I asked him about the value of working with others: "At One More Child, we know that we don't own anything. Every resource or blessing we receive, we share. It all belongs to Jesus. It doesn't make sense not to work with people we might not agree with 100 percent of the time when we will live with them one day forever in eternity. Everyone together can do so much more."

For example, One More Child has evolved through one hundred-plus years of history to do more and do it more effectively. They have grown exponentially from group homes for children to foster parent homes and resourcing, antitrafficking, single-mom homes, and feeding millions of children across America and around the globe. Dr. Haag and the leadership would tell you that all of this is only possible through viable, sustainable relationships and partnerships with churches and other parachurch organizations.

---

[1] "Hope Street," One More Child, accessed July 16, 2021, https://onemorechild.org/hopestreet.

Student Leadership University (SLU) has partnered with the North American Mission Board (NAMB) to create the Inside Out Strategy in order to train underresourced students to become influencers for change in their communities.[2] We believe that the change in these cultures has to come from the very students who live there, and we wanted to equip and empower them to succeed as young men and women committed to Christ and a sure biblical worldview. Though we were sure this was a great idea, we also knew we needed a strong partner. NAMB was quick to come alongside us and has been a great support.[3]

Now in our twenty-sixth year, SLU was founded upon and continues to operate on the belief that training others to understand that the future belongs to those who are prepared is the most important ministry we can do.[4] For more than two decades, I traveled the globe preaching in stadiums, schools, universities, churches, and even the streets, sharing the good news of salvation. God blessed the crusades with thousands of decisions, schools opened their doors widely to a strong message of hope, and I thought that would be my life for the next two or more decades. But God began to do a work in me, and though it was a big change, I listened and accepted the risk.

In my heart, the Lord planted an idea: teach students to be leaders so that they can become influencers for the kingdom. I remember vividly calling my wife to the dining table one day with the words, "I have an idea, but I don't know where to start." She listened as I unfolded the vision God had placed in my heart, and together a plan evolved for a "test" week that would eventually bring almost a quarter of a million students, educators, and student ministers to

---

[2] "The Inside Out Strategy," Student Leadership University, accessed July 16, 2021, https://www.slulead.com/slu-inside-out.

[3] North American Mission Board, accessed July 16, 2021, www.namb.net.

[4] Student Leadership University, accessed July 16, 2021, www.slulead.com.

Student Leadership University programs. I did not do this alone. God brought a wonderful board of directors alongside me, some of whom have been my friends and mentors for several decades. I have learned that if you can accomplish a dream by yourself, most likely that dream did not come from God.

My good friend Dr. George Barna, director of research for the Cultural Research Center at Arizona Christian University, conducted a new survey about the worldview of Americans. His survey shows:

- Although seven out of ten consider themselves to be Christian, just 6 percent actually possess a biblical worldview.
- Only one-fifth of those attending evangelical Protestant churches (21 percent) have a biblical worldview, as compared to one-sixth of those attending charismatic or Pentecostal churches (16 percent). The study finds even smaller proportions in mainline Protestant (8 percent) or Catholic (1 percent) churches.
- The number of American adults holding a biblical worldview has declined by 50 percent over the past quarter century.
- Regarding the next generation, the numbers are even more startling. A mere 2 percent of those eighteen to twenty-nine years old possess a biblical worldview.[5]

These statistics lead us to believe that campus evangelism and discipleship are vital to the strategies of a growing student ministry.

---

[5] Arizona Christian University Cultural Research Center, "American Worldview Inventory 2020—At a Glance: CRC Survey Shows Dangerously Low Percentage of Americans Hold Biblical Worldview," Arizona Christian University Cultural Research Center, March 24, 2020, https://www.arizonachristian.edu/wp-content/uploads/2020/03/CRC_AWVI2020_Report.pdf.

Having spoken in ten thousand public school assemblies, I can tell you, hands down, that the First Priority Club of America is the most effective strategy for reaching students, where they are, that I have ever seen.

The public school is an undiscovered country for most student ministries, but for too long we have been held back by incorrect thinking about taking the Bible into US public schools. As you read more about the success of First Priority Clubs (FPC), you will see a different story. The mission of First Priority is to network with the church for a common cause of sharing the gospel on middle and high school campuses. Student leaders are equipped to start student-led FPCs on middle and high school campuses, and these clubs create a relational environment on the school campus where the gospel is shared. During one school year, First Priority trained 3,600 Christian students to lead a FPC, and these became forty-one First Priority Chapters around America serving 877 schools. Out of this, 10,108 students came to know Christ. Now, I was never very good at math, but this I get. Success begets success. Inspiration breeds inspiration. There are more than 300,000 churches in America[6] and only 43,850 middle and high schools;[7] the workers are in place to change America and certainly to impact the next generation. Perhaps the culture of America would be of a different kind if our churches looked at their youth group as servant leaders and missionaries, praying and supporting as they go. This could be the game changer we hope for.

---

[6] Greg Stier, "Over 300,000 Churches in America; Do We Really Need More Church Plants?" *Christian Post*, February 16, 2016, https://www.christianpost.com/news/church-planting-growth-pastors-evangelicals-ministry-america.html.

[7] *U.S. News & World Report*, "Find the Best High Schools," accessed April 2, 2020, https://www.usnews.com/education/best-high-schools.

This group is a great example to all of us about how to adapt rather than give in to circumstance. When the coronavirus pandemic closed schools, they quickly morphed into virtual clubs, knowing students would be looking to the internet for companionship and hope. As a result, salvations in the FP circles skyrocketed. Challenge accepted. God is exalted.

There are almost 50.8 million students in America's public schools, making our schools a prime opportunity to minister to students.[8] Who do you think can reach a fourteen-year-old student? Probably a fourteen-year old student with a biblical worldview, assurance of salvation, and strong discipleship background. It might be messier and take a little longer, but instead of reaching one student, you train students to reach multiple students. Students are relational and performance-oriented; let's train them to go and do.

Youth pastors, teachers, and volunteers can sign up for training at https://firstpriority.club and get all the necessary resources to get ministry going on a school campus. If you are educated about separation of church and state and organized in your efforts, there is opportunity to influence this generation with the most powerful book in the universe.

The Equal Access Act of the United States is a federal law passed in 1984 to compel federally funded secondary schools to provide equal access to extracurricular clubs. According to the U.S. Department of Education, "The Act applies to: (1) any public secondary school [middle or high school] (2) that receives federal funds (3) and . . . allow[s] one or more noncurricular student groups to meet on its premises (4) during noninstructional time. Schools meeting these criteria are forbidden to prevent access or deny fair opportunity

---

[8] Maya Riser-Kositsky, "Education Statistics: Facts About American Schools," January 3, 2019, https://www.edweek.org/ew/issues/education-statistics/index.html.

to," or discriminate against, "students who wish to hold meetings on school grounds. . . . because of the 'religious, political, philosophical, or other content of the speech at [the group's] meetings.'"[9] In layman's terms, if a school has a debate club or a chess club or any other club, it cannot deny a Christian club. "'Access' refers not only to physical meeting spaces on school premises, but also to recognition and privileges afforded to other groups at the school, including, for example, the right to announce club meetings in the school newspaper, on bulletin boards, or over the public address system. Noninstructional time is 'time set aside by the school before actual classroom instruction begins or after actual instruction ends,' and covers student meetings that take place before or after school as well as those occurring during lunch, 'activity periods,' and other noninstructional periods during the school day."[10]

American students have religious freedoms:

- The right to meet with other religious students
- The right to identify your religious beliefs through signs/symbols
- The right to talk about your religious beliefs at school
- The right to distribute religious literature at school
- The right to pray at school
- The right to carry or study your Bible at school
- The right to do papers, speeches, and projects with religious themes
- The right to be exempt

---

[9] U.S. Department of Education, "Legal Guidelines Regarding the Equal Access Act and the Recognition of Student-Led Noncurricular Groups," U.S. Department of Education, accessed August 29, 2021, 1, www2.ed.gov/policy /elsec/guid/secletter/groupsguide.doc.

[10] U.S. Department of Education, "Legal Guidelines Regarding the Equal Access Act and the Recognition of Student-Led Noncurricular Groups," 2.

- The right to celebrate or study religious holidays at school
- The right to meet with school officials

The best way to implement any new strategy is to share the vision with as many people as possible. Mark Robbins, executive director of First Priority of America, says, "The more people you get involved, the more people you get involved. We are convinced that most students in the schools across this great land have not rejected the message of the gospel, they simply have not heard it."[11]

The bridge from ministry outside the church to bringing students into the church can be a shaky one. While we do not believe in building your youth group by offering entertainment alone, we also know that the reality of what the culture offers students and what is available to them 24-7 through streaming can be a tough competitor to gathering students for worship and building commitment to your small groups. For most of my early ministry, I could not afford to put on a stellar event. I know from talking with thousands of student pastors over the years that the majority of you face the same issue.

The SLU ministry exists to help you build a core team of leaders who can exponentially grow your leadership and your student ministry with confident, bold students who know and own their biblical worldview. We believe our end goal is to empower every student to be able to "always be ready to give a defense to everyone who asks you for a reason for the hope that is in you" (1 Pet 3:15 NKJV). Everything we create and facilitate is to equip student pastors, educators, and parents to remain faithful and focused in the journey of Christian citizenship as influencers for the kingdom. Foundationally, students and leaders need to experience three fundamental elements to make a student event successful in its end goal:

---

[11] Marty Robbins, personal communication, February 20, 2020.

- Engaging Scripture through biblical teaching
- Exalting Christ through Christ-centered worship
- Equipping students with the necessary tools needed to be salt and light for their generation

To provide this for thousands of students nationwide at an affordable cost, we created the LIFT Tour, a weekend of discipleship and evangelism. By providing strong biblical content, the best of worship, and bringing students together across the community, they are inspired to face daily pressures of the culture with confidence. The LIFT Tour is a theme-based weekend experience, where life-change takes place. This is our evangelistic arm of the ministry, as we see many come to decisions for Christ after a clear gospel presentation every Friday evening of the tour.

Relationships and partnerships with trusted parachurch organizations is key to expanding your ministry. Ben Trueblood, director of student ministry for Lifeway Christian Resources, partners with us on the LIFT Tour so that churches can also partner with us as we all have the same mission to equip and reach students. He says:

> In the Christian life, our race is meant to be run alongside other believers in community rather than alone. You need other people in your life to encourage you, challenge you, to listen to you, and to share your burdens. In many ways, your ministry can have these same benefits as you choose to partner with parachurch organizations who are built to come alongside you and whose heart is to serve the church.[12]

The second big component after evangelism and being on the campus is your personal growth as a leader and building leadership

---

[12] Ben Trueblood, *Student Ministry That Matters* (Nashville: B&H, 2016).

within your youth group. Often student pastors find themselves desperate for a bit of inspiration, some resources, and leadership training but simply do not have the financial means to attend conferences. I dare say all of us have had that experience. We all know that youth ministries are frequently at the bottom of the budget. Less training, less money, less staff, and sometimes less opportunity. So we created a way for you to leverage resources and relationships to expand the influence and effectiveness of your ministry.

Our Youth Pastor Summits (YPS) were founded in 1996, more than two decades ago. When the Lord spoke to me about YPS, he also told me that it had to be *free*. This was a daunting task, but through partnerships, we raised hundreds of thousands of dollars to provide a program that mirrored one of our core values—*all things in excellence.* The YPS experience includes sessions from world-renowned pastors, authors, leaders, and communicators as well as other exciting elements unique to the location. Even though our registration often fills in twenty-four hours, we knew that at least 10 percent would forget to show. This is something you might experience with students. After twenty years, we added a small registration fee of $10 solely because people don't always value commitment that is "free," and a small registration fee makes the participant value the commitment to attend, learn, and grow. Consider this as you plan.

These intensive two days of inspiration, training, creativity, and resourcing are spread throughout the country so that anyone can access them. Get yourself registered today at www.slulead.com /youth-pastor-summit or find more resources on our web page.

Beyond the classroom, I would ask you to give your students a global perspective. Mission trips are an important part of this. At Student Leadership University, we realize that while not every student can go on a mission trip, we can bring the world to everyone through true stories. For this reason, we partner with Open Doors, founded by Brother Andrew.[13]

As a new Christian, I read his book *God's Smuggler*. The stories lit a fire in me to share the gospel that has never been quenched. Open Doors describes Brother Andrew as "our chief adventurer and lead risk taker."[14] He's best known, in fact, for courageously putting his life on the line to smuggle Bibles behind the Iron Curtain at the height of the Cold War. His infamous prayer was: "Lord, in my luggage I have Scripture I want to take to your children. When you were on earth, you made blind eyes see. Now, I pray, make seeing eyes blind. Do not let the guards see those things you do not want them to see." Years later, my daughters and I stuffed small New Testaments into our heavy coat pockets as we made our way together to China to share the good news there. We prayed that prayer also, and they have never forgotten the adventure.

Open Doors team members still take on risks to resource these Christians living in hostile regions and continually work against persecution wherever it exists. They spend time getting to know persecuted believers on the ground, in their communities, and in the midst of great hardship. SLU invites our participants to become part of the extended Open Doors family by reading the firsthand stories of persecuted Christians on their website, praying for the persecuted church around the globe, and writing letters to encourage these believers. Giving these stories to your students will quickly take them from "I'm bored" to an adventure boiling inside them to go against the culture, against the popular way, and to dare to stand up for what they believe in. Suffering brings compassion. Our students might

---

[13] Open Doors USA, accessed July 16, 2021, https://www.opendoorsusa .org/.

[14] Open Doors USA.

not know suffering today, but they will. Understanding what others who have gone before us have learned will bring them through with bold faith.

Through the Open Doors World Wide Watch List,[15] we stay connected to the realities of global persecution. My favorite example of this ministry's ability to help our students connect to current world news happened while we were actually in the midst of an SLU program session. We were told that Boko Haram kidnapped young girls the age of our students and took them to rape camps. Open Doors gave us the first names of many of the girls and made it possible for our students to send immediate messages to the parents with prayers for those who were abducted. In the midst of terror, these parents were receiving notes of prayer with their daughter's own name in each one, and our students were instantly filled with compassion and understanding of both suffering for Christ and intercessory prayer. True stories instill adventure and give birth to the desire to serve.

It is my prayer that all of these examples will reinforce a strategic lesson I live by. There is always a way

- to reach my campus, regardless of available resources,
- to get the training I need,
- to expand my influence through training and inspiring others, and
- to give my students opportunities to serve locally and abroad.

One of the reasons I have been asked to contribute this appendix is because I have for forty years been a leader in my denomination of Southern Baptists, serving most of that time in a parachurch capacity. Obviously, we don't want to get involved with a ministry

---

[15] "The World Watch List," Open Doors USA, accessed July 16, 2021, https://www.opendoorsusa.org/christian-persecution/world-watch-list/.

outside of church whose doctrine is not consistent with our biblical worldview. We don't want to be involved with leaders of ancillary ministries who are not churchmen or churchwomen. SLU ministry and all of those I wrote of in this chapter serve and support the local church. We believe in the body of Christ as defined and founded by Jesus during his earthly ministry. Everything we do is to equip the local church as they reach and keep the next generation. Be careful whom you align with. Test the character and the theology; inspect the fruit. Whom do they align with?

Over the years, I have served alongside various ministries. One of those I continue to work with because of their integrity and successful practices is Scott Dawson Evangelistic Association.[16] Scott's camps, conferences, training, and events are built around his belief that parachurch ministries are never to come across as a competitor of the church. He says, "The local church is not a good suggestion, the local church is the only answer. A nonprofit must be a tool of the local church. You might have a family physician, but sometimes you have to go to a specialist. Nonprofits are not a cure-all but are specialists in their areas. Evangelism, mission trips, feeding the hungry, etc. Together we can do more."

We believe in youth camps. In fact, we partner with Lifeway, Scott Dawson, and others to share the good news about camps that are based on biblical worldview, affordable, and run with integrity. But after decades of ministry, I began to look for a way to extend the thrilling camp experience into ongoing leadership as students go back to the realities of life. This is a generation that has been told by its surrounding culture that there are no definitive boundaries for thought patterns and decisions other than to love everyone as they

---

[16] Scott Dawson Evangelistic Association, accessed July 16, 2021, https://scottdawson.org.

are. A biblical worldview certainly agrees with the latter phrase of love supported by the example of Jesus. But what a great majority of our students do not know and understand are the boundaries of the moral code outlined in absolutes through the pages of the Scriptures.

Please allow me to conclude this appendix with an explanation of why I believe you can build an effective youth group if you have student leaders who *know* what they believe. Not Mom and Dad's faith, but their own. Not what they think might be true, but what they know and experience in Scripture. SLU is an intensive, interactive week where students begin to be fully convinced in their own minds to build their lives and eternity on God's Word. We prepare students for the bridge to the university setting where they will face questions from those whose mission is to pull up by the root all that students have been taught about their faith and their God. In fact, the very first thing students will hear from me at the start of SLU 101 is: "It's time for the little boy to sit down and the young man to stand up. It's time for the little girl to sit down and the young woman to stand up."

The sessions and experiences of SLU include:

- Rules and tools of leadership
- Time and life management skills training
- Developing a biblical worldview
- Relational skills
- Personality testing and understanding
- Theology of imagination and discovering your dream

Students, parents, student pastors and leaders, and educators take these skills combined with great inspiration back to their local church and begin to train others. When youth groups are built on student leaders rather than one leader, they thrive. Your middle school students will be the leaders or the lid of your group when they reach the eleventh or twelfth grade. We invest in them now to give them a head start so they can turn around and model how to follow through on goals, ideas, dreams, and character.

We see that students will rise to the level you present to them. For that reason, our leadership training is based on a biblical worldview first, but also using the same leadership skills I have taught to corporate entities including Walmart, NASA, Johnson and Johnson, and to many professional sports teams. As of now, we have SLU alum across the globe serving in ministries, businesses, communities, churches, and even in the White House. Most importantly, these have a biblical worldview intact and are spreading that word to others as they go and as they grow.

I believe and teach that you will be the same person five years from now, except for the places you go, the books you read, the people you meet, and the Scripture you memorize. We built the various stages of SLU programs around that premise.

At SLU 201 in Washington, DC, students are challenged to think about the role their faith has played and will continue to play in the public square and the development of this country. We explore how to think Christianly about some of the pressing moral and ethical issues our country is facing. The interactive experiences continue as they understand the power of evil as they walk through the Holocaust Museum and learn about sacrifice at a private wreath laying in Arlington Cemetery. Through these experiences, students develop a spirit of gratitude and respect as well as an understanding that freedom is not free.

The SLU 301 Journey takes students to another time and place. Sitting in the same pew in Holy Trinity Church where C. S. Lewis was inspired to write the *Chronicles of Narnia*. Walking on Omaha Beach and standing on the cliffs of Point Du Hoc. Venturing through the halls of the Louvre. Hearing character studies at the graves of John Wesley and John Bunyan. Touring Westminster

Abbey and the graves of Wilberforce, Newton, Dickens, and Darwin. Contemplating the major decisions of life in front of *The Thinker* at Rodin's Sculpture Garden. We take leadership to a whole different level by jumping into history, inheriting the past, and imagining how to transform the future.

The final step of the SLU Journey takes place in the Holy Land. SLU works with Arab students in Nazareth, Bethlehem, and Jordan through East–West peace initiatives. We take our fourth-year students to Israel and Jordan for the greatest leadership lesson of all time: *Leadership begins at the feet of Jesus.* Every student leader must understand that because Jesus walked the road, they can run the race.

In closing, allow me to share a story from Dr. James Dobson. It seems a great effort of time and money was put into an evangelistic event some years ago and out of it only one person came publicly to faith in Christ. Of course, the organizers were distraught, feeling that God had not blessed their efforts. But the "one" happened to be Dr. Dobson's father, who went on to teach his son, James, the precepts of Scripture and a sure biblical worldview. He once told a reporter that he learned to pray before he learned to talk, and says he gave his life to Jesus at the age of three, in response to an altar call by his father.[17] And, as you know, Dr. Dobson has ministered to millions upon millions through Focus on the Family, books, radio, print, TV, and now through Family Talk Radio over a span of more than four decades and counting.

Remember: Don't despise small beginnings. Believe your ministry is bigger than the number you see.

---

[17] Paul Apostolidis, *Stations of the Cross Adorno and Christian Right Radio* (Durham, NC: Duke University Press, 1980), 22.

So that a future generation—children yet to be born—might know. They were to rise and tell their children so that they might put their confidence in God and not forget God's works, but keep his commands.

Then they would not be like their ancestors, a stubborn and rebellious generation, a generation whose heart was not loyal and whose spirit was not faithful to God. (Ps 78:6–8 NIV)

NAME & SUBJECT INDEX

SCRIPTURE INDEX